Approaches to Teaching Masterpieces of World Literature

Joseph Gibaldi, Series Editor

Approaches to Teaching Chaucer's *Canterbury Tales*

Joseph Gibaldi

Consultant Editor

Florence H. Ridley

The Modern Language Association of America   1980

Copyright © 1980 by The Modern Language Association of America

Library of Congress Cataloging in Publication Data

Gibaldi, Joseph, 1942–
    Approaches to teaching Chaucer's Canterbury tales.

    (Approaches to teaching masterpieces of world literature; 1)
    Bibliography: p.
    Includes index.
    1. Chaucer, Geoffrey, d. 1400. Canterbury tales. 2. Chaucer, Geoffrey, d. 1400—
Study and teaching. I. Ridley, Florence H. II. Title. III. Series.
PR1874.G5   821′.1   80–22909
ISBN 0–87352–476–4
ISBN 0–87352–475–6 (pbk.)

Published by The Modern Language Association of America, 62 Fifth Avenue,
New York, New York 10011

CONTENTS

The Chaucer Course: General Overviews

The Chaucer Course: Specific Approaches

Survey Courses for Nonmajors

Teaching the Backgrounds

PREFACE TO THE SERIES

In his thoughtful and sensitive book, *The Art of Teaching* (1950), Gilbert Highet wrote, "Bad teaching wastes a great deal of effort, and spoils many lives which might have been full of energy and happiness." All too many teachers have failed in their work, Highet argued, simply "because they have not thought about it." It is our hope that the Approaches to Teaching Masterpieces of World Literature series, sponsored by the Modern Language Association's Committee on Teaching and Related Professional Activities, will not only improve the craft—as well as the art—of teaching but also enhance in these years of a "publish and/or perish" mentality an awareness of the importance of teaching in our profession and encourage serious and continuing discussion of the aims and methods of our teaching.

The principal objective of the series is to collect within each volume a number of points of view on teaching a particular work of world literature that is widely taught at the undergraduate level. The preparation of each volume will begin with a survey of diverse philosophies of and approaches to teaching the work in question, thus enabling us to include in the volume the thoughts and methods of scores of teachers with considerable experience in teaching the work at the undergraduate level. The result will be a source book of material, information, and ideas on teaching the work to undergraduates.

Approximately one-half of each volume will be devoted to a presentation and analysis of the information and issues emerging from the survey and will include a discussion of such matters as preferred editions, suggested background materials, useful teaching aids, and so on. In the remainder of the volume, twelve to fifteen teachers will discuss their particular approaches to the work.

We expect a wide-ranging audience for the series, for each of its volumes will be intended to serve both the inexperienced and the experienced teacher of a literary work at the undergraduate level, those who wish to learn new ways of teaching as well as those who wish to compare their own approaches with the approaches of colleagues in other schools. Of course, no volume in the series could ever serve as a substitute for erudition, intelligence, creativity, and sensitivity in teaching. We hope merely that each book will point readers in useful directions; at most each will offer only a first step in the long journey to successful teaching.

We live in a time that increasingly demands a rededication to undergraduate teaching of the humanities, a time, in fact, that presents us with almost daily struggles for the survival of the humanities and of the idea of a liberal education. It may well be that our sometimes divided and fragmented profession will rediscover in its concern for and commitment to teaching a sense of purpose, unity, and community that many believe it presently lacks.

We hope that the Approaches to Teaching Masterpieces of World Literature series will serve in some small way to refocus attention upon the importance of teaching and to improve undergraduate instruction. We may perhaps adopt as keynote for the series Alfred North Whitehead's observation in *The Aims of Education* (1929) that the essence of a liberal education "proceeds by imparting a knowledge of the masterpieces of thought, of imaginative literature, and of art."

Joseph Gibaldi
Series Editor

PREFACE TO THE VOLUME

It seems only fitting that the first volume in the Modern Language Association's Approaches to Teaching Masterpieces of World Literature series should be devoted to the first great English poet. On the one hand, no other literary figure continues to generate more enthusiasm and dedication in teachers and students alike than Geoffrey Chaucer does. On the other hand, because of the decline of the study of both language and history in contemporary American education—and the corresponding decline in contemporary American life of linguistic and historical interest or even awareness—no other major English author is in as much danger of having his work either completely eliminated from the standard curriculum or so watered down and "simplified" as to be eliminated in all but name only.

This volume, like all others in the series, primarily concerns itself with teaching at the undergraduate level. It is offered to all teachers of Chaucer; in order to reach as wide an audience as possible, however, the publication is of necessity pitched at the beginning (and future) instructor and the nonspecialist. Experienced teachers and Chaucerians will probably find much that seems elementary. Yet, there is much here, particularly in the second half of the volume, that should be of interest even to the specialists. It is our fondest hope, too, that many Chaucer scholars will deem the volume important enough to be placed in their students' hands along with other valuable research and pedagogical tools.

The volume begins with an introduction by consultant editor Florence H. Ridley on the challenge of teaching *The Canterbury Tales*. The body of the work is divided into two parts, respectively entitled "Materials" and "Approaches." The first deals with such questions as editions for teaching *The Canterbury Tales*, required and recommended student readings, aids to teaching (recordings, films, and so on), and "The Instructor's Library" —that is, reference works, background studies, and critical and linguistic studies. The discussion in the first part is based on information supplied by the more than one hundred teachers of Chaucer throughout the United States and Canada who participated in the survey that preceded the preparation of this volume.

For the second part we have invited fifteen Chaucer teachers to discuss their approaches to teaching *The Canterbury Tales*. We offer these essays not as the "Fifteen Best Ways to Teach Chaucer"—there is simply no way of judging which approaches are the "best"—but rather as descriptions of approaches that are representative and/or at least interesting, at best inspiring. An appendix of participants in the survey, a list of works cited, and an index complete the book.

I am pleased to acknowledge the important roles that a number of persons have played in the preparation of this work. First and foremost, I wish to thank the teachers and scholars who participated in the survey that proved the foundation and the impetus for the volume. A special thanks must also be given to Florence H. Ridley, who served as the consultant editor of the book, lending useful, timely, and much appreciated moral support and editorial assistance throughout the development of the project. Emerson Brown, Jr., David C. Fowler, and Charles Muscatine generously read drafts of the work. Their perceptive and very helpful comments and suggestions for revision were, almost always, incorporated in the final manuscript. Finally, I am grateful to Bege Neel for her careful copy-editing of the manuscript; to the members of the Association's Committee on Teaching and Related Professional Activities for their strong endorsement and official sponsorship of the Approaches to Teaching Masterpieces of World Literature series; and to Walter S. Achtert, Joel Conarroe, Judy Goulding, and my other colleagues on the MLA staff for their encouragement and support of the project from its inception to its completion.

In preparing the volume, I have striven to remain faithful to the vision set forth in the Preface to the series. I hope the reality has not fallen too far short of the ideal. I will deem this pioneering effort a true success not only if it proves useful and stimulating but also, and more important, if it paves the way for the preparation and publication of an even better volume—or a series of such volumes—that will eventually replace it.

JG

INTRODUCTION

THE CHALLENGE OF TEACHING
THE CANTERBURY TALES

Florence H. Ridley

At the beginning of every course on *The Canterbury Tales*, some under-graduate is sure to ask (even if silently), "What has Chaucer to do with me?" Why indeed should we continue to teach the works of a poet who has been dead for half a millennium? Why in the age of jet travel be concerned with fourteenth-century riders on the road to Canterbury? Be-cause, as Matthew Arnold says, Chaucer's "power of fascination, however, is enduring; his poetical importance does not need the assistance of the historic estimate; it is real. He is a genuine source of joy and strength, which is flowing still for us and will flow always."[1] His contemporaries and early successors—John Gower, Thomas Hoccleve, John Lydgate, John Skelton—who reads them now? Today Chaucer is read and studied and subjected to the same analytical techniques as a Faulkner or a T. S. Eliot. And while one might find fault with the quality of much of the annual outpouring of critical commentary on Chaucer's poetry and rail with Dorothy Wellesley at the

> Vultures infernal
> Tearing internal
> Poets eternal
>   and so on and so on,[2]

the sheer bulk of such commentary attests to the poet's importance. There are as many reasons for the outpouring as there are readers, for in Chaucer's work each person seeks and finds something different; I believe, however, there are, in the main, three basic characteristics that account for the continuing popularity of Chaucer's poetry.

The first characteristic is its visuality. Chaucer's medium is specific, physical detail. As Hazlitt says, he seemed "obliged to inspect things for himself, to look narrowly, and almost to handle the object."[3] Chaucer writes as if he were using a painter's brush or a sculptor's chisel, and the surface of his work has a concrete, tactile finish. Hazlitt and Lamb sense this resemblance between the arts when they speak, respectively, of "the effect of sculpture" his work has on the mind, of "the strokes of Chaucer's pencil," his "canvass" crowded with "so many diverse yet cooperating materials," or when they compare his depictions to "portraits," to "physiognomical studies," or to those of Hogarth.[4] It is largely this graphic quality of Chaucer's art that enabled Dryden to "see . . . all the Pilgrims in *The Canterbury Tales*, their humours, their features, and their very dress, as distinctly as if I had supped with them at the Tabard in Southwark."[5]

The second reason for the continuing appeal of Chaucer's work appears to be an intentional ambiguity, one that teases, inveigles the reader into the creative process. Charles Lamb took Chaucer's biographer, William Godwin, to task for his "conjecturing spirit," his "fondness for filling out the picture by supposing what Chaucer did and how he felt where the materials are scanty."[6] But which one of the numberless persons who have read the poet's work has not done the same? At some point the materials are always "scanty," and the reader's conjecturing spirit is stirred to fill out the picture. Chaucer almost never tells us specifically what he means; instead, he leaves us with an open-endedness that invites endless divergent interpretations of his poetry. In what way should we answer the *demande d'amour* of the Knight, or of the Franklin? How unravel the ambiguities of the Prioress—saintly simpleton or irreligious sadist? The Monk, are his opinions good or bad? The Merchant, prosperous or secretly in debt? The Man of Law, legal eagle or pompous dunce whose words alone are wise? And what of the Pardoner, that demiman, whose pardons damn rather than save? The question is the hallmark of Chaucer's craft. As Virginia Woolf says, "Questions press upon him; he asks them, but . . . leaves them unsolved, uncramped by the solution of the moment, and thus fresh for the generations that come after him."[7]

I believe, finally, that Chaucer's poetry achieves its timeless life because it embodies what we today might call a constant of mammalian motivation. Beryl Rowland points out that "those characteristics which are common to most mammals do in fact control human behavior. . . . [T]he motivations of behavior upon which the artist draws in order to achieve the illusion of truth are fundamentally timeless, and as a result, his creation may survive into this century as a recognizable individual."[8] Chaucer is endeared to us not by a humanity that is "unreservedly" of his own time and place[9] but, rather, precisely because he rises above such limitations, as Blake and Dryden and thousands of others have recognized.

Thus, despite varying degrees of resistance on the part of our students, the contributors to this book are unanimously agreed that Chaucer's poetry should be taught. Its truth to universal human reactions, its vivid visuality, and what Donald Howard calls its "artistic inconclusiveness"[10] will without doubt continue to prompt widespread response as the pilgrims "ryden forth hir weye" through the minds of readers yet to come.

But for the present-day undergraduate, that pilgrimage presents problems. Last year a California student lamented with blunt honesty:

> I came into this class with no background in Middle English or Chaucer whatsoever. I think it would help students if *right away* students are introduced to the characters. This would be better than starting off with an explanation of how to pronounce Middle English because from my own experience I could hardly follow the explanation and I didn't feel it was crucial anyways [sic], as I was reading silently to myself in my head. I caught on to words and sentences easy enough, but that didn't really help because I had *no idea* what the *CT* were about. I had a hard time making the characters connect to each other and even to their own characterizations. I actually thought they *were* all truly "worthy" like Chaucer said. I think it would be helpful to explain on the very first day of class that Chaucer never means what he says. I started my readings the first night of class and continued confused until after 3 weeks into class. By that time I had completely changed my mind about the characters and I had to reread the Gen. Prologue all over again to get on the right track. Maybe it is necessary to give a *short* background on Chaucer's life and time, but telling every detail about John of Gaunt, and Chaucer's travels in Italy and France was very boring and hasn't helped me at all. I think pointing out Chaucer's occupations, his travels, who he was influenced by and historical events like the crusades, and the black death would be sufficient. And the most helpful thing I've found and interesting is for the teacher to explain customs, beliefs, folklores, architecture, painting, politics, music and religion and Chaucer's sources and his friends and experiences when they come up in the text.

Had we but world enough and time.

This anonymous *cri de coeur* makes clear, though perhaps inadvertently, the essential difficulties of teaching *The Canterbury Tales* to today's undergraduates. The ambiguity and irony we have to accept as given. For Chaucer, as for Swift, it will always be necessary "to explain on the very first day" that he rarely means what he says—at least not literally. But the other barriers, unique for comprehension of this particular poet, of time, place, and language, we must attempt in various ways to overcome.

Students grasp readily enough Chaucer's historic importance as the first to write literature of any moment in English, and as the "first fyndere of oure faire language," who brought about an influx of coinages from Latin, French, even Yiddish. But for them to realize his artistic accomplishment and understand his poetry, they must somehow be helped to cross a wide temporal gulf and enter his world and see and feel why he is a literary giant, at least the equal of Cervantes and Dickens if not of Shakespeare and Milton (though the latter point is arguable), and why he clearly surpasses Pope and Johnson and Swift and the "Americanists" of the nineteenth and twentieth centuries.

Even if today's struggling instructors do not tell "every detail about John of Gaunt, and Chaucer's travels in Italy," they must, usually within a restricted period of time, convey a wealth of information about Chaucer's life and times. What is a Pardoner? What is a Reeve? Why does the Squire fight in France, the Knight in faraway places? Why shouldn't Madame Eglentyne wear a gold brooch and weep over her pet dogs? Why does Alice despise the Friar? And just who is the "privee theef men clepeth Deeth, / That in this contree al the peple sleeth"? These and an appalling number of other questions must be dealt with if the literal meaning, much less the nuances and significance, of the poetry is to be made comprehensible.

Bertrand Bronson once wrote something about Conrad that seems to me peculiarly applicable to Chaucer as well:

> Great writers do not remain static identities. Their stature is per-
> petually altering; they take on something of the color and ap-
> pearance of every age through which their works travel. The
> reassessment of a great author by a new generation of readers is a
> mutually creative act. It is the duty of every age to find its own
> truth; and in the field of literature, to try to see, without falsifying
> the evidence, what was unnoticed by its predecessors because from
> their stretch of the road it was concealed.

As teachers we are faced with the challenge of enabling our students to see how Chaucer's poetry passes the ultimate test of the world's greatest literature, to see that it says something about human behavior true then, true now, and that it was, indeed, written *sub aspicies eternitatis*. But in leading them to see, we have to be very careful not to falsify the evidence of the moral, social, political, and intellectual milieu of the late fourteenth century, for that milieu shaped the poetry and is itself reflected therein.

Then there is the challenge of the language. A Harvard undergraduate once wrote on an examination: "Chaucer might have been a good enough poet if only he hadn't chosen to write in this filthy Middle English"—overlooking in lordly fashion the fact that the poet could not have chosen modern English, however "cleanly" that might be, which is at least debatable. Chaucer probably did write poetry in Latin and French, but none has ever been found; and we can thank our lucky stars that he chose to entrust his greatest literary accomplishments to English, though it be Middle. So our students must grapple with his language. Interestingly enough, he knew that they would have to, for Chaucer had a clear comprehension of the transitoriness of language and of the fact that his own vernacular was changing. He says as much in *Troilus and Criseyde*: "You know that within a thousand years there is change in form of speech, and words which were once deemed apt and choice now seem to us wondrous quaint and strange; and yet they spoke them thus once, and succeeded as well in love by doing so as men do now." And the very words in which he couched this idea express by their difficulty the idea itself:

> Ye knowe ek that in forme of speche is chaunge
> Withinne a thousand yeer, and wordes tho
> That hadden pris, now wonder nyce and straunge
> Us thinketh hem, and yet thei spake hem so,
> And spedde as wel in love as men now do . . .
>
> (II.22–26).

He realized that our students, and we, would have trouble. But he earnestly prayed that his poetry not be lost. At the end of *Troilus and Criseyde*, he writes of his own little book:

> And for ther is so gret diversite
> In Englissh and in writyng of oure tonge,
> So prey I God that non myswrite the,
> Ne the mysmetre for defaute of tonge.
> And red wherso thow be, or elles songe,
> That thow be understonde, God I biseche!
>
> (V.1793–98).

Chaucer's work is understood; it is loved; and it has a very great deal to say to people of every generation in their turn. For almost six hundred years, readers have experienced Chaucer's characters and their behavior with an instant response, a sudden electric shock of recognition. It is our duty and happiness as teachers of English literature to make such experience possible for students today. It is our challenge to find the means of doing so.

Notes

[1] This passage from Arnold and some of the following quotations are taken from Caroline F. E. Spurgeon, *Five Hundred Years of Chaucer Criticism and Allusion, 1357–1900*, The Chaucer Society, Ser. 2, Nos. 48–50, 52–56, 7 vols. (London: Oxford Univ. Press, 1914–25). For Arnold, see III, 126.

[2] "Dorothy Wellesley to W. B. Yeats," in William R. Crawford, *Bibliography of Chaucer, 1954–63* (Seattle: Univ. of Washington Press, 1967), [p. vii].

[3] From "On Chaucer and Spenser," *Lectures on the English Poets*, Lecture 2, 1818, in J. A. Burrow, ed., *Geoffrey Chaucer* (Middlesex, Eng.: Penguin, 1969), p. 88.

[4] Burrow, p. 87; Spurgeon, I, 54, and II, 105.

[5] Burrow, p. 6.

[6] Spurgeon, II, 10.

[7] Burrow, p. 125.

[8] "Chaucer's Dame Alys: Critics in Blunderland?" in *Studies Presented to Tauno F. Mustanoja on the Occasion of His Sixtieth Birthday, Neuphilologische Mitteilungen*, 73 (1972), 383.

[9] Cf. Albert Friedman, "The Prioress' Tale and Chaucer's Antisemitism," *Chaucer Review*, 9 (1974), 120.

[10] "Literature and Sexuality: Book III of Chaucer's *Troilus*," *Massachusetts Review*, 8 (1967), 455.

Part One

MATERIALS

Joseph Gibaldi

EDITIONS

Introduction

Although instructors are probably loath to admit it, textbook selection determines in a number of different ways the nature and progress of a literature course. Unfortunately, for the various reasons described below, there is at present no standard teaching edition of *The Canterbury Tales*. As one of the contributors to this volume has remarked, "Clearly, a really sound school text is needed."

What we present below is an objective guide to the editions now being used for teaching *The Canterbury Tales*, as reported by participants in the survey of teachers of Chaucer that preceded preparation of this volume. Attention is given to such matters as completeness of text, commentary and notes supplied, and physical format. Included, too, are both favorable and unfavorable comments of instructors who have had experience in using the texts in the classroom. Since instructors must themselves select the edition that is most suitable for their particular pedagogical situation and purposes, we offer no recommendations here but hope instead to supply information that will lead to appropriate text selections.

Chaucer texts seem naturally to fall into four categories—editions of the works of Chaucer, editions of *The Canterbury Tales* alone, dual-language editions and translations, and anthologies. These categories, therefore, determine the organization of the following discussion. (See the List of Works Cited for full bibliographical information for each work.)

Works of Chaucer

For many years F. N. Robinson's edition *The Works of Geoffrey Chaucer* (2nd ed., 1957) served as the standard text for both teaching and scholarship devoted to Chaucer. Time, however, has effectively undermined the preeminent position of the Robinson edition as a teaching text in two important ways: the proliferation of Chaucer scholarship over the more than two decades since the publication of the second edition of Robinson, on the one hand, and the apparent decline in the linguistic awareness and preparation of college students, on the other, have made it difficult for many undergraduate teachers of Chaucer to continue using the Robinson edition.

It is nonetheless incontestable that Robinson is still the most widely used edition of Chaucer's works. Of course, the virtues that recommended the edition at its publication remain: its accuracy, objectivity, and comprehensiveness. It has been described as an edition that is "relatively free of error" and one that "rides no hobby-horse." Robinson's useful introduction includes sections on the life of Chaucer, the canon and chronology of Chaucer's writings, his language and meter, and the text used. The complete *Canterbury Tales* is printed first in the edition and is followed by *The Book of the Duchess, The House of Fame, Anelida and Arcite, The Parliament of Fowls, Boece, Troilus and Criseyde, The Legend of Good Women*, the short poems, *A Treatise on the Astrolabe*, and *The Romaunt of the Rose*. The works are published in a double-column format. No glosses or notes appear on the page.

After the text of Chaucer's works, Robinson presented a relatively modest bibliography—just over one hundred titles—which, of course, takes into account only works published up to 1957. The bibliography is divided into the following topics: general references; life of Chaucer; editions; canon and chronology; literary sources; medieval history, life, and thought; history of Middle English literature; general criticism; language and meter; and dictionaries. A list of abbreviations precedes two separate sections of notes on the text: 234 pages of explanatory notes and a 46-page section of textual notes. A glossary and a list of proper names conclude the book.

Robinson's notes have been praised for being "unusually extensive" and "the most objective comprehensive notes." Many find the glossary "full" and adequate for their teaching needs. The placement of the notes and glossary at the back of the book has, of course, troubled a considerable number of teachers in recent years, but several instructors argue that the separation of text from glosses—if not from explanatory notes—is actually pedagogically advantageous. Some believe that glosses on the page discourage learning and that students learn Middle English vocabulary better when they have to "look it up" every time they fail to remember a word. One advocate of Robinson cogently points out that a glossary following the text gives students the full sense of a word's meaning although she admits that her "most recent students have been having trouble just reading Chaucer" and she is therefore considering using another edition.

Indeed, the many present-day critics of the Robinson edition as a teaching text concur that the edition is very difficult for undergraduates precisely because there are no annotations on the page and there is simply not enough help with the language. As one instructor strongly and succinctly puts it, the edition is "impossible for beginning students because of the arrangement of notes and glossary." Some also criticize the small print used for the book and find the double-column format cluttered.

In addition to the arrangement and design of the book, the second major reason for the decline in the use of Robinson as a classroom text is its out-of-dateness. Many teachers of Chaucer report that they have switched to another edition simply because Robinson is "getting too old." One instructor remarks that he used the edition for some time primarily "for sentimental reasons" but now thinks its scholarship "out-of-date and mostly irrelevant." Another regrets relinquishing Robinson but is unable to justify—"to undergraduate students especially"—the "obsolete notes" and outdated bibliography of the edition.

There are other criticisms of Robinson. The glossary, which some believe satisfactory, others judge "far from perfect" and even "poor." the notes, which some find comprehensive, others think sometimes "fussy and dead-end." It is clear, too, that many instructors use the Robinson edition for reasons of convenience rather than sound pedagogy. More than one Chaucer teacher has candidly remarked, "I'm familiar with it since I did all my Chaucer studies from Robinson." As has been observed before, many teachers are usually less than eager to transfer their marginal notes and comments from one teaching text to another.

But, as a teacher of upper-division English majors correctly states, Robinson is still the "standard quoted edition" and the one students probably will use should they continue their work on Chaucer after the course. Many instructors seem to be coming to the conclusion that Robinson's edition is a "must" for serious students and advanced work, particularly in graduate courses, but that other editions are in truth more helpful for undergraduates. This situation may soon change, however, for a new edition of the works of Chaucer, now in preparation, is being referred to as "Robinson[3]." The work, undertaken by Robert Pratt and others, will be a completely new edition prepared in the "spirit" of the late Professor Robinson. Notes and bibliography will be updated, and one assumes that the new edition will be more attractive physically than the old edition. Houghton Mifflin will again be the publisher; the projected publication date is 1983.

The only edition to match—or even surpass—Robinson's in terms of completeness is John H. Fisher's recently published *The Complete Poetry and Prose of Geoffrey Chaucer* (1977). In fact, the edition is so recent that it is much too early to evaluate its reception by teachers of Chaucer, many of whom readily admit that they have not yet used it although a good number say they plan to test its usefulness in the classroom within the near future.

In addition to all of the works included in Robinson, Fisher's edition also offers *The Equatorie of the Planets*, now widely believed to be Chaucer's work. Fisher provides an introduction to each work and furnishes three brief concluding essays, "The Place of Chaucer," "Chaucer in His Time," and "Chaucer's Language and Versification." The bibliography comprises an impressive 1,570 entries listed under dozens of useful headings and subheadings (see discussion below for its relationship to other Chaucer bibliographies). A glossary (added for the second printing of the book) rounds out the volume.

In terms of design and organization, the Fisher edition consciously aims to be a teaching text. The endsheets of the work (i.e., its inside covers and their facing pages) contain a "Chaucer Chronology" and a guide to the pronunciation of Chaucer's language. All notes and glosses appear at the bottom of the page. The following are typical comments of teachers who favor the Fisher edition: "up-to-date and helpful to students"; "easily readable (good type, same-page glosses)"; "copious notes, attractive format, editorial apparatus, bibliography, not to speak of completeness of Chaucerian corpus"; "well-printed (adequate margins)"; "footnotes are much handier for student use than Robinson's endnotes"; "brighter page and less intimidating for students."

Of course, not everyone has embraced the Fisher edition as the solution to the problem of choosing a suitable classroom text for teaching Chaucer. An advantage to some is a disadvantage to others. Because the work is intended as a classroom text to be priced as inexpensively as possible for a student market and because Chaucer scholarship over the past quarter century has been so abundant, Fisher acknowledges in his preface that he could not make his explanatory notes as all-encompassing as those editions published in a previous generation. Thus, some find his notes only "fairly decent" or "adequate"; others think them "meager" or "incomplete." The linguistic apparatus has similarly been labeled less than complete. As one instructor writes, "Beginning students need a more thoroughly glossed text." Needless to say, those who prefer that the text be separated from the notes find the Fisher edition "critically obtrusive" or believe the placement of the glossary at the bottom of each page an unnecessary crutch that prevents students from learning Middle English vocabulary more quickly.

Two other widely used editions of Chaucer's works are Albert C. Baugh's *Chaucer's Major Poetry* (1963), and E. Talbot Donaldson's *Chaucer's Poetry: An Anthology for the Modern Reader* (2nd ed., 1975). As its title indicates, the Baugh edition omits all of Chaucer's prose, including the two prose treatises in *The Canterbury Tales*: *The Tale of Melibee* and the Parson's Tale. It offers its readers the "critical texts of all of Chaucer's poetry except the *Romaunt of the Rose*, the fragmentary *Anelida and Arcite*, and a few of the short lyrics." Baugh's annotations appear on the same page as the text. His introduction includes information on Chaucer's life and on his language and versification. The edition also has a bibliography (eighty-four items) and a glossary.

The Donaldson edition offers *The Canterbury Tales* (also omitting the prose tales), *Troilus and Criseyde, The Book of the Duchess, The Parliament of Fowls,* the Prologue to *The Legend of Good Women,* the Proem and Invocation to Book I and all of Book II of *The House of Fame,* and a selection of the short poems. The second part of the volume contains about 165 pages of commentary on Chaucer's language (20 pages), life (10 pages), and works (135 pages). Donaldson also presents a table of pronunciation, a glossary, and a bibliography of sixty-two titles. What is distinctive about the editing of this collection is its editor's standardization of Chaucer's spelling in the hope of attaining "the great readability that is possible without sacrificing either the phonological values or the general appearance of Middle English orthography."

The two editions have certain advantages and disadvantages in common. Both are less complete than either Robinson or Fisher; some instructors particularly bemoan the omission of the prose sections of *The Canterbury Tales.* Many choose these editions over Robinson, however, because they are more recent and because each utilizes a format (large type size, single-column texts, footnotes rather than endnotes, and so on) that is easier for students to use. The Baugh edition is praised for its helpful notes and introductions, easily readable notes, and "excellent glossary." One Chaucer teacher lauds its "compassionate glossing of lexical and syntactical difficulties." It should be pointed out, however, that Baugh, persuaded by the arguments of Robert A. Pratt and others, has incorporated into his arrangement of the tales the so-called "Bradshaw shift," which is discussed below in the description of Pratt's edition, *The Tales of Canterbury.*

Donaldson's edition is also thought to be useful as an undergraduate text with accessible notes, glossary, and commentary. One advocate of the edition praises it for its "tasteful but full annotation, and a commentary that offers the student some purchase on the tone and value of each poem"—in short, he thinks it "a genuinely supportive edition" that helps students to overcome their "initial resistance to so foreign a text." Donaldson's commentary is frequently cited as the edition's greatest virtue. One scholar thinks Donaldson's the "best critical discussion" of Chaucer's works available; another calls Donaldson's annotations and commentary "irreplaceable." From a pedagogical point of view, Chaucer teachers have remarked that it contains "good, workable, sane teachable material" and, in general, that it is helpful for students "to begin with Donaldson's

commentary as a way into the poetry." In comparing Baugh and Donaldson, an instructor who has used both editions reports that Donaldson's
text is the easier to read and his essays "provocative." "Baugh's text,"
though, he writes, "is more extensive, has a better glossary, and more
extensive notes."

Critics of the Donaldson edition point to what they deem a neglect of
certain important background materials, claiming that its notes give less
explanatory information than students need and that some basic information (e.g., sources) must be supplied by the instructor. Needless to say,
whereas some praise Donaldson's standardization of Chaucer's spelling,
others condemn it. And, of course, those scholars—apparently very few in
number—who disagree with Donaldson's interpretations may find, as one
person did, that he has "an ax to grind" in the edition.

The Canterbury Tales

Instructors who teach only *The Canterbury Tales* often select as classroom texts editions containing just the masterwork itself. One widely used
edition is Robert A. Pratt's *The Tales of Canterbury* (1966). The edition
includes an introduction, a bibliography of fifty-seven entries, all the tales,
twenty-one excellent illustrations, a section of variant readings, a basic
glossary, and on both endsheets a useful map depicting the route of the
journey to Canterbury. Glosses are in the margins to the right of the text;
substantive notes are at the bottom of the page. Those who use the Pratt
edition praise it for completeness of text, convenience of notation, and
inclusion of helpful reading materials (e.g., map and illustrations).

Pratt arranges the tales according to the order suggested by Henry
Bradshaw and not, as Robinson and most other editors of Chaucer have
arranged them, according to the order of the best manuscripts (including
the Ellesmere) that have come down. Basing his arrangement on certain
geographical references in the work, Pratt thus inserts the tales of Robinson's Fragment VII—Shipman, Prioress, *Sir Thopas, Melibee*, Monk, and
Nun's Priest—between the tales of the Man of Law (Fragment II) and
the Wife of Bath (beginning of Fragment III). (For a full statement of
the argument in favor of the arrangement, see Robert A. Pratt, "The
Order of *The Canterbury Tales*," *PMLA*, 66 [1951], 1141–67.) Anyone
familiar with Chaucer scholarship is aware that the so-called "Bradshaw
shift" has been a subject of considerable controversy for decades. Needless to say, those who deem the Bradshaw shift indefensible or hold any
such rearrangement of the tales unacceptable reject the Pratt edition out
of hand. "I refuse to use a text which incorporates the Bradshaw shift" is

not an uncommon remark, but those who advocate the Bradshaw shift and those who are not primarily concerned with the arrangement of the tales may find Pratt's edition a viable classroom text.

When cost is an important factor in the choice of a text for teaching *The Canterbury Tales*, instructors may turn to one of a number of fine editions published in paperback. A. C. Cawley's edition (rev. ed., 1975) follows Robinson closely and presents *The Canterbury Tales* "complete and unabridged." Cawley includes a short introduction, a selected bibliography, and brief appendixes dealing with pronunciation, grammar, and versification. Cawley's glosses appear in the margins, his explanatory notes at the bottom of the page.

The price of Donald R. Howard's justly popular *The Canterbury Tales: A Selection* (1969) is about half that of the Cawley edition. Howard's edition includes the following selections: the General Prologue, the Knight's Tale, the Miller's Prologue and Tale, the Reeve's Prologue and Tale, the Shipman's Tale, the Prioress' Prologue and Tale, the Prologue and *Tale of Sir Thopas*, the Monk's Prologue, the Nun's Priest's Prologue and Tale, the Wife of Bath's Tale, the Clerk's Prologue and Epilogue, the Merchant's Prologue and Tale, the Franklin's Prologue and Tale, the Pardoner's Prologue and Tale, the Parson's Prologue, and Chaucer's Retraction. Howard also offers a useful introduction, a discussion of the pronunciation of Chaucer's English (which includes a discography of recordings of Middle English readings), a Chaucer chronology, a selected bibliography, and a glossary of basic words.

Daniel Cook's The Canterbury Tales *of Geoffrey Chaucer* (1961) presents fewer selections than either Cawley or Howard: the General Prologue and the tales of the Miller, Wife of Bath, Pardoner, Prioress, and Nun's Priest. (Omitted tales are briefly summarized.) The edition does boast a very readable format, however. The text of the poems is printed in relatively large type only on left-hand pages; annotations are given on facing right-hand pages. There is an introduction but no bibliography.

Also available in paperback is Charles W. Dunn's *A Chaucer Reader: Selections from* The Canterbury Tales (1952). Dunn's selections include the General Prologue, Prioress' Tale, *Tale of Sir Thopas*, excerpts from the Monk's Tale, Nun's Priest's Tale, Wife of Bath's Tale, Franklin's Tale, Pardoner's Tale, and Chaucer's Prayer. Curiously enough, three tales— those of the Reeve, Clerk, and Canon's Yeoman—appear at the end of the book in prose translation. Completely missing from the edition are such often taught tales as those of the Knight, Miller, and Merchant. As in Cook's edition, omitted tales are summarized. Dunn's edition has an introduction, a selected bibliography, and an appendix on the pronunciation of Chaucer's language. Glosses are printed in the right margins; explanatory comments appear as footnotes.

Dual-Language Editions and Translations

The question of whether to teach *The Canterbury Tales* in the original Middle English or in modern English translation is by far the most controversial and sensitive matter to be touched upon in this volume. Opinions on the subject are apt to be strongly, decisively, and, occasionally, colorfully expressed. In response to a query concerning the teaching of *The Canterbury Tales* in modern English translation, the following responses were among those received from teachers who advocate teaching the work strictly in Middle English:

> I do not believe that *The Canterbury Tales* should be taught in modernized versions.

> I certainly do not teach *The Canterbury Tales* in modern English translation. I object to those who do.

> Never!

> Never! "Poetry is what evaporates in translation," as Frost said. In translation, Chaucer seems trivial intellectually and flabby prosodically!

> Never, never, never: an offensive condescension to both Chaucer and the students.

> People who teach *The Canterbury Tales* in modern translation are to be pitied.

> Horrors!

Those who teach *The Canterbury Tales*, or a part of it, in modern English translation argue that their students, particularly in lower-division survey courses for non–English majors, come without the adequate linguistic preparation or the sufficient motivation needed to study the work in its original language. As one teacher sadly remarks, "Freshmen at [name of school] would not be interested in Chaucerian Middle English." Such teachers are often content merely to acquaint their students, however superficially, with the author and his poem. Even those teachers inclined to teaching Chaucer only in Middle English find that survey courses, particularly of the *"Beowulf* to Robert Burns" or *"Beowulf* to Virginia Woolf" variety, just do not allow enough time to do so.

Solutions to the problem—short of teaching *The Canterbury Tales* exclusively in modern English translation—vary. Some instructors have their students read a translation first, then study the work in class in the original language. Others, because of the limits of time, read the General Prologue in Middle English and then switch to a translation for the tales or read some of the tales in Middle English and some in translation. Still others encourage or tacitly permit students to use a translation as an aid to reading the work in Middle English. One teacher remarks, "I don't forbid their using a trot as a way of getting into the original."

Teachers who find that their students do need linguistic assistance report success in using one of the dual-language paperback editions of *The Canterbury Tales* now available. Perhaps the most popular dual-language edition now being used is A. Kent Hieatt and Constance Hieatt's reasonably priced *Canterbury Tales/Tales of Canterbury* (1964). The volume contains the General Prologue and the tales of the Knight, Miller, Wife of Bath, Merchant, Franklin, Pardoner, Prioress, and Nun's Priest. The Middle English text appears on left-hand pages with modern English translation on facing pages. The editors' introduction covers biographical, critical, and linguistic matters, but there are no substantive notes in the edition. A glossary is printed at the end of the book; glossed words are indicated by an asterisk in the text.

Another dual-language edition used is Vincent F. Hopper's *Chaucer's Canterbury Tales (Selected): An Interlinear Translation* (1948). After a brief introduction, the edition offers the General Prologue and the tales of the Knight, Prioress, Nun's Priest, Pardoner, Wife of Bath, and Franklin. There are about a half dozen pages of notes in the back of the book. Not all teachers, however, like the idea of working with an interlinear translation. Some find it distracting and thus impossible to use in teaching; some find that students tend to read only the lines containing the translation.

The most widely used translations of *The Canterbury Tales* are those of Nevill Coghill (1952) and Robert M. Lumiansky (1948), both of which, interestingly enough, adopt the Bradshaw shift. Coghill offers a verse translation that follows Chaucer's metrical forms and rhyme schemes. It includes almost the complete works; only the two prose tales, *The Tale of Melibee* and the Parson's Tale, are given in synopsis form. There is an introduction, and notes are printed in the back of the book. Teachers who use the Coghill translation praise such qualities as its generous selection of tales, readability, accuracy, fidelity to its source, and liveliness—"its breezy, racy rhymed lines," in the words of one instructor who argues thus for the superiority of a verse to a prose translation: "I like students to get some idea of the concision and wit of Chaucer's rhymed lines—and they can't do that in prose."

Lumiansky's is a modern English prose translation. The volume includes a brief preface by Mark Van Doren as well as an introduction by the translator. It contains all of *The Canterbury Tales* except for the Prioress' Tale, *The Tale of Melibee*, the Monk's Tale, and the Parson's Tale, each of which is summarized. Although no notes are given, the inclusion, at the end of the book, of the General Prologue and the Nun's Priest's Tale in Middle English makes the volume pedagogically useful. A teacher who favors the Lumiansky translation finds it the most appropriate for use by nonmajors, "for whom narrative rather than language" is of primary importance, in his opinion. In comparing prose and verse translations, one instructor comments that Lumiansky succeeds in giving "the texture and color" of Chaucer's poem: "Even though he's translating from poetry to prose, the language is much closer to Chaucer's own than, say, Coghill's versified modernization." One strong advocate of teaching Chaucer only in Middle English suggests Lumiansky to students "if they feel compelled to consult a translation" for this reason: "At least that way they aren't misled into thinking that they are reading poetry."

Another translation sometimes used is that found in *The Portable Chaucer*, edited and translated by Theodore Morrison (rev. ed., 1975). Like Coghill's this is a poetic translation that attempts to reproduce Chaucer's verse forms and rhyme schemes. The volume's selections from *The Canterbury Tales*, arranged according to Bradshaw's order, include the General Prologue; the tales related by the Knight, the Miller, the Reeve, the Prioress, Chaucer the Pilgrim (*Sir Thopas* only), the Nun's Priest, the Wife of Bath, the Friar, the Summoner, the Merchant, the Franklin, and the Pardoner; and, finally, Chaucer's Retraction. The edition has rounded out the section with prologues and epilogues to other tales and with summaries of omitted tales. In addition to selections from *The Canterbury Tales*, this volume contains translations of *Troilus and Criseyde*, selections from other longer works (*The Book of the Duchess*, *The House of Fame*, *The Parliament of Fowls*, and *The Legend of Good Women*), and four short poems. One wonders, though, why any teacher who would take the time and effort to teach the minor works would wish to teach them in translation rather than in the original Middle English. The Morrison volume offers an introduction and a selected bibliography but no notes.

Anthologies

In choosing textbooks for survey courses that cover long periods of time and several literary periods (e.g., the ubiquitous *"Beowulf* to Burns" course), the instructor must decide between using a number of paperbacks and using an anthology of literary works. (Often, there is no choice, because a department requires a certain text.) The advantages of using a paperback edition of *The Canterbury Tales*, or any other work for that matter, rather than an anthology are obvious. As one person notes, the use of paperbacks "permits the teacher to choose what he thinks is important rather than what the anthologist thinks is important." Teachers are quick to point out that anthologies "don't have enough of Chaucer usually" and that they present only "snippets of text" and "frequently the wrong excerpts." "I would have selected some other tales," and "It doesn't offer enough flexibility so that I can combine tales I'd like to discuss together" are common complaints concerning anthologies.

But there are definite economic and pedagogical advantages to using an anthology. "An anthology is cheaper than a set of paperbacks and won't go out of print," one Chaucer scholar remarks. Another adds, "Only one book to carry." An anthology also helps the teacher and student place a writer in a certain "historical/literary context" and "in direct relationship to other poets of his period."

All reports indicate that the anthology most frequently used in English literature survey courses is the two-volume *Norton Anthology of English Literature* (4th ed., 1979), the general editor of which is M. H. Abrams. The Middles Ages section of Volume I is edited by E. Talbot Donaldson. The selections from *The Canterbury Tales*, printed in Middle English, include the General Prologue, Miller's Tale, Wife of Bath's Tale, Franklin's Tale, Pardoner's Tale, Nun's Priest's Tale, Prologue to the Parson's Tale, and Chaucer's Retraction. The Chaucer section also includes excerpts from *The Parliament of Fowls* and six short poems. There is an introduction, and biographical and bibliographical information is printed in the back of the book. Glosses appear in the margin, substantive comments in footnotes.

In spite of the usual complaints concerning anthologies (e.g., quarrels with the selection of tales), comments on the *Norton Anthology of English Literature* and its medieval section in particular are generally positive, although by no means universally so. Many teachers consider the *Norton Anthology* "the best anthology available." To some, the section on the Middle Ages is "excellent"; to others, it is "variable" in quality. A number of teachers think the introduction, notes, and glosses are good or suited to the needs of survey students or at least adequate. But some find that the supplementary aids are "not quite adequate" in helping students read Chaucer in the original with little preparation. "Too few words are glossed," says a teacher who has used the section; "Reading pace is thus slowed."

One advantage of the medieval section in the opinion of some Chaucer teachers is that Donaldson is the editor. (Nevertheless, critics of Donaldson's standardization of Middle English spelling in his edition of *The Canterbury Tales* complain about his continued application of that practice in the *Norton Anthology*.) The price and convenience also make the anthology attractive for classroom use. Most important of all, some instructors feel, the anthology gives students "sufficient exposure to the Middle English text" to allow them to become at least "marginally competent readers." An unfortunate aspect in the design of this particular anthology (and in the design of other Norton anthologies) is that little visual support is given to students in their initial efforts to tackle the Middle English verse. One instructor laments, "The density of format (crowded pages, etc.) makes the Middle English harder to read for some (many?) students."

Other multivolume anthologies commonly used in survey courses are the *Oxford Anthology of English Literature*, edited by Frank Kermode and John Hollander (1973); *Major British Writers*, edited by G. B. Harrison (1959); and *British Literature*, edited by Hazelton Spencer, Beverly J. Layman, and David Ferry (1974). As might be expected, the selections from *The Canterbury Tales* appear in the first volume of each.

The medieval literature section of the *Oxford Anthology* was prepared by J. B. Trapp, who has included the General Prologue to *The Canterbury Tales*, the Miller's Tale, the Nun's Priest's Tale, the Wife of Bath's Tale, the Franklin's Tale, the Pardoner's Tale, and Chaucer's Retraction— all in Middle English. A unique feature of the section is Trapp's inclusion of supplementary readings intended to enhance the reader's understanding and appreciation of some of the tales. Thus, the edition prints in conjunction with the Nun's Priest's Tale two excerpts from a fifteenth-century bestiary and an excerpt from William Caxton's *History of Reynard the Fox*, and along with the Wife of Bath's Tale an appropriate excerpt from the *Gesta Romanorum*. Some teachers, however, would prefer that the space allotted to the supplementary readings be used instead to include another of Chaucer's tales, such as the Knight's Tale or the Clerk's Tale. In addition to selections from *The Canterbury Tales*, the section also contains selections from *The Parliament of Fowls*, *Troilus and Criseyde*, and *The Legend of Good Women* as well as a few short poems. To assist the student reader, the section offers an introduction, useful illustrations, marginal glosses, and explanatory footnotes.

Edited by Charles W. Dunn, *The Canterbury Tales* selections in the *Major British Writers* anthology begin with the General Prologue, conclude with Chaucer's Prayer, and contain the tales of the Pardoner, Prioress, Miller, Wife of Bath, Clerk, Franklin, and Nun's Priest. Dunn also offers a brief introduction, a note on Chaucer's language, suggestions for further reading, and commentary in footnotes.

Like those in the *Oxford Anthology of English Literature* and *Major British Writers*, the Chaucer selections in the *British Literature* anthology appear in the original Middle English. The Chaucer section, edited by Hazelton Spencer and Beverly Layman, offers five tales—those of the Miller, Wife of Bath, Franklin, Pardoner, and Nun's Priest—as well as four of the shorter poems. An introduction precedes the selections; notes appear at the foot of the page.

A final anthology widely used at the undergraduate level, particularly in world literature survey courses, and thus deserving mention here is the two-volume Norton anthology *World Masterpieces* (4th ed., 1979), the general editor of which is Maynard Mack. The Middle Ages section in Volume I of the anthology is edited by John C. McGalliard, who offers an introduction to the period as well as biographical and bibliographical information on each author in the section. Selected from *The Canterbury Tales* are the General Prologue, Miller's Tale, Pardoner's Tale, and Nun's Priest's Tale, all in the verse translation by Theodore Morrison. Notes are printed at the bottom of the page, and, as a useful pedagogical aid, the first eighteen lines of the General Prologue are also included in Middle English. Despite this last feature of the section, which allows the teacher at least to introduce students to Chaucer's language, some teachers are unhappy with the decision of the anthology's editors to use a translation of *The Canterbury Tales*. Such teachers think the practice "an unnecessary 'simplification' for college students," who may well have read and enjoyed a portion of the work in Middle English in high school. The obvious advantage of the *World Masterpieces* anthology, as teachers of world literature survey courses continue to argue, is that it does collect major texts in a single inexpensive book and does place Chaucer and his literary masterpieces properly in the context of international literature—for the anthology contains, in addition to *The Canterbury Tales*, not only *Sir Gawain and the Green Knight*, *Everyman*, and excerpts from *Paradise Lost* but also selections from the Bible, Classical Greek and Roman literature, Augustine's *Confessions*, Dante's *Divine Comedy*, and Boccaccio's *Decameron*.

REQUIRED AND RECOMMENDED STUDENT READINGS

The works that teachers most often require their students to read in conjunction with *The Canterbury Tales* and other works of Chaucer are primarily the materials classified as the poet's "sources." All these are hap-

pily available in translation in paperbound editions. (Consult the List of
Works Cited for detailed publication information.)

In addition to the Bible, Boethius' *Consolation of Philosophy* and the
Roman de la Rose by Guillaume de Lorris and Jean de Meun are most
often required. Other diverse influences on Chaucer that are also brought
to the attention of students include those of courtly love, Christian theology, and popular medieval literature—as reflected, respectively, in Andreas Capellanus' *Art of Courtly Love*, Augustine's *On Christian Doctrine*
and *Confessions*, the recent anthology *The Literary Context of Chaucer's
Fabliaux: Texts and Translations* prepared by Larry D. Benson and Theodore M. Andersson, and T. H. White's *Bestiary*. Boccaccio's *Decameron*
and Dante's *Divine Comedy* are frequently introduced to indicate the
Italian influence; Vergil's *Aeneid* and Ovid's *Metamorphoses* and *Art of
Love*, the classical influence. Often, in lieu of requiring the complete texts
of Chaucer's sources, teachers use as a classroom textbook, side by side
with Chaucer's poetry, the convenient paperback edition of Robert P.
Miller's *Chaucer: Sources and Backgrounds* (1977).

Teachers of *The Canterbury Tales* also regularly require or recommend
scholarly and critical works to supplement their students' reading and
understanding of Chaucer. The brief survey that follows includes the
works most often cited; all titles given below are currently available in
paperbound editions. (For a more extensive treatment of these works, see
the section "The Instructor's Library.")

Many students are required to read a biography of the poet, usually
John Gardner's *The Life and Times of Chaucer* (1977) or Marchette
Chute's *Geoffrey Chaucer of England* (1946), or a monograph devoted
to the "life and works"—e.g., D. S. Brewer's *Chaucer* (3rd ed., 1973) or
Chaucer in His Time (1963), Muriel Bowden's *Reader's Guide to Geoffrey
Chaucer* (1964), Nevill Coghill's *The Poet Chaucer* (2nd ed., 1968), and
the useful *An Introduction to Chaucer* (1965) by Maurice Hussey, A. C.
Spearing, and James Winney.

Some instructors ask their classes to use the collection of introductory
essays specifically intended for a student audience, *Geoffrey Chaucer*
(1975), edited by George Economou. Graduate students and English
majors are often required to have on hand as reference guides Beryl Rowland's *Companion to Chaucer Studies* (2nd ed., 1979) and the selected
bibliography, *Chaucer* (2nd ed., 1977), compiled by A. C. Baugh.

Required and recommended works dealing with the intellectual, artistic,
historical, social, and economic background to Chaucer's poetry vary considerably and depend on individual teacher preference. C. S. Lewis' *The
Discarded Image* (1964) is widely used although Johan Huizinga's *The
Waning of the Middle Ages* (1924) and Robert Ackerman's *Backgrounds*

to Medieval English Literature (1966) are frequently suggested, as are Eileen Power's *Medieval People* (10th ed., 1963) and *Medieval Women* (1975), Barbara Tuchman's *A Distant Mirror* (1978), R. W. Southern's *The Making of the Middle Ages* (1953), G. G. Coulton's *Medieval Panorama* (1949), A. R. Myers' *England in the Late Middle Ages* (1966), G. M. Trevelyan's *England in the Age of Wycliffe* (1900), and Emile Mâle's *Gothic Image* (1913).

The anthologies of criticism that are clearly required and recommended most frequently are Richard J. Schoeck and Jerome Taylor's *Chaucer Criticism* (1960) and Edward C. Wagenknecht's *Chaucer: Modern Essays in Criticism* (1959). Of course, students are guided to all major critical works and linguistic studies (see appropriate discussion in the section "The Instructor's Library" below). Among this group, the five that are placed in students' hands most often are E. Talbot Donaldson's *Speaking of Chaucer* (1970), D. W. Robertson's *Preface to Chaucer* (1962), Charles Muscatine's *Chaucer and the French Tradition* (1957), Donald R. Howard's *The Idea of the* Canterbury Tales (1976), and Bernard Huppé's *A Reading of the* Canterbury Tales (1964).

AIDS TO TEACHING

The subject of audiovisual aids in the teaching of literature is still a controversial one. Some instructors simply dismiss the topic with comments such as "I have absolutely no truck with this stuff," or "That's all Sesame Street stuff, and a sub-intellectual retreat from words." The majority of college teachers, though, seem to feel that recordings, illustrations, and films, if properly used, can enhance the learning experience. For teachers of Chaucer, a useful guide to these aids is Frederick E. Danker's "Teaching Medieval English Literature: Texts, Recordings, and Techniques," published in *College English* (1970). For a listing of bibliographies and indexes to such material, see Lorrayne Y. Baird's *A Bibliography of Chaucer, 1963–1973* (1977), pages 245–58. The discography in Donald Howard's paperback edition of *The Canterbury Tales* evaluates several recordings.

A surprising number of instructors prepare their own tapes of readings of *The Canterbury Tales*. These tapes are often played in class or left in the school's language laboratory or audiovisual center for independent student use. In some schools it is even possible for students to have access to such tapes over the telephone.

In addition, professionally produced records are often used as a corrective or complement to the instructor's own reading of Middle English. Recordings that provide a valuable overview of the development of the

English language are Diane Bornstein's three-record set, A *History of the English Language* (1973), and the two-record A *Thousand Years of English Pronunciation* (1963) prepared by Helge Kökeritz. The famous Swedish linguist also recorded selections from the General Prologue, the Wife of Bath's Prologue, the Prioress' Tale, and *Troilus and Criseyde* on one side of the 1957 recording, Beowulf *and Chaucer Readings.*

Even more helpful for classroom use is Niel K. Snortum and Daniel Knapp's three-record anthology, *The Sounds of Chaucer's English,* issued in 1967 by the National Council of Teachers of English. The recording contains excerpts from the General Prologue, Knight's Tale, Reeve's Tale, Wife of Bath's Tale, Pardoner's Tale, Nun's Priest's Tale, and some of the minor works. A script of the record is included in the accompanying fifty-two page pamphlet, additional copies of which may be purchased separately from NCTE at a nominal cost.

Several other recordings in Middle English of selections from *The Canterbury Tales* deserve mention for teaching purposes. In the 1960s, J. B. Bessinger, Jr., made two recordings of Chaucer readings for Caedmon Records. The first has excerpts from the General Prologue, the Prologue to the Parson's Tale, and Chaucer's Retraction; the second contains the Miller's Tale and the Reeve's Tale. During the same decade, that great popularizer of Chaucer, Nevill Coghill, also helped make a number of recordings of *The Canterbury Tales.* Chief among these are his readings on Argo Records of the General Prologue and Nun's Priest's Tale (with Norman Davis, Lena Davis, and John Burrow) and on Spoken Arts Records of the General Prologue and Pardoner's Tale (with Norman Davis). Caemon produced a 1952 recording of the Pardoner's Tale and the Nun's Priest's Tale read in Middle English by Robert Ross, and a similar repertory appears on Victor L. Kaplan's *Chaucer: Readings from the* Canterbury Tales (1966) on Folkways/Scholastic Records, a recording that includes selections from the General Prologue, Pardoner's Tale, and Nun's Priest's Tale as well as two of the minor poems.

Those instructors who teach *The Canterbury Tales* in modern English translation may be interested in two Caedmon recordings that boast the talents of three celebrated British actors. The first record, issued in 1961, presents Peggy Ashcroft reading the Wife of Bath's Tale in the J. U. Nicolson translation. On the other record, produced in 1962, Michael MacLiammoir and Stanley Holloway read, respectively, the Pardoner's Tale and the Miller's Tale in Theodore Morrison's translation.

An even more popular approach to Chaucer is found in Capitol Records' original cast recording of the London and Broadway musical version of *The Canterbury Tales.* The ubiquitous Coghill wrote the lively lyrics and coauthored with Martin Starkie the book for the show; Richard

Hill and John Hawkins composed the music. For more serious musical compositions based on Chaucer's poetry, see Darius Milhaud's *Cantate sur des poèmes de Chaucer*, a 1963 composition for mixed choir and orchestra, and *Four Fragments from Caunterbury Tales* (1958) by the American composer Lester Trimble. The Trimble work is available on Columbia Records.

Instructors who wish to give students a sense of the music of Chaucer's time have a wealth of material from which to choose. The catalogs of the Musical Heritage Society, Nonesuch Records, and other recording companies that specialize in early music offer a number of excellent titles. Carl Orff's well-known *Carmina Burana* presents another modern musical setting of medieval verse.

Visual aids related to Chaucer and his age are also being increasingly introduced into the classroom. Some instructors find this an effective means to present the social and artistic background of the period; others wish through illustrative material to introduce their students to medieval iconography and Gothic style—the unique mixture in medieval art of symbolism and realism. The form of such instruction ranges from the use of self-made films and slides to the showing of professionally produced films. Colleagues in art departments are sometimes invited to lecture. Not uncommon, too, are class visits to libraries and museums to see medieval books (e.g., breviaries, prayer books, editions of the Bible) and works of art (paintings, sculpture, stained-glass windows, reliquaries, and so on).

Several publications contain valuable visual material that many instructors find helpful in teaching *The Canterbury Tales*. For example, the famous Ellesmere pilgrim portraits are included in the pamphlet *The Ellesmere Manuscript of Chaucer's* Canterbury Tales, prepared by Herbert C. Schulz and published by the Huntington Library. (One may also obtain slides of the pilgrim portraits directly from the Huntington Library in San Marino, California.) An interesting complement to the Ellesmere portraits is William Blake's depiction of the group in his engraving *Pilgrimage to Canterbury*, which was the poet-artist's largest plate. Roger S. Loomis' *A Mirror of Chaucer's World* (179 illustrations) and Maurice Hussey's *Chaucer's World* (125 plates) are excellent aids for helping students visualize the life and times of Chaucer. Examples of medieval iconography may be found in D. W. Robertson's *Preface to Chaucer* (118 illustrations) and John V. Fleming's *The* Roman de la Rose: *A Study in Allegory and Iconography* (42 illustrations).

In addition, many fine films are available to teachers of Chaucer. The programs "The Great Thaw" and "Romance and Reality" in Kenneth Clark's eye-filling BBC series *Civilisation* provide a wide-ranging background to the age. The Encyclopedia Britannica's production entitled *The*

Medieval Mind is also a fine introduction to the period. A good number of instructors report that they use Mary Kirby and Naomi Diamond's first-rate 1969 film, *From Every Shires Ende: The World of Chaucer's Pilgrims* (see Donald Howard's comments in his essay in Part Two). An older film that still finds its way into many classrooms is the Encyclopedia Britannica's thirty-minute *Chaucer's England* (1958), which includes a presentation of the Pardoner's Tale. The University of Michigan Television Center has produced film versions of ten of the tales, each thirty minutes in length: the Pardoner's Tale, Knight's Tale, Shipman's Tale, Prioress' Tale, Wife of Bath's Tale, Friar's Tale, Clerk's Tale, Merchant's Tale, Franklin's Tale, and, in a single film, both the Nun's Priest's Tale and Manciple's Tale. Of interest, too, are two useful sound filmstrips prepared by Educational Audio-Visual entitled *The Time, the Life, the Works of Geoffrey Chaucer* (1968) and *Chaucer's Canterbury Pilgrims* (1970), the latter of which contains the Ellesmere portraits.

Finally, Ingmar Bergman's *Seventh Seal* (1956), a profoundly modern re-creation of the age, may be studied in conjunction with Chaucer with illuminating results. An English translation of the script was published in 1960. More directly related to the works of Chaucer is Pier Paolo Pasolini's radical interpretation of Chaucer in the film *Racconti di Canterbury* (1971).

THE INSTRUCTOR'S LIBRARY

Introduction

Proper preparation for teaching *The Canterbury Tales* is the product of a serious commitment to scholarship and pedagogy. No bibliography, no essay, no book, no course can replace the wide reading and the critical and creative thinking required to teach the poetry of Chaucer successfully.

What we will attempt here is to present something of a checklist of the essential reference works, background material, and critical and linguistic studies that the teacher of Chaucer, ideally, should not only know about but also have access to for future consultation. The choice of works has been guided by the titles most frequently mentioned in the survey of teachers of *The Canterbury Tales* as "essential."

Because of the exigencies of space, we have for the most part suggested works that have been published in book form. These include, of course, important essays and articles that have appeared in book-length collections. Needless to say, many important journal articles have not yet found their way into collections of criticism and commentary. Some of these articles are mentioned here and in the essays in the second part of the volume; many, however, have of necessity been omitted. The reader, therefore, is encouraged to go beyond the limits of this volume to explore bibliographies and reviews of criticism to seek out the major journal articles devoted to *The Canterbury Tales*. The nonspecialist reader is also urged to keep up with current Chaucer scholarship by consulting recent numbers of the *Chaucer Review: A Journal of Medieval Studies and Literary Criticism* (Robert W. Frank, Jr., Editor, Pennsylvania State University, University Park, Pennsylvania 16802) and *Studies in the Age of Chaucer: Yearbook of the New Chaucer Society* (Roy J. Pearcy, Editor, University of Oklahoma, Norman, Oklahoma 73019), as well as other journals, like *PMLA*, that frequently publish articles on the poet of *The Canterbury Tales*. Both teachers and scholars of Chaucer will also be interested in the *Chaucer Newsletter*, published twice yearly by the New Chaucer Society, and *RALPH: A Newspaper for Undergraduate Teaching: Medieval and Renaissance Humanities*. The *Chaucer Newsletter*, edited by Donald M. Rose, J. Lane Goodall, and Lynne H. Levy (University of Oklahoma, Norman, Oklahoma 73019) is "devoted to the publication of factual information: reports on the major research projects in medieval literature and language; reports on experiments in teaching methodology and pedagogy in classroom instruction of Chaucer and other courses in medieval studies; the announcement of the program for the International Congress; the list of current members in the Society; and the report of the Annual Chaucer Lecture delivered at the International Congress." *RALPH*, edited by Robert V. Graybill and Robert L. Kendrick (Department of English, Central Missouri State University, Warrensburg, Missouri 64093), publishes "contributions from teachers of medieval and Renaissance art, history, literature, music, philosophy, and theology on topics such as the following: (1) unusual course syllabi; (2) available resources: media materials, films, recordings, paperbacks, etc.; (3) calendars of regional events; (4) bibliographies of readily available materials; (5) continuing surveys of medieval and Renaissance materials read or used by students and teachers."

Finally, the reader will find in the pages below few extended evaluations and elaborate descriptive summaries. This path has been chosen partly because Beryl Rowland's *Companion to Chaucer Studies* (2nd ed., 1979) makes such an approach unnecessary and partly because this author strongly wishes that the present volume not be used as a substitute for actual confrontation with the works themselves. In short, the aim of this section is to isolate "essential" works for present and prospective teachers of Chaucer.

Reference Works

The field of Chaucer studies has been well served by modern bibliographers. The pioneering efforts of Caroline F. E. Spurgeon, *Five Hundred Years of Chaucer Criticism and Allusion, 1357–1900* (1925), and Eleanor P. Hammond, *Chaucer: A Bibliographical Manual* (1908), were followed by Dudley David Griffith, *Bibliography of Chaucer, 1908–1953* (1955), William R. Crawford, *Bibliography of Chaucer, 1954–63* (1967), and Lorrayne Y. Baird, *A Bibliography of Chaucer, 1964–1973* (1977). The bibliography in John H. Fisher's edition *The Complete Poetry and Prose of Geoffrey Chaucer* (1977) is also intended as a continuation of the Crawford bibliography, for it includes all relevant books and articles published between 1964 and 1974 as well as some two hundred important titles published earlier than 1964 and later than 1974. Albert C. Baugh's *Chaucer* (2nd ed., 1977) is a selected bibliography "intended for graduate and advanced students who desire a convenient guide to scholarship on Chaucer and related subjects." Containing some 3,200 entries, this bibliography is not annotated, but its compiler has placed asterisks next to works of "special importance." For more recent scholarship, scholars and teachers must consult the annual bibliographies published in the *Chaucer Review* and the *MLA International Bibliography*.

Among biographical and historical materials, the exhaustive compilation *Chaucer Life-Records* (1966), edited by Martin M. Crow and Clair C. Olson, contains all contemporary documents relating to Chaucer's life and activities. A useful companion work is the earlier *Chaucer's World* (1948), compiled by Edith Rickert and edited by Olson and Crow, which includes excerpts from medieval records, documents, and literature that help bring to life the age and its concerns.

Linguistic aids begin with the *Oxford English Dictionary (OED)*. The excellent *Middle English Dictionary (MED)*, edited by Hans Kurath, Sherman M. Kuhn, and others, modeled on the *OED*, has been published since 1952 by the University of Michigan Press in a series of fascicles, each about 128 pages in length. As of this writing, the letters A through N have appeared in print in fifty-four fascicles. When completed, the MED will contain approximately ten thousand pages.

Fortunately, John S. P. Tatlock and Arthur Kennedy's *A Concordance to the Complete Works of Geoffrey Chaucer* has been available since 1927. Another reference work of long-standing merit is *Sources and Analogues of Chaucer's* Canterbury Tales (1941), edited by William F. Bryan and Germaine Dempster. Robert P. Miller's more recent *Chaucer: Sources and Backgrounds* (1977) may be used as a classroom text. Its "textual supplements" include selections drawn from works that Chaucer is known to have used and works that represent significant attitudes toward matters with which Chaucer concerned himself. Unlike the Bryan and Dempster volume, which gives sources and analogues in their original language, Miller offers translations of such authors as Ovid, Macrobius, Jerome, Augustine, Boethius, Andreas Capellanus, Jacobus da Voragine, Dante, Petrarch, and Boccaccio.

Other reference works of interest to Chaucer scholars and teachers include *A Chaucer Gazetteer* (1961) by Francis P. Magoun, Jr., which lists and discusses all geographical names used by Chaucer; Bert Dillon's *A Chaucer Dictionary: Proper Names and Allusions, Excluding Place Names* (1974); and A. F. Scott's *Who's Who in Chaucer* (1974). Of great value is the *Companion to Chaucer Studies* (2nd ed., 1979), edited by Beryl Rowland. This fine review of Chaucer scholarship, to which we will refer at various points below, includes some two dozen essays on such topics as "Chaucer the Man," "Chaucer and Fourteenth-Century Scholarship," "Chaucer's Prosody," "Chaucer's Imagery," "The French Influence on Chaucer," "The Italian Influence on Chaucer," "The Influence of the Classics on Chaucer," "The General Prologue," "The Tales of Romance," and "The Fabliaux." Its contributors include such well-known Chaucerians as Albert C. Baugh, Robert O. Payne, Robert M. Jordan, Paul G. Ruggiers, Richard L. Hoffman, Chauncey Wood, Charles A. Owen, J. Burke Severs, D. S. Brewer, Robert P. Miller, Rossell Hope Robbins, D. W. Robertson, and John H. Fisher. The new edition also includes a convenient index, a feature strangely missing from the first edition.

Finally, two large-scale Chaucer projects should be mentioned here: the Chaucer Library and the Variorum Chaucer. Progress reports on both projects appeared in the summer 1979 issue of the *Chaucer Newsletter*. The purpose of the Chaucer Library is to present, with accompanying English translations, "the works that Chaucer knew, translated, or made use of in his writings in versions that are as close as possible to those in existence, circulating, and being read by him and his contemporaries." Since 1970 the Chaucer Library, now under the general editorship of Robert E. Lewis, has had a formal publishing agreement with the University of Georgia Press. Two volumes have appeared in the series: Paul M. Clogan's edition of Statius' *Achilleid* (1968) and Robert E. Lewis' edition of Lotario dei Segni's treatise, *De Miseria Condicionis Humanae* (1978). Sigmund Eisner's edition of Nicholas of Lynn's *Kalendarium* is scheduled to be the next published volume in the Chaucer Library. Included among the many other volumes now in progress are editions of the Chaucerian text of Boccaccio's *Teseida*, the *Summa de Virtutibus Abbreviata*, and sixteen medieval alchemical texts.

The Variorum Chaucer intends to publish a series of facsimiles of the principal manuscripts on which the Chaucer textual tradition is based and a series of commentaries on each of Chaucer's works, drawn from a survey of almost six hundred years of scholarship. Volumes in the series are published under the general editorship of Paul G. Ruggiers by the University of Oklahoma Press. In 1979, the first Variorum Chaucer volume was published: *A Facsimile of the Hengwrt Manuscript of the* Canterbury Tales. Next to be published in the series is the two-volume *A Commentary on the Minor Poems of Geoffrey Chaucer*, edited by George Pace and Alfred David. Other volumes in the final stages of preparation include commentaries on the General Prologue (Charles Moorman), Manciple's Tale (Donald Baker), Physician's Tale (Helen Corsa), *Tale of Sir Thopas* (Thomas Garbáty), and Miller's Tale (Thomas Ross).

Background Studies

Useful studies that attempt to show Chaucer in the context of his time and place include G. G. Coulton's *Chaucer and His England* (5th ed., 1930), D. W. Robertson's *Chaucer's London* (1968), and A. R. Myers' *London in the Age of Chaucer* (1972). Similar works that offer a wealth of visual materials are *A Mirror of Chaucer's World* (1965), by Roger S. Loomis, and *Chaucer's World: A Pictorial Companion* (1968), by Maurice Hussey.

Among the more general studies of the period, Barbara Tuchman's recent bestseller, *A Distant Mirror: The Calamitous Fourteenth Century* (1978), despite certain minor errors regarding Chaucer and his works, makes excellent reading. Noteworthy are R. W. Southern's *The Making of the Middle Ages* (1953) and James W. Thompson's *History of the Middle Ages, 300–1500* (1931). Perhaps the best single-volume history of England during the age of Chaucer is May McKisack's *The Fourteenth Century, 1307–1399* (1959), the fifth volume in the Oxford History of England series. Also of considerable assistance are the collection *The Reign of Richard II: Essays in Honour of May McKisack*, edited by F. R. H. DuBoulay and Caroline Barron, and such studies as A. R. Myers' *England in the Late Middle Ages* (1966), Austin L. Poole's *Medieval England* (rev. ed., 1958), Coulton's *Medieval Panorama: The English Scene from Conquest to Reformation* (1949), and G. M. Trevelyan's *England in the Age of Wycliffe* (1900). *The Pastons and Their England* (2nd ed., 1932) by H. S. Bennett and *The Court of Richard II* (1968) by Gervase Mathew are two more specialized but highly respected studies.

There are many very helpful works that treat the social and economic conditions of the age. A good starting point is perhaps a comprehensive study such as Trevelyan's *English Social History: A Survey of Six Centuries* (3rd ed., 1946) or James W. Thompson's *Economic and Social History of the Middle Ages* (1928). Significant among more recent medieval scholarship are Marc Bloch's *Feudal Society* (1961), Christopher Brooke's *The Structure of Medieval Society* (1971), and Eileen Power's *Medieval People* (10th ed., 1963) and *Medieval Women* (1975). Worthy of perusal, too, are Mary E. Whitmore's *Medieval English Domestic Life and Amusements in the Works of Chaucer* (1937) and *A History of Everyday Things in England* (1918) by Marjorie and C. H. B. Quennell, the first volume of which covers the years 1066 to 1499. Of special interest to scholars and teachers of *The Canterbury Tales* are such works as J. J. Jusserand, *English Wayfaring Life in the Middle Ages* (4th ed., 1888); D. J. Hall, *English Mediaeval Pilgrimage* (1965); Jonathan Sumption, *Pilgrimage: An Image of Medieval Religion* (1975); Johannes Nohl, *The Black Death: A Chronicle of the Plague* (1926); George Deaux, *The Black Death, 1347* (1969); Philip Ziegler, *The Black Death* (1969); Sidney Painter, *French Chivalry: Chivalric Ideas and Practices in Mediaeval France* (1940); Cecil Roth, *A History of the Jews in England* (3rd ed., 1964); Lynn White, Jr., *Medieval Technology and Social Change* (1962) and *Medieval Religion and Technology: Collected Essays* (1978); W. E. Mead, *The English Medieval Feast* (2nd ed., 1967); and Madeleine P. Cosman, *Fabulous Feasts: Medieval Cookery and Ceremony* (1977).

A good grasp of the economic picture of the age is offered in two companion volumes: *The Commercial Revolution of the Middle Ages, 950–1350* (1971), by Robert S. Lopez, and *The Economy of Early Renaissance Europe, 1300–1460* (1969), by Harry A. Miskimin. Students of medieval England need also to consult, among other studies, *The Merchant Class of Medieval London, 1300–1500* (1948), by Sylvia L. Thrupp, and M. M. Postan's *Medieval Economy and Society: An Economic History of Britain in the Middle Ages* (1972).

The Medieval Library (1957), by James W. Thompson and others, offers a helpful glimpse into what was being read in the Middle Ages. Yet, for literary scholars perhaps the best introduction to medieval thought is C. S. Lewis' *The Discarded Image* (1964), which is in fact subtitled *An Introduction to Medieval and Renaissance Thought*. Johan Huizinga's *The Waning of the Middle Ages* (1924) is another now-classic study dealing with the intellectual life of the period. The following are among the many works that give a comprehensive view of medieval philosophy and theology: Gordon Leff, *Medieval Thought: St. Augustine to Ockham* (1958); Armand Maurer, *Medieval Philosophy* (1962); Henry O. Taylor, *The Medieval Mind* (4th ed., 1962); David Knowles, *The Evolution of*

Medieval Thought (1964); Heiko A. Oberman, *The Harvest of Medieval Theology* (rev. ed., 1967); and John V. Fleming, *An Introduction to the Franciscan Literature of the Middle Ages* (1977).

Thanks in large part to George Lyman Kittredge's identification of the "Marriage Debate" theme in *The Canterbury Tales*, Chaucer's attitude toward love and marriage has attracted considerable scholarly attention. A fine introduction to the subject is provided in the papers by Norman E. Eliason, Edmund Reiss, R. E. Kaske, James I. Wimsatt, and others in *Chaucer the Love Poet* (1973), edited by Jerome Mitchell and William Provost, a volume containing the proceedings of a conference on that topic held at the University of Georgia. Another volume that contains papers from a relevant conference is *The Meaning of Courtly Love* (1968), edited by F. X. Newman and including essays by D. W. Robertson, Charles S. Singleton, and W. T. H. Jackson, among others. Also to be consulted are *In Pursuit of Perfection: Courtly Love in Medieval Literature* (1975), edited by Joan M. Ferrante and George D. Economou; Roger Boase's *The Origin and Meaning of Courtly Love: A Critical Study of European Scholarship* (1977); C. S. Lewis' chapter on Chaucer in *The Allegory of Love* (1936); and Henry A. Kelly's specialized treatment of "clandestine marriage" in his *Love and Marriage in the Age of Chaucer* (1975).

Scholarship devoted to Chaucer and medieval science has increased in recent times to such a degree that a chapter on the subject (written by Chauncey Wood) is included in Rowland's *Companion to Chaucer Studies*. The two major books on Chaucer and contemporary science are W. C. Curry's *Chaucer and the Mediaeval Sciences* (2nd ed., 1960) and Wood's own *Chaucer and the Country of the Stars: Poetic Uses of Astrological Imagery* (1970).

Similarly, interest in Chaucer's imagery and his use of allegory has prompted among scholars a corresponding interest in the visual arts of the age. Studies by Emile Mâle and Erwin Panofsky are probably the most widely read and cited by historians and scholars of medieval art. Fortunately, two of Mâle's indispensable works are now available in English translation: *The Gothic Image: Religious Art in France of the Thirteenth Century* (1913) and *Religious Art in France: The Twelfth Century* (1978). Equally invaluable for the student of medieval and Renaissance art is Panofsky's *Studies in Iconology* (1939). More recent works of considerable interest include *The Living Theatre of Medieval Art* (1967), by Henry Kraus, and *Literature and Art in the Middle Ages* (1970), by Frederick Pickering.

Literary histories can usually be relied on to set authors in their proper literary context. For Chaucer, such histories include H. S. Bennett's *Chau-*

cer and the Fifteenth Century (1947), the first part of Volume II of the Oxford History of English Literature; the second volume of the Cambridge History of English Literature, *The End of the Middle Ages* (1908), edited by A. W. Ward and A. R. Waller, particularly the essay "Chaucer," by George Saintsbury (pp. 156–96); and *The Age of Chaucer* (1954), edited by Boris Ford, Volume I of the Pelican Guide to English Literature. Two works that help illuminate Chaucer's relationship to his native tradition are John A. Burrow's *Ricardian Poetry: Chaucer, Gower, Langland, and the* Gawain *Poet* (1971) and A. C. Spearing's *Criticism and Medieval Poetry* (1972). Presenting a broader, more international background for the study of Chaucer are H. J. Chaytor's *From Script to Print: An Introduction to Medieval Vernacular Literature* (1945) and Robert W. Ackerman's *Backgrounds to Medieval English Literature* (1966). A very useful presentation of two sides of the debate over the value of patristic exegesis for understanding Chaucer's poetry is contained in *Critical Approaches to Medieval Literature* (1960), edited by Dorothy Bethurum. The Bethurum volume offers six informative and stimulating essays. Three specifically concern the subject of patristic exegesis in criticism of medieval literature—E. Talbot Donaldson taking the opposition, R. E. Kaske the defense, and Charles Donahue presenting a summation. The remaining essays treat "Folklore, Myth, and Ritual" (Francis L. Utley), "Classical Fable and English Poetry in the Fourteenth Century" (Richard H. Green), and "Chaucer and Dante" (Howard Schless). Two other landmark studies necessary for placing Chaucer against the artistic, esthetic, and intellectual backdrop of his age are Ernst R. Curtius' classic *European Literature and the Latin Middle Ages* (trans. Willard R. Trask, 1953) and D. W. Robertson's *A Preface to Chaucer: Studies in Medieval Perspectives* (1962), the latter doubtless the most controversial and influential Chaucer study published in this generation.

For Chaucer's relationship with classical and continental literature, it is helpful to begin with the three essays in Rowland's *Companion to Chaucer Studies* on the influence on Chaucer of French literature (Haldeen Braddy, pp. 143–59), Italian literature (Paul Ruggiers, pp. 160–84), and the classics (Richard L. Hoffman, pp. 185–201). Five book-length studies that treat Chaucer's indebtedness to Roman literature are Hoffman's *Ovid and the* Canterbury Tales (1967), John M. Fyler's *Chaucer and Ovid* (1979), Edgar F. Shannon's *Chaucer and the Roman Poets* (1929), Howard R. Patch's *The Tradition of the Goddess Fortuna in Roman Literature and in the Transitional Period* (1922), and George D. Economou's *The Goddess Natura in Medieval Literature* (1972). In exploring the French influence on Chaucer, we have, first and foremost, Charles Muscatine's masterly and highly respected *Chaucer and the French Tradition*

(1957). Of use, too, are Larry D. Benson and Theodore M. Andersson's *The Literary Context of Chaucer's Fabliaux: Texts and Translations* (1971), Thomas D. Cooke's *The Old French and Chaucerian Fabliaux: A Study of Their Comic Climax* (1978), Janette Richardson's *"Blameth nat me": A Study of Imagery in Chaucer's Fabliaux* (1970), and Dean S. Fansler's *Chaucer and the* Roman de la Rose (1914). There is at present a great need for a comprehensive study of Chaucer and the Italian tradition. Unfortunately, the only book-length work in the area is the very outdated *The Indebtedness of Chaucer's Works to the Italian Works of Boccaccio* (1916), by Hubertis M. Cummings. See Robert J. Clements and Joseph Gibaldi's *Anatomy of the Novella: The European Tale Collection from Boccaccio and Chaucer to Cervantes* (1977) for an attempt to treat *The Canterbury Tales* in the context of the European novella tradition.

Finally, other studies useful for perceiving Chaucer's indebtedness or contribution to different literary genres, traditions, and forms include Jill Mann's *Chaucer and the Medieval Estates Satire: The Literature of Social Classes and the General Prologue to the* Canterbury Tales (1973); G. R. Owst's *Preaching in Medieval England: An Introduction to Sermon Manuscripts of the Period, c. 1350–1450* (1926) and *Literature and Pulpit in Medieval England* (1966); Beverly Boyd's *Chaucer and the Liturgy* (1967); Ann S. Haskell's *Essays on Chaucer's Saints* (1976); Mortimer J. Donovan's *The Breton Lay: A Guide to Varieties* (1969); Maurice Valency's *In Praise of Love: An Introduction to the Love Poetry of the Renaissance* (1961); Rosemond Tuve's *Allegorical Imagery: Some Mediaeval Books and Their Posterity* (1966); James J. Murphy's *Medieval Eloquence: Studies in the Theory and Practice of Medieval Rhetoric* (1978); and George A. Kennedy's *Classical Rhetoric and Its Christian and Secular Traditions from Ancient to Modern Times* (1980). Of significant use and interest, too, are Stith Thompson's *The Folk Tale* (1951)—as well as his monumental *Motif-Index of Folk Literature* (rev. ed., 1966)—T. H. White's *The Bestiary: A Book of Beasts* (1954); Michael Curley's translation (1979) of the early bestiary *Physiologus*; and Beryl Rowland's *Blind Beasts: Chaucer's Animal World* (1971), *Animals with Human Faces: A Guide to Animal Symbolism* (1973), and *Birds with Human Souls: A Guide to Bird Symbolism* (1978).

Critical and Linguistic Studies

Several biographies and monographs offer a one-volume introduction to the study of Chaucer. Marchette Chute's biography, *Geoffrey Chaucer of England* (1946), read by countless students since its publication, soon may be replaced in popularity by the recent best seller, *The Life and Times of Chaucer* (1977), a fictionalized account by the novelist-critic John Gardner. Among the several commendable monographs providing general introductions to the life and works of the poet are the following: Derek Brewer's *Chaucer and His World* (1978), *Chaucer* (3rd ed., 1973), and *Chaucer in His Time* (1963); S. S. Hussey's *Chaucer: An Introduction* (1971); Nevill Coghill's *The Poet Chaucer* (2nd ed., 1968) and *Geoffrey Chaucer* (rev. ed., 1969); M. W. Grose's *Chaucer* (1969); *An Introduction to Chaucer* (1965), by Maurice Hussey, A. C. Spearing, and James Winney; Muriel Bowden's *Reader's Guide to Geoffrey Chaucer* (1964); and the venerable *A Chaucer Handbook* (2nd ed., 1947), by Robert D. French.

The extensive notes in the Chaucer editions by W. W. Skeat (2nd ed., 1899), John M. Manly and Edith Rickert (1940), and F. N. Robinson (2nd ed., 1957) all give useful cross sections of critical thought up to their dates of publication. Similar samplings of Chaucer criticism may be obtained from one or more of the various anthologies of critical essays devoted to the works of Chaucer. Three such collections were published around 1960. The most widely used of the three is probably *Chaucer Criticism* (1960), edited by Richard J. Schoeck and Jerome Taylor, published in two volumes—the first on *The Canterbury Tales,* the second on *Troilus and Criseyde* and the minor poems. In addition to appreciations by E. E. Cummings and Henry Wadsworth Longfellow, the first volume contains sixteen critical essays, including several classic papers, by scholars such as E. Talbot Donaldson ("Chaucer the Pilgrim"), Ralph Baldwin ("The Unity of the *Canterbury Tales*"), George Lyman Kittredge ("Chaucer's Discussion of Marriage"), J. S. P. Tatlock, Robert P. Miller, Charles Muscatine, John M. Manly, and Roger S. Loomis. The volume *Discussions of the* Canterbury Tales (1961), edited by Charles A. Owen, Jr., offers early comment on Chaucer by Spenser, Milton, Dryden, Coleridge, and Arnold, as well as sixteen modern essays by, among others, Donaldson, Baldwin, Kittredge, Muscatine, E. M. W. Tillyard, Kemp Malone, Bertrand H. Bronson, Morton W. Bloomfield, John L. Lowes, and Owen himself. Edward C. Wagenknecht's *Chaucer: Modern Essays in Criticism* (1959), with twenty-six essays, contains pieces by many of the same critics—Manly, Muscatine, Kittredge, Owen, Bronson, Tatlock—as well as by other Chaucerians such as J. Leslie Hotson, Walter C. Curry, Paul G. Ruggiers, and Howard R. Patch.

Other critical collections include *Chaucer and His Contemporaries* (1968), edited by Helaine Newstead and now unfortunately out of print, and A. C. Cawley's *Chaucer's Mind and Art* (1969), published in Edinburgh. The Newstead volume offered two "contemporary voices" (Boccaccio's description of the plague in Florence and Froissart's account of the Peasants' Revolt), several background essays (e.g., C. S. Lewis on imagination and thought in the Middle Ages, Lynn White on technology and invention in the age, and Gervase Mathew on marriage and courtly love in fourteenth-century England), and critical articles by Bronson, Coghill, Donaldson, Brewer, William W. Lawrence, and others. The ten essays in Cawley's collection are grouped under the rubrics "Chaucer and the Modern Mind," "Chaucer and the Medieval Mind," and "Aspects of Chaucer's Art." Cawley, Brewer, Donald R. Howard, Francis L. Utley, Janette Richardson, and Dorothy Bethurum Loomis are among the scholars represented in the volume.

Over the past two decades, Derek Brewer has compiled two anthologies of modern Chaucer criticism—*Chaucer and Chaucerians: Critical Studies in Middle English Literature* (1966) and *Geoffrey Chaucer* (1974)—both of which were published by American university presses. The former, containing nine essays, presents the work of Muscatine, Brewer, Coghill, Derek Pearsall, and others; the latter offers twelve essays by such scholars as Donaldson, James I. Wimsatt, Peter Dronke and Jill Mann, V. A. Kolve, and Larry D. Benson.

Special mention must be made of Brewer's *Chaucer: The Critical Heritage* (1978) and George Economou's *Geoffrey Chaucer* (1975). Published in two volumes, *Chaucer: The Critical Heritage* is a collection of commentary on Chaucer from 1385 to 1933. In the first volume, the comments of Gower, Lydgate, Skelton, Spenser, Sidney, Pepys, Dryden, Pope, Johnson, Wordsworth, Byron, Blake, and Coleridge are among the 103 excerpts reproduced. The fifty-two authors excerpted in the second volume include Emerson, Thoreau, Ruskin, James Russell Lowell, Frederick J. Furnivall, Arnold, Hopkins, Swinburne, Kittredge, Pound, Aldous Huxley, Virginia Woolf, C. S. Lewis, G. K. Chesterton, and T. S. Eliot. The Economou volume contains original essays intended to introduce students to Chaucer and his poetry. Authors of the useful and very readable essays include Emerson Brown, Jr., Robert W. Hanning, and Esther C. Quinn.

Finally, a number of *Festschriften* also merit mention here because they reflect recent trends in not only Chaucer criticism but also medieval scholarship in general. These include *Studies in Medieval Literature* (1961), edited by MacEdward Leach; *Chaucer und seine Zeit: Symposion für Walter F. Schirmer* (1968), edited by Arno Esch; *The Learned and the Lewd: Studies in Chaucer and Medieval Literature* (1974), edited by Larry D. Benson; and *Chaucer and Middle English Studies in Honour of Rossell Hope Robbins* (1974), edited by Beryl Rowland.

When asked to compile for novice teachers and nonspecialists a list of essential critical studies, Chaucer scholars and teachers tend to cite more frequently than other titles two works already mentioned: D. W. Robertson's *A Preface to Chaucer* (1962) and Charles Muscatine's *Chaucer and the French Tradition* (1957). Among works published before 1960 that continue to attract the attention of Chaucerians are, in addition to Muscatine, George Lyman Kittredge's *Chaucer and His Poetry* (1915), Robert M. Lumiansky's *Of Sondry Folk: The Dramatic Principles in the* Canterbury Tales (1955), John M. Manly's *Some New Light on Chaucer* (1926), Ralph Baldwin's *The Unity of the* Canterbury Tales (1955), and John L. Lowes' *Geoffrey Chaucer and the Development of His Genius* (1934).

Many critical studies devoted to Chaucer were published during the 1960s. Those that scholars and teachers appear to consult most often include, besides Robertson's *Preface*, Robert O. Payne's *The Key of Remembrance: A Study of Chaucer's Poetics* (1963), Muriel Bowden's *A Commentary on the General Prologue to the* Canterbury Tales (2nd ed., 1967), Bernard F. Huppé's *A Reading of the* Canterbury Tales (1964), Paul G. Ruggiers' *The Art of the* Canterbury Tales (1965), Robert M. Jordan's *Chaucer and the Shape of Creation: The Aesthetic Possibilities of Inorganic Structure* (1967), and Trevor Whittock's *A Reading of the* Canterbury Tales (1968).

It is doubtless too early to determine which studies published in the 1970s will prove of lasting value, but the two works that seem to have elicited the most critical enthusiasm are E. Talbot Donaldson's *Speaking of Chaucer* (1970) and Donald R. Howard's *The Idea of the* Canterbury Tales (1976).

Many other titles may be recommended to the nonspecialist. The List of Works Cited at the back of this volume contains the titles of dozens of critical works mentioned by participants in our survey of teachers and scholars of Chaucer. To gain a sense of the trends and directions in recent Chaucer scholarship, one might consult the following articles: Beryl Rowland, "Contemporary Chaucer Criticism," in *English*, 22 (1973); and Florence H. Ridley, "The State of Chaucer Studies: A Brief Survey," in *Studies in the Age of Chaucer*, 1 (1979).

Similarly, for a review of linguistic scholarship devoted to Chaucer, one should peruse Tauno F. Mustanoja's essay "Chaucer's Prosody" in Rowland's *Companion to Chaucer Studies* (pp. 65–94). An excellent introduction to the language of Chaucer's time is provided in *A History of the English Language* (3rd ed., 1978), by Albert C. Baugh and Thomas Cable. Two standard linguistic studies with which Chaucer teachers and students should be familiar are Bernhard ten Brink's *The Language and Metre of Chaucer* (1901) and Helge Kökeritz' *A Guide to Chaucer's*

Pronunciation (1961). Also informative and useful is Paull F. Baum's discussion of meter, prosody, and rhythm in *Chaucer's Verse* (1961), as is the collection *New Views on Chaucer: Essays in Generative Criticism* (1973), edited by William C. Johnson and Loren C. Gruber. Among more recent book-length linguistic studies are Ian Robinson's *Chaucer's Prosody* (1971), Norman E. Eliason's *The Language of Chaucer's Poetry: An Appraisal of the Verse, Style, and Structure* (1972), and Ralph W. Elliot's *Chaucer's English* (1974).

Part Two

APPROACHES

INTRODUCTION

The following essays illustrate how fifteen experienced Chaucer instructors approach their teaching of *The Canterbury Tales*. The essays represent something of a cross section of pedagogical philosophies espoused and techniques employed by teachers in the United States and Canada who devote entire courses or portions of courses to teaching Chaucer.

It will be noted at once that most of the essayists are trained and published Chaucerians—many eminent in their field—who regularly teach courses solely on Chaucer or *The Canterbury Tales*. Although this is by no means the way in which most North American students encounter Chaucer, a full two-thirds or more of this part of the volume is allotted to Chaucer specialists simply because they have much more experience in teaching *The Canterbury Tales* than do the nonspecialists. They have thought about the subject more, have attempted a wider diversity of approaches, and, therefore, have more to impart than those of us who teach the work primarily as a part of a larger survey course. All the essayists, however, are concerned with the teaching of Chaucer's poetry.

The section begins with an essay by John H. Fisher, who reminds us, among other things, that any literature course centers on the confrontation of student with text and that the teacher's chief role is as mediator between the two. Next, Thomas J. Garbáty, Donald R. Howard, Emerson

Brown, Jr., and Mary J. Carruthers offer general overviews of their Chaucer courses. Robert M. Jordan, William Provost, Terrie Curran, and Thomas W. Ross outline more specific approaches. The next three essays deal with teaching *The Canterbury Tales* as part of courses for non-majors. Michael D. West and Stephen R. Portch discuss their approaches in the English literature survey course at, respectively, a four-year and a two-year undergraduate school; and Susan Schibanoff describes her more specialized comparative course on women in medieval literature. The final section, on backgrounds of *The Canterbury Tales*, includes three essays: D. W. Robertson's survey of the many fields of knowledge that must be brought to bear on Chaucer's poetry to convey its rich complexity; Ernest N. Kaulbach's description of his Tradition of Western Literature course; and Julia Bolton Holloway's account of her seminar The Medieval Pilgrimage.

Limitations of space prevent us from including sustained treatment of the many other English, comparative literature, and interdisciplinary courses in which Chaucer is prominently featured. These would include, for example, courses devoted to genre (e.g., The Medieval Romance, The Romance Narrative, The Novella, Satire, Short Fiction), period (e.g., Medieval English Literature, The Middle Ages), and theme (e.g., The Hero in Literature, The Dream Vision in Literature).

Although the essays were all written independently of one another, the reader will nonetheless discern in them collectively an informative discussion of the major issues and problems confronting the teacher of *The Canterbury Tales*. John Fisher rightly remarks that Chaucer's writings do not lend themselves to study by monolithic approaches. Still, instructors lend a conscious or unconscious focus to every individual course or unit on *The Canterbury Tales*. Fisher himself is interested in the narrative voices in the poem. Robert Jordan gives his course a rhetorical and structural emphasis. The "Boethian unity" of *The Canterbury Tales* attracts William Provost. Thomas Ross stresses Chaucer's language, while D. W. Robertson, Terrie Curran, and Michael West, all in very different ways, stress the cultural context. Ernest Kaulbach sees Chaucer as "scholiast and etymologizer," and, following the nature of their particular courses, Susan Schibanoff concerns herself with Chaucer's depiction of women, and Julia Holloway concentrates on the pilgrimage metaphor in *The Canterbury Tales*.

The organization of each course or unit also differs from instructor to instructor. The syllabuses appended to some of the essays below graphically document how some of the essayists organize their courses. As readers will note, some instructors begin with the language of *The Canterbury Tales*, others with the historical or literary background. Another approach is to start immediately with the poetry itself and let linguistic and historical considerations follow. Thomas Garbáty prefers to teach the minor works as an introduction to the art and thought of *The Canterbury Tales*. Most Chaucer teachers, using either the Ellesmere or Bradshaw arrangement of the tales, work their way from the General Prologue through the tales to Chaucer's Retraction. Donald Howard and Robert Jordan are among those who discuss the Parson's Tale early in the course to give students a structural overview of the whole work at the outset. The historical nature of most survey courses encourages a chronological organization of such courses although here, too, there are interesting variations.

Two crucial areas that all teachers of Chaucer must encounter are the poet's language and the cultural context of his work. The contributors to the volume offer several different techniques for teaching Middle English. Thomas Ross's discussion of his use of the International Phonetic Alphabet in teaching Chaucer's language is the most sustained treatment of the subject. But others also describe their approaches to teaching Middle English, including the use of recordings and tapes, daily oral readings by the instructor, and considerable student recitation. (Some readers may be surprised at the apparently widespread use of memorization in teaching the language of *The Canterbury Tales*.) All teachers of Chaucer agree on the importance of introducing students to the cultural context of the *Tales*, but methods are never identical. D. W. Robertson urges extensive outside reading; Mary Carruthers assigns a few background books; Emerson Brown introduces the cultural context through lecture and distribution of a wealth of supplementary material. John Fisher and Thomas Garbáty are among those contributors who touch on methods of incorporating the works of scholars into classroom study.

Of significant interest, too, in these essays are the pedagogical techniques variously employed in teaching *The Canterbury Tales*. On the one hand, Donald Howard advocates instruction almost totally through lecture. On the other, Stephen Portch, teaching nonmajors, actively encourages class discussion and student involvement. Thomas Garbáty and others consciously, even systematically, alternate lecture with discussion. Terrie Curran fosters student participation through the assignment of oral background reports. A common pedagogical technique is the use of supplementary material or "handouts" supplied by the instructor (see particularly Emerson Brown and Thomas Ross). Handouts sometimes provide students with reading guidelines that not only assist them in their out-of-class assignments but also prepare them for the next day's discussion (see especially Portch). Fisher, Garbáty, Howard, and Carruthers are among the many who make use of audiovisual aids. (Note, however, that their methods of doing so differ quite markedly. For instance, Carruthers shows students the Ellesmere portraits early in the course whereas Garbáty uses the portraits as an effective conclusion to his course.) The dedication of many a Chaucer teacher also extends to activities outside the classroom that are usually of a social as well as an intellectual nature. Chaucer seems to stimulate more such activities than does any other English author. In the essays below, extracurricular efforts range from Emerson Brown's Tuesday Afternoon Chaucer Society to Terrie Curran's annual campus-wide medieval feast.

We turn, finally, to the matter of testing and evaluation. Our survey of Chaucer teachers generally indicates traditional practices in this area. Research papers and examinations (midterm and/or final) that combine identification questions, translation exercises, and essays are common. One or two interesting trends are discernible. Many instructors, it would seem, are inclining toward a number of short papers or reports rather than a single extended paper and toward frequent quizzes to supplement comprehensive exams. There also appears to be an increasing emphasis on creative assignments intended to enhance the student's understanding and appreciation of Chaucer and his age (see especially Curran and Portch).

The essays that follow, therefore, are presented more to raise important questions than to answer them. What gives them unity and coherence is not just the common issues they treat but also the energy and love that their authors continue unselfishly to devote to their study and teaching of Chaucer.

JG

THE STUDENT AS READER OF CHAUCER

SCALA CHAUCERIENSIS

John H. Fisher

The ideas put forward by proponents of the transactional theory of literary criticism have helped me to understand the reactions of my students to the reading of Chaucer. For example, in her recent book, *The Reader, the Text, the Poem* (1978), Louise Rosenblatt drew together a good deal of recent critical and psychological thinking to argue that there is no poem until the reader becomes actively involved. The "text" (which was of such concern to critics of the 1940s and 1950s) is merely

> the printed signs in their capacity to serve as symbols. . . . The poem must be thought of as an event in time. It is not an objective or ideal entity. It happens during a coming-together, a compenetration, of a reader and a text. The reader brings to the text his past experience and present personality. Under the magnetism of the ordered symbols of the text, he marshalls his resources and crystallizes out of the stuff of memory, thought, and feeling a new order, a new experience, which he sees as the poem. (p. 12)

What experience, memory, and personality does a twenty-year-old reader from a middle-class family, educated in a public high school in the United States, bring to the reading of poetry intended for an English court audience in the fourteenth century?

39

For many years the New Critics enabled us to bypass this question by insisting that the text should not be taught in the context of either author or reader. It was the formal expression that mattered, the internal resonances and dissonances. In the sense that, until the 1930s, English literature had been taught as acculturation to English cultural history, viewed as the precursor of the cultural history of the United States, the New Critical declaration of independence from matters outside the text may have been useful—at least it is understandable. But this approach cut the study of English literature off from its roots, and by the 1960s the result became evident. English literature is no longer considered an indispensable subject in the "core curriculums" of either high school or college, and when elected it is usually taught as "masterpieces of literary expression" (like the works of Homer or Dante) instead of as an introduction to the student's own cultural background.

This "masterpiece" philosophy presents a problem for the "transactional" reading of English literature because the student brings to the recreation of the poem experience and personality quite different from those envisaged by the author. Walter Ong's brilliant "The Writer's Audience Is Always a Fiction" in *PMLA* (1975) speaks of the mask that the reader of a written message must assume in order to respond properly to the writer's message. In order for the transaction to be successful, the mask assumed by the reader must accommodate itself to the mask assumed by the narrator. The voice and techniques employed by the *oral* narrator speaking to an immediate collective audience are very different from those needed by the *literary* narrator speaking to an abstract individual reader. It has taken centuries for the literary narrator's technique to develop, and each generation of readers must learn anew to recognize and respond to the signals. Ong uses the opening lines of Hemingway's *A Farewell to Arms* to illustrate the intimate relationship assumed by the narrator and shared by the reader:

> In the late summer of that year, we lived in a house in a village that looked across the river and the plain to the mountains. In the bed of the river there were pebbles and boulders, dry and white in the sun, and the water was clear and swiftly moving and blue in the channels.

Ong points out how the writing conveys the assumption that the reader already knows what year, what plain, and what mountains. The scene is treated as recalled—as shared. The you-and-me effect is achieved largely by the use of the demonstrative and the article: "*that* year," "*the* river," "*the* plain," "*the* mountains." In distancing their objects, both *that* and *the* tend to bring together the speaker and the one spoken to. They implement the shared relationship that the reader experiences in Hemingway's novels.

Ong sees this intimate relationship as the end result of a long development in written narrative. Classical rhetoric details devices that the oral narrator uses to direct the attention of an immediate collective audience. Such devices play on mob psychology. It has taken centuries for the literary narrator to develop other techniques for addressing the disembodied individual reader. One of the earliest devices for instructing the reader how to react was the introduction (as in Dante and the *Roman de la Rose*) of the persona narrator, who seldom occurs in oral narrative. Another is the frame story, through whose links the writer can signal the reader how to react to the individual tales.

In my classes I have often compared the opening lines of *A Farewell to Arms* with the opening lines of the General Prologue as an example of the continuity of tone and technique, the way in which, by using very concrete details, the author directs the attention of the reader through a universalized description. It would appear that as he wrote the opening lines of *A Farewell to Arms*, Hemingway had in the well of his unconscious the opening lines of the General Prologue:

> Whan that Aprill with his shoures soote
> The droghte of March hath perced to the roote,
> And bathed every veyne in swich licour
> Of which vertu engendred is the flour . . .
>   Bifil that in that seson on a day
> In Southwerk at the Tabard as I lay . . .

The word *that*, by which Hemingway helps signal the shared nature of the experience of "*that* year," is in Chaucer merely an adverbial complement—"Whan *that* Aprill." The second *that* in "Bifil that in *that* seson" refers not to a shared experience but to the spring season mentioned above; it does not ask the reader to share the memory of a specific spring. Yet, "Southwerk" and "*the* Tabard" invite the same shared relationship as "*a* village" and "*the* river."

It says much for the continuity of the literary (or empathic) experience that modern readers get as much out of the General Prologue as they do, and progressively more as they grow familiar with the idiom and the allusions. One reason is that by adopting the persona, Chaucer has already made the transition from addressing a mass "audience" to addressing an individual "reader." Authors near to the oral tradition keep the persona first-person (I-Dante or I-Geffrey), as the speaker of an oral narrative might do, in a self-deprecating fashion. It is only much later that we find the third-person persona, Gulliver or Marlowe. As I see it, the principal challenge in helping students to read Chaucer is leading them to recognize the indirection of the narrative and the different voices and points of view. If they can do this, they will become more sophisticated readers of any literature.

On the one hand, Chaucer is very much the omniscient narrator. He tells us things about the Knight, the Prioress, the Wife of Bath, the Reeve that could not by any stretch of the imagination have been gleaned from a chance encounter at the Tabard. Yet the delight of reading Chaucer is the abrupt shifting of tone and point of view, so often loosely characterized as "Chaucerian irony." He writes, for instance,

of the Prioress: "And al was conscience and tendre herte."

of the Monk: "And I seyde his opinioun was good. / What, shold he studie and make hymselven wood?"

of the Summoner: " 'Purs is the ercedekenes helle,' seyde he. / But wel I woot he lyed right in dede."

of Alysoun in the Miller's Tale: "She was a prymerole, a pyggesneye, / For any lord to leggen in his bedde, / Or yet for any good yeman to wedde."

of Troilus riding from battle in Book II, seen from Criseyde's point of view (in which *that* is nearly as suggestive as Hemingway's): "For bothe he hadde a body and a myght / To don *that* thing, as wel as hardynesse / . . . For of her owne thought she wex al red."

And how are we to take the voice of the Franklin in his headlink and in his tale, or the voices of Justinus and Placebo in the Merchant's Tale?

As a professional performer reading his poems to the court, Chaucer must have dramatized all the different voices, as Charles Dickens did in reading from *David Copperfield*, or as Robert Manson Myers does in reading from his *Children of Pride*. What would we not give for a tape of Chaucer's performance! None of the recordings on the market is adequate in this respect. Nevill Coghill's musical succeeded much better in its own way. The instructor who is uninhibited enough to dramatize his or her rendition to the class will go far toward sensitizing students to the innuendo in Chaucer's lines. If the instructor, moreover, can bring the students to the same sort of dramatic reading and to discussion of the appropriate voices for different passages, he or she will have gone far toward making them sophisticated readers.

The students' chief obstacle to fluent reading of Chaucer's language seems to be less difficulty with the actual pronunciation than self-consciousness about making those strange sounds. (Foreign language teachers say the same thing about teaching American students to speak French or German.) In order to confront the language problem, I have made two-track tapes that are on file in the language laboratory. On them I have read a line and left time for the student to read the line aloud after me. My part of the tape cannot be erased; the student's part is erased and used again and again. After a class discussion of the principles of pronunciation and some classroom practice, I send the students to the laboratory. It is miraculous how quickly they master the rudiments of pronunciation. In voluntary extra sessions, those who wish have an opportunity to read more extensively and achieve some fluency in expression. But they must all read aloud to me before they can pass the course.

I stress oral performance and recognition of voices because these seem to me the sine qua non for appreciating Chaucer's poetry. How far and in what direction one goes beyond this depend on the situation. I do not find that Chaucer's writings lend themselves—as Shakespeare's plays do so admirably—to exploring different critical approaches: historical, formalist, psychoanalytic, mythic, Marxist, structuralist, semiotic, and so forth. The plays are similar enough in structure that each may be usefully treated in various ways. The tone and texture of Chaucer's tales and poems vary so much that I cannot employ them usefully for such comparative criticism. This is not to say that it is not enlightening to explore the different modes of Chaucer criticism, beginning with the historical and cultural explications of George Lyman Kittredge, John Livingston Lowes, John Matthews Manly, and more recently J. A. W. Bennett and Derek Brewer; the psychological and philosophical criticism of such critics as C. S. Lewis, Howard Patch, and Morton Bloomfield; the exegetical criticism of D. W. Robertson, Bernard Huppé, Robert Kaske, and others; the rhetorical criticism of Charles Muscatine, Robert O. Payne, and James Murphy; the structuralist interpretations of Paul Ruggiers, Robert Jordan, and Donald Howard; the social interpretations of Margaret Schlauch, Sheila Delany, and Will Héraucourt. But it does not seem to me profitable to compare the results of subjecting (say) the Clerk's Tale or *Troilus* to (say) cultural and exegetical interpretations as it does with *Hamlet* or *Measure for Measure*. Too much attention directed toward critical method appears to lead the reader away from Chaucer's text instead of providing greater illumination.

Seminars on Chaucer can from time to time provide valuable experience in paleography, editorial method, and the use of documents. Facsimile editions of the Ellesmere and the Hengwrt manuscripts; easy access to microfilms of the other manuscripts; the Chaucer Society transcripts; the collations of Manly and Rickert, Root, Koch, and others; the Chaucer life-records; and the indexed calendars of the Public Record Office, county historical societies, and the Victoria County Histories—all make it possible to set editorial exercises and to trace members of the Chaucer circle or possible originals for the characters in Chaucer's writings.

Seminars in Chaucer's intellectual milieu are less easy to organize. It is deplorable that there is no recent monograph on Chaucer's own reading. One must still go all the way back to Lounsbury's *Studies in Chaucer* (1892, rpt. 1962) for an attempt at a unified survey although the essays in the collection entitled *Geoffrey Chaucer* (1974), edited by Derek Brewer, provide valuable specialized introductions to Chaucer's knowledge of Latin, French, Italian, and other literatures. There are also excellent supplementary readers, such as D. W. Robertson's *The Literature of Medieval England* (1970) and Robert P. Miller's *Chaucer's Sources and Backgrounds* (1977). I am not forgetting Bryan and Dempster's still invaluable *Sources and Analogues* (1941) or Beryl Rowland's *Companion to Chaucer Studies* (2nd ed., 1979). Nevertheless, it is no small task to assemble the editions, translations, and interpretations of the major authors and intellectual currents leading up to Chaucer that would make possible the sort of exploration of primary materials in the intellectual and esthetic realms that it is so easy to achieve in connection with manuscripts and records.

The final stage is the most difficult—merely to set Chaucer in his own time. In order fully to appreciate Chaucer's achievement, one must know John Gower, William Langland, the *Pearl* Poet, John Wycliffe, the romances, the lyrics, the homilies, the penitentials, as well as Guillaume de Machaut, Eustache Deschamps, Jean Froissart, Dante, Petrarch, and Boccaccio. This stage is difficult partly because it implies reading in Latin, French, and Italian, as well as in Middle English. Eventually, one must know all that Chaucer's contemporaries thought and read and wrote in order to be aware of the extent to which Chaucer himself was original and the extent to which he was derivative. This is a never-ending task, which means, finally, that we all remain students of Chaucer throughout our lives. Not everything can be achieved at any stage.

My own sense of sequence is, first, reading *The Canterbury Tales*, mastering the oral performance, and recognizing the different voices; second, reading *Troilus* and Chaucer's other works; then, learning something about Middle English dialects and other Middle English literature; exploring Chaucer's reading and his intellectual milieu; considering critical methodologies; learning textual and diplomatic method; and developing fuller acquaintance with contemporary culture (both English and continental) and Chaucer's contemporaries. We should be conscious of some such hierarchy as we plan courses and programs of study.

Limitations of resources make it increasingly difficult to provide separate courses in all these areas. Fortunately, Chaucer studies, like all medieval studies, lend themselves well to independent reading. If students in the introductory course can be given a vision of the possibilities and of the various stages of development and if instructors have enough time and energy, those students who wish to go further may do so independently. I see great merit in having as many students as possible read *The Canterbury Tales*. The *Canterbury* collection is delightful in and of itself, and it is the beginning of modern literature in English. But there is decreasing value in encouraging many students to pursue the more advanced stages of philology and medieval studies. Success here must be counted in quality, not quantity. Fortunately, the Middle Ages just now seem to be attracting excellent students who are willing to learn the languages and eager to master the methodologies. There is no reason to be pessimistic about the state of Chaucer studies.

THE CHAUCER COURSE: GENERAL OVERVIEWS

AND GLADLY TECHE THE TALES OF CAUNTERBURY

Thomas J. Garbáty

The inaugural conference of the New Chaucer Society in Washington, D.C., in 1979 was a great success, I thought. Although in sharing the crowded Hyatt Regency with another convention of some sort of staid professionals we had had neither world enough nor time, we did achieve much. Groups of us had heard reports on the Variorum Chaucer and other projects, discussions of Ricardian aspects and Chancery script. A few had watched a colleague intently explain his model of the astrolabe, and most had listened raptly to a Donaldsonian luncheon address. Some of the best Chaucerian minds in the world had gathered and fed one another. As I hurried, somewhat euphoric, through the lobby to catch my plane, I overheard behind me three delegates of the other convention remark with unfeigned astonishment at "all those people belonging to a Chaucer Society."

"I didn't know the man wrote that much," said the first. "Just a few dirty stories," replied the second; and the third added, "In *The Canterbury Tales*, wasn't it?" Thoroughly deflated, I fled the hotel and flew away.

But I had been given food for serious thought. For us, as teachers and scholars, it is a truth not universally acknowledged that there are people in this world who neither know nor care about Chaucer. To be sure, we cannot teach those who never come to us, and I suppose these three delegates, probably successful achievers in their world, had never heard about Chaucer from a teacher. At least I hope not. But once students come to us, whether willingly, in an elective course, or unwillingly, in a required one, it is our job—and one that must be fulfilled intently, lovingly, and wisely—to teach them the whole Chaucer, the work and the man. And here we dare not fail, for the poet's sake and ours. A dull Chaucer course unquestionably defines a dull instructor.

Depending on the scope of their high school curriculum, students come with a varied preparation to our courses. Most have read the General Prologue, the Pardoner's Tale, and Wife of Bath's Tale. Occasionally, a fabliau has been thrown in for spice. More often than not, the Nun's Priest's Tale, a sophisticated, complicated masterpiece, has been lauded by an enthusiastic teacher to an uncomprehending class. Generally, students come with an anticipation of finding in Chaucer "realism," bawdiness, and quaintness. The anticipation is ground to plant on, albeit perhaps none too fertile.

Ideally, my objective in a Chaucer course is to involve the students in a revelation of the life's work of an unusually brilliant and humane man, a revelation that leads always to an enjoyment, often, I hope, to a deeper understanding, and occasionally even to a kind of love. The most important step for the teacher to take first is to distill method out of emotion: to recognize Chaucer's method of attaining his results, and to choose the most fitting method of explaining them. A vital gift of Chaucer's is his ability to characterize deftly, sharply, and in depth. Another is his transfiguration of medieval stereotypes into "round" characters of life, with all their frustrating ambiguities and inconsistencies. These methods achieve Chaucer's view of the human comedy. Instructors must engage themselves totally, take their work very seriously, but never so themselves. All teachers, I am sure, have some preconceived view of Chaucer to which they fit their own personalities and their approaches. Thus an effective symbiosis ought to be reached between Chaucer, instructor, and student. And if gentle, benign irony is Chaucer's trademark, it would be helpful if this trait were not neglected in the teaching.

With an advanced class in *The Canterbury Tales*, I sometimes preview the main work with a reading of *The Book of the Duchess* or *The Parliament of Fowls*. In both works one can notice the early Chaucer's close ties to the Dream Vision tradition, and the relatively stiff allegorical conventions of the French school from which the young Chaucer learned. Yet one can see already the seeds of genius for lively colloquial dialogue, for the shorthand descriptions of the foibles of animal and man that come to fruition on the pilgrimage to Canterbury. At the same time, attention to Chaucer's personae reveals the development from the earlier, prosaically logical mask to the later naive pilgrim Chaucer, the evolution of the intensification of Chaucer's self-directed humor.

In general, however, I start at the beginning. Let us be relaxed at the start, have fun reading in Middle English, attempting to translate and understand everything that goes on. I don't like to spend too much time in pronouncing Middle English. For one reason, there is no one around any more who can tell us if we are really right; for another, it slows us down and we find out that the student often doesn't remember what has been read—if she or he knew it in the first place. After a while we leave the Middle English pronunciation to recordings heard after class. But we still proceed slowly, explaining all terms, from *April* (spring, renewal) to *Zephyr* (small rains, Westron Wind, Christ, fertility, pilgrimage). We cannot afford to forget the "whit wal" or tabula rasa that the students may be afraid to display.

The General Prologue is of course crucially important, both in itself and for an understanding of the whole *Canterbury Tales*. For Chaucer's descriptive method it is the tip of the iceberg. The surface pictures, explicit and at times deceptively objective, that we get of the Pardoner, for instance, or the Wife, the Clerk, the Franklin, and so many others are enhanced implicitly in the links and in the tales the pilgrims tell. Chaucer's manner of fitting teller to tale is a very complex phenomenon that includes not only the fact that the Prioress must tell a religious tale (and that the Miller must not) but also the style and manner in which she tells it. Her tale is as poetically beautiful as she is: what a lovely way to describe an auto-da-fé! The Prioress is good grist for the teaching mill. Students, with a little nudging, see her plain and are ready (or at least less unprepared) later for her tale. At the same time they have seen the pilgrim Geoffrey and can follow his amiable and unwavering approbation among a series of scoundrels. In our reading and discussions, the students are shown the dynamics of the General Prologue; the secular gradation of Knight, Squire, and Yeoman with the contrasting aspects of chivalry and service represented; Chaucer's serious regard for the older man and his approval of all three, tempered with humor at the son. Again, although line counting is a bore, it does not take much to see that the presentations of the portraits of Prioress and Monk are nearly equal in length—two sides of the same coin—and to follow the parallels from then on. Among the church-attached figures there is increasing sharpness, ending in an unhealthy duet of Pardoner and Summoner, and saved only by the grace of the Parson. Much goes on between the lines.

An examination of the process of characterization leads to an understanding of how flat types are transfigured, how an archetypal spinning white witch may evolve into an old bawd, to be suddenly called Alisoun, and how the polemic against generally corrupt friars, as in Langland's *Piers Plowman* for instance, is changed to a not unappealing picture of knavery in Hubert. I like to use the results of my own research wherever possible. Students seem to listen suddenly more intently (or do I only think so?), and I am sure that I am personally more engaged. Thus, when explaining Chaucer's stylistic trick in the General Prologue of building up to a punch line effect in the last three to four lines of a description (the Cook's "mormal," the Friar's name, and ignorance of the Merchant's), I can discuss the importance of the Reeve's home town of Baldeswelle as a source of rustic immigrants to London in Chaucer's time, an association that would have called up a knowing smile or chuckle in the poet's listeners. Or, in reading about the Summoner's disease, I can point out that Chaucer does not waste ink merely on a realistic description of ugliness but rather highlights the irony of a venereal disease in a member of the Church's vice squad. Although I often must give information such as the results of the Manly-Rickert school of historical identification, I attempt to move to the broader questions of why—why Harry Bailly and Thomas Pynchbeke, for instance, as models for the Host and Man of Law—and what results these personal pictures produced among Chaucer's contemporary audience. Nor is physiognomy neglected, but I cannot use it as an incentive for discussion. Basically, I want the class to recognize, through my interest, that Chaucerian research is neither a dry nor a useless task.

Yet, I never finish discussing the General Prologue—although, of course, the students must finish reading it. Important pilgrims like the Merchant, Clerk, Franklin, Wife of Bath, Miller, and several others I leave for the later discussion of the tales so that the student can see how the iceberg technique of the General Prologue really works, how in fact we probe and see more and more deeply into the pilgrim as we move from the General Prologue to the link, to the prologue of the tale, and finally to the tale itself (as with the Franklin or Wife of Bath, for instance), always within a wider circle of characterization.

It is very early on that I start my system of alternating lectures with discussion, usually one lecture per week, in preparation for the larger issues that will face us in the tales. Generally, the lectures are scheduled so as to preview themes that appear in the reading. The lectures provide the theory, background, and raw material; later the students recognize how the theory is put into practice, the background highlighted, and the raw source material refined and developed in the works themselves. In this way students first receive information passively, then recognize it in discussion, and actively produce it again. In fact, I start the course with a lecture. If *The Canterbury Tales* is only part of a general early survey, the lecture is on Chaucer's life, a kind of intense and far-ranging life-and-works one-hour flash that I often give in high schools as guest lecturer. But in the regular *Canterbury Tales* semester I take the bull by the horns. Since it is Chaucer's language that scares most students, I start with a background on language, the historical reasons for a shift from Anglo-Norman to English, the social and cultural aspects of the various languages. Here, too, I mention the verse forms Chaucer uses, the earlier and later, the French and native traditions. Basically, it is pleasant when the students no longer talk of reading Chaucer in "Old English." After the lecture, the lines make more sense, and the Prioress' linguistic affectation is self-explanatory.

Very early in the course, in conjunction with information on Chaucer criticism and essay collections, I even venture a bibliographic background lecture. Admittedly, there is a bit of self-indulgence here because the lecture gives me a chance to talk widely of Frederick J. Furnivall, his achievements in the British Museum Reading Room with scholars and on the Thames with assorted working girls; of Kittredge's accomplishments and terror; of Manly and Rickert, the "Chicago Gang," as the Public Record Office employees called them in the 1930s, when, rumor has it, they even shared a first-class cabin on the Queen Mary. My purpose, of course, is to introduce students to a whole tradition and lineage of Chaucerians, a background of intimacy and congeniality that so many scholars have shared under the aegis of this great man.

A vital lecture, which is still scheduled during the reading of the General Prologue, is the one on courtly love. All my colleagues will recognize how important this lecture is and how difficult the topic. Needless to say, I try to cover everything—C. S. Lewis, Capellanus and the Courts of Love, Albigensians, Cathari, Catalan poetry, *Dolce Stil Nuovo* —and every second word of mine is *cave!* For what we are all the time interested in, and have information about, is only a literary tradition, which by Chaucer's time was evoking skepticism and satire. For better or for worse, however, after this lecture nothing that Chaucer does regarding "Honest Love" in *The Canterbury Tales* ought to slip by the student unawares.

After a concentrated discussion of Boethius, the medieval sympathy for the renunciation of false felicities, and Chaucer's ever recurrent interest in the subject, we are ready to start with the Knight's Tale. After this I can relax since most of the spade work has been done, and I can schedule the lectures without fear of being passed over by the reading before the class is prepared. One of my great pleasures starts after we begin the tales, and that is the group of lectures I call the Life Series. These five lectures travel leisurely, like a red thread, through the whole course. In the process I can touch on everything that connects Chaucer's life with our own reading and the poet's other works. The theory of national origin (French, Italian, English) is mentioned and examined, and so are the personal literary influences on Chaucer, his adventures in France, Spain, and Italy, and his friends, wife, and children (and I am careful to mention that Skeat's conjecture concerning precocious "Litel Lewis" Chaucer and Cecily Chaumpaigne is rumor not to be passed on). In spite of the rather timeworn New Criticism, this historical kaleidoscope has proved invaluable in providing life to the times. Sometimes, with luck, we can end the Life Series, per schedule and as appropriate, on the day Chaucer died, 25 October.

At this point it does not matter when the "Genre-Anthology" lecture occurs, because the students are ready to take an active part in recognizing the various medieval forms of narrative. As A. C. Baugh pointed out long ago, *The Canterbury Tales* is an anthology of almost every type of literary entertainment and instruction. We start with the romance, the origin of the word, the classification into Matters (France, Britain, Rome the Great, and England), examples of these, and a discussion of what types of romance have been found in Chaucer so far. Then, we proceed to the parody of romance and by natural sequence to the Breton lay and the fabliau. If by this time we have read the Miller's Tale and discussed the parodic features in "quiting" the Knight, then the class knows a bit about some aspects of this genre, the difference between "high" and "low" style, the necessity for fast pacing, quick action, and lower-class milieu. Whenever the works have appeared on the syllabus before the lecture, the students will contribute information here. Where the reading is still ahead of them, they will recognize the genre (beast fable, saint's legend, exemplum, miracle of the Virgin, tragedy, sermon, classical legend) when they come to it. This lecture, like the one on courtly love, may extend beyond the one hour assigned to it since I never like to pass questions by; I encourage all of them—no matter how bizarre.

By this time, I should have a fair idea of the intellectual capacity of the class, their interest, and their willingness and ability to digest material whose importance they may not immediately grasp. Depending on my evaluation of their capacity and interest, I mention problems of revision and the sequence of the tales, pointing out that the Ellesmere order, which I follow in teaching, is only one of several possible lines. I might even, with solemn preparation, initiate them into the mystic rite of the Bradshaw Shift—because some of them, indeed, might ask why, at the top of the pages of Robinson's edition, we have Roman numerals and alphabetical letters. To put it bluntly, I grab at the opportunity to teach. If the students give me only a little finger of interest, I will return them a handful of information.

All other matter is brought in during the class discussion of the tales themselves. Here I base myself on the collected efforts of my fellow Chaucerians, providing the class with examples of all of the major schools of criticism. In the Knight's Tale I follow Muscatine in pointing out how style (slow, ritualistic pacing, tapestrylike descriptions) represents theme —rigid order covering a potential chaos of despair. Boethian ideas are again thoroughly explored, the interchange of "high" and "low" styles (the latter in Theseus' speech "The God of Love, a *benedicite*" and especially in Part IV) should be recognized, and alliteration (and the reasons for it) noted. To counter an atavistic feeling toward Chaucer as a kind of medieval Pollyanna, the Knight's Tale is an especially effective antidote. The description of the Temple of Mars can shock some students, especially a line like "The sowe freten the child right in the cradel" (A 2019). This is an image that Chaucer could not possibly have got in any reading of romance, or chronicle, or book of arms. Undoubtedly, it is something he saw in France as a young man—a farm burned, the parents killed, and the baby left unattended, a prey to pigs who would eat anything when starved—one of the rare flashes of personal experience in the poet's works. I do not neglect to point out to my students that this is a true picture and that some years ago the University of Michigan hospital admitted for plastic surgery a young man from Greece whose face had been chewed away by pigs when he was an infant. I stress these facts because I agree with Talbot Donaldson in wanting to emphasize to students that Chaucer's geniality, humor, and wise humanity may have been dearly bought.

In contrast to the Knight's Tale, the following fabliaux do not broach serious problems, and the students can readily see the difference as well as the satiric mirroring in which all three completed tales of Group A are connected. The "low" fabliau style is that of the General Prologue, and the description of Nicholas—"This clerk was named hende Nicholas"— could easily be inserted among those of the other pilgrims. I think there is no need here to explain all the points that go into the discussion of the tales: the *aubade* in the Reeve's Tale, the anti-intellectualism of the Carpenter and the Miller, the use of *occupatio*, and so on. Most of these aspects can be read in Chaucerian criticism and notes. Suffice it to say that antifeminism, its virulence and Church sanction, needs to be carefully explored in any discussion of the Wife of Bath or "Marriage

Group"; gentilesse, appearance and reality in the Franklin's Tale; bitter irony and sarcasm in the Merchant's encomium on marriage and general smudging of the refined aspects of *fin amor* in his tale.

All the while, the drama of the pilgrimage must not be forgotten, and although I cannot cover all the links in depth, I point out to the students that the portrait of one pilgrim, the Host, is psychologically developed only in the links, especially in terms of his approach to the women on the trip and in the tales. In fact, the dynamics of the Wife, Host, and Pardoner trio, because of the tensions produced by their interaction, can provoke some of the most interesting discussions in class.

The tales should give no trouble as long as the instructor has made it clear from the start that Chaucer never wholly shows his cards and that there is no one correct interpretation but several, at times even conflicting, interpretations. Life is relative after all, and Chaucer holds the mirror up to life. But possibly the Clerk's Tale may be a tough nut for some. Here the late Francis Utley helped me greatly, in showing that the Clerk's Tale is puzzling in part because it shifts in genre from folk tale, to fabliau, to symbolic literature, to exemplum, and certainly to drama in taking up the Wife's gauntlet. In addition, the range of the story makes it possible to introduce the students to the four levels of scriptural exegesis here, for the tale lends itself willingly to this kind of intellectual gymnastics. In sum, the complexity of the Clerk's Tale can cause grief only to those instructors who teach Chaucer as a simple and straightforward writer. And I suspect there are few of us who do this. Chaucer is a slippery fish, not easily hooked or pinned down. I am sure he kept his mouth closed at many a diplomatic function.

Finally, I use the Nun's Priest's Tale as a kind of Ph.D. orals in which the whole class participates. By the end of the semester, this brilliant tour de force ought to be understood completely by anyone who has stayed the course. As Muscatine has pointed out, all Chaucer's favorite themes come together here: Boethian discussion of fate, dreams, herb lore, courtly love, tragedy, comedy, antifeminism, high and low styles, mock heroic, and the deflation of a cocky human ego. I like to end the course on a note that does not jar. We have passed our Prioresses, Summoners, Pardoners, and Merchants, their tales, and those of the Knight. We have seen glimpses of what Donaldson calls Chaucer's dark night of the soul. The Nun's Priest's Tale confirms, yet again, that for Chaucer the sun always rises.

And so we come to the last day but one. The lights are turned out and the Ellesmere slides appear on the screen. The Huntington Library's copies of these are inexpensive but extraordinarily rewarding. The first slide is a photo of the first MS page. Students can practice a bit of reading and admire the luxury of the illumination. Then the identifying of the pilgrims starts, and I proceed with a mock examination. The student puts down the pilgrim on paper, and then we all work out the answer together. There is no cheating because there is no grading, just end-of-the-semester relaxation. I am constantly amazed, however, how these small miniature illustrations bear up under unusually high magnification. Everything is seen clearly: the Cook's mormal and ladle, the starry eyes of Hubert, the flask of the Manciple, the accoutrements of the Pardoner, and the Summoner's "whelks." All the horses are different, taking on the character of their riders. Of great interest is Alisoun, with her spurs and her little whip, and she herself riding astride. The other ladies are side-saddle, a fashion evidently started under Queen Ann of Bohemia. I arrange the slides so that the easier ones come early, but, by process of elimination, all the pilgrims can be identified. Last is the picture of Geoffrey Chaucer himself, and with the Ellesmere MS dated 1400–10 this is the earliest portrait we have, probably the closest to life. For the class I can sense that there is a moment of truth here, some kind of epiphany. The face surprises many; it was not quite what they expected, that shrewd, knowing look. This is good. We must all be aware (and constantly!) that Chaucer is master of the unexpected.

By now it is hard to accept the inevitable, the final day of the course, and the last hour is always a sad one. My attempt to sum up is not closely planned; it stems less from method now than from emotion, from a conviction of the merit of what we have learned during the semester. The Chaucerian character has come through so intensely during the past weeks that it is almost superfluous to point out to the class the poet's relativist view of mankind, ironic, at times wry, but always unwaveringly charitable, which makes Chaucer so appealing and immediately modern. His great power is that he elicits not only an intellectual response from students but an intensely emotional one as well, a response that the instructor must foster by attempting to achieve a close rapport with the class. If there is occasionally anguish at the final leave-taking, I comfort my friends with the thought that Chaucer's *Troilus* will provide them hours of future pleasure.

By the looks in their eyes I am certain of one thing at the end of the course: at another conference, under similar circumstances, there would be several students in that class who would not deny Chaucer. They would break a spear for him, stand their ground at the risk of missing their flight, and give those three staid professionals a lecture—certainly unprofessional, probably even un-Chaucerian, but to the point.

Appendix

COURSE SYLLABUS

Geoffrey Chaucer, *The Canterbury Tales*

Course Description: The course consists of background lectures, reading and discussion in class, records, and slides. The text is the standard scholarly edition of Chaucer's works by F. N. Robinson, 2nd ed., 1957. Always bring this book to class.

Scheduled written work required for the course will be one outside paper on topics to be assigned or chosen after discussion with the instructor, of a minimum of twelve pages, and a final examination.

Except for the General Prologue, which will be read in class, all other tales should be read ahead of the day assigned. Possible brief quizzes may occur on such days. *All* tales, prologues, and "links" must be read, with the exception of the Parson's Tale and the *Melibee* (the pilgrim Chaucer's second tale), which are optional. Only a grasp of their content is required. The student is therefore responsible for all tales, including those not on this list.

As clerks you should use "translations" only in the privacy and secrecy of your own cloistered cells. Use of such officially forbidden works, however, since they are heretical, damned, perhaps even of Lollard origin (forbidden because of perversion and unorthodoxy of text), must be publicly confessed to the Superior, and his penance must be accepted with grace and joy. We are mild in chastising the body: the hair shirt is welcome, but self-flagellation is interdicted.

Assignments and Lecture Schedule

MEETINGS

1   Lecture: Introduction and Language
2–3 Readings in General Prologue
4   Lecture: Philology and Meter
5–6 Readings in General Prologue
7   Bibliography
8–9 Readings in General Prologue

THE IDEA OF A CHAUCER COURSE

Donald R. Howard

There is probably such a thing as the idea of a Chaucer course, but if so it exists not in people's heads as real ideas do but in a supramundane realm, where one assumes the students are very good. Such a course would, I feel certain, last throughout the academic year and cover all of Chaucer's works in chronological sequence. The students would get the hang of Middle English right away, and all the discourse would be on an unremittingly high plane. The complexity and turbulence of late medieval culture and the depth and variousness of Chaucer's works would communicate themselves by a cumulative process, as would the poet's development and the excellence of each poem. And each of the students would end up possessing his or her own Chaucer: an interiorized presence whose wit and learning, whose humor, whose rage, whose love of life and contempt for the world would nourish and liberate. Such a course would render the teacher unnecessary, but he (by which I mean "he or she") would go on attending for the joy of it and because it would never for a moment cross his mind that teaching is a thankless task.

The realm in which Chaucer courses are taught is, however, the fallen world we live in, where there are quarters or semesters, programs, administrations, compulsive talkers, and few if any perfect textbooks. In this world of compromises, one ten- to fifteen-week Chaucer course may be all that is possible. If so, it must be devoted in large measure to *The Canterbury Tales*. This means that one must begin with the General Prologue at a time when students do not read Middle English at all well. *The Canterbury Tales* is an unfinished whole whose wholeness is endowed by the General Prologue. Treating the General Prologue first gives it the prominence it was meant to have, not to say the place. But in all texts it is the most heavily footnoted selection: everything here—the Miller's wart, the Guildsmen's daggers, the Prioress' brooch—*everything* needs a footnote. Students should be encouraged to let curiosity be their guide and to skip some footnotes but to come back, as they read the tales, to the individual pilgrims. Good portions should be read aloud unless the teacher is hopelessly without histrionic ability, and perhaps even then. Having students read aloud individually in class should, I think, be avoided. It is embarrassing to the reader and boring to all, and it does Chaucer a cruel violence. Reading (or repeating) in unison on the first few days is perhaps useful—as is listening, with books closed. But more than a little of this sort of exercise is a waste of class time in our day of double-track cassettes, recordings, language laboratories, and listening rooms.

The Rubicon of any course about *The Canterbury Tales* comes after the General Prologue. Here one finds the Knight's Tale, just where it belongs. *The Canterbury Tales* as a whole, let alone the Miller's and Reeve's tales that follow, does not have its intended effect if the Knight's Tale is displaced, and omitting it is unthinkable. It is a high-minded, ceremonious romance that bespeaks the grand old ideals of the medieval knighthood—the ideals of the just ruler, of warfare in a just cause, of servitude in love, of resignation to Fortune, of "glory." What a falling-off is to come after it! And what an irony is established *in* it by that curious voice that can tell us "I nam no divinistre." But that falling-off and that ironic voice are lost on any reader who skips to the Miller's offering. To do so is to miss the point. Still, the Knight's Tale is a long struggle for students at this stage of their linguistic expertise, and high-mindedness makes large demands on one's emotional attention span. Anything that can clear the student's path is useful. I encourage them to read the Knight's Tale in a normalized-spelling version (Donaldson's or my own in the Signet paperback), and I read aloud to them some glorious pàssages like the descriptions of the temples under the entirely hypocritical guise of telling them what they might omit: such set pieces can be omitted without damage to the plot, but in truth the work, for all its seeming length, is a jewel of concision—nothing can be omitted.

Once past the Knight's Tale, one only has to decide what to do in the classroom and what order to put the tales in.

What to do in the classroom? Lecture. Let students ask questions and ask *them* questions at any appropriate juncture, but do not fool with the "Socratic" method. It is one of the pieties of our profession that a good teacher, instead of "lecturing away," gets students to speak their thoughts. But Chaucer does not in my experience lend himself to the discussion method: his age is too distant from ours, there are too many facts to be learned, the language presents too many difficulties. At least one person agrees with me, for I once asked B. J. Whiting how he taught Chaucer at Harvard. "Read to them and comment," was his reply.

"You don't have discussion?"

"Not at all. Their remarks are always jejune. And there is too much else to do."

"So essentially you read aloud from the text."

"It's what Chaucer did."

Since discussion doesn't work, it follows that large enrollments are no problem in a Chaucer course; there can still be questions, so the audience may as well be as large at least as the court of Richard II.

For a while, I thought showing slides in the classroom was a way to deal with the strangeness of medieval culture, but the effort was not a success. There is scarcely a humanities classroom in the country adequately equipped for a smooth transition from the matter at hand to the slides and back to the matter at hand, and humanities faculties are too craven to demand such facilities. Time is wasted with the mechanics of the thing. The teacher must sacrifice some remnant of dignity groveling for switches and plugs. The introduction of the machine into the room sets up an air of expectancy; there is foot scuffing until the slides are shown, and when the lights go on there is glumness in the air. If one *must* show slides, there should be no more than eight; they should be unimpeachably germane to the day's topic; and they should be shown first, and perhaps again last.

There is, however, one "audiovisual aid" that well deserves a class hour: the splendid film, available in sixteen millimeter or video cassette, made by Mary Kirby and Naomi Diamond for Pilgrim Films: *From Every Shires Ende: The World of Chaucer's Pilgrims* (1969). When it comes to the cultural background, here is God's plenty. There is not a moment of phoniness in this film: everything is an authentic artifact of Chaucer's day, the commentary is informative and scholarly, the music is medieval music handsomely performed, and the cinematography never calls attention to anything but the subject matter. It lasts thirty-eight minutes, leaving time for questions. The commentary with a list of sources —that is, things photographed and their whereabouts—is available. (The commentary is magnificently pronounced by Robert Lang, but in a somewhat mushmouth British accent with souped-up resonance, so have the projectionist go heavy on the treble.)

What order to put the tales in? Any order that does not violate Chaucer's clear intentions. I like to show students the Parson's Prologue in the first week to give them an overview of the pilgrimage metaphor, but that's just a preview. At some point I explain the problem of order with a few words about manuscript transmission and a list of the MS fragments and the groups of tales. Obviously Chaucer meant the General Prologue and the group Knight-Miller-Reeve-Cook (Fragment I) to go first; obviously he meant the group Second Nun-Canon's Yeoman-Manciple-Parson (Fragments VIII–X) to go last. Between these, not counting the solitary Man of Law's tale (Fragment II), there are three interior groups: Wife-Friar-Summoner-Clerk-Merchant-Squire-Franklin (Fragments III–V); Physician-Pardoner (Fragment VI); and Shipman-Prioress-*Sir Thopas*-*Melibee*-Monk-Nun's Priest (Fragment VII). Since I am committed to the view that each group has some sort of dramatic propriety and thematic unity, however mysterious, I feel deeply about keeping each group intact. But the three groups could be presented in any order.

From a pedagogical viewpoint, however, I believe there is a reason why the order given above, the Ellesmere order, is best. It puts the Nun's Priest's Tale as close to the end as it can come without doing violence to Chaucer's plain intentions. The Nun's Priest's Tale should come toward the end not because it is the most Chaucerian in spirit of all the tales, what Muscatine calls *"The Canterbury Tales* in little," though this is reason enough. It should come toward the end because it is the hardest tale to teach. So, at least, I have always found. Its shimmering wit is directed at so many features of medieval culture that it is almost a universal satire. But to understand it, one must know all those features: courtly love, rhetoric, Geoffrey of Vinsauf on the death of Richard I, medicine, astrology, dreams—you name it. The poor teacher must struggle to explain all this background, and nothing spoils a joke more than explaining it. I have never felt I taught the tale with success. The first time, years ago at Ohio State, was a disaster: on the evening of that terrible day I met the famous Germanist and humanist Oskar Seidlin, who asked how my course in my specialty was going. When I bemoaned the day's mishap, he smiled: "And you are still worried about it? How young you are."

I think I see a way to succeed with the Nun's Priest's Tale, though I have yet to manage it. It would involve making a list of everything the student would need to know in order to possess the riches of the tale. One would take the list and parcel out items throughout the course as they were relevant to earlier tales. Such a list would be a serviceable introduction to medieval culture. And then the Nun's Priest's Tale would itself serve as a droll review. Chaucer said in the *Treatise on the Astrolabe* that it is better to explain something twice than have the student forget it once, and he hit on a good practice when at one point he said, "Now have I told thee twice." If one could manage to touch on each point twice and remind students the second time around that it has been covered before, perhaps they would know all background matters well enough when they got to the Nun's Priest's Tale to recognize them with little prompting. Then the tale would communicate its own effect by itself, and that is best, I wol you nat deceive.

I wanted this little treatise to have some touch of majesty, but I see it has descended to the practical. I may as well add two more of my personal crotchets. One is the "narrator." Explaining the narrator has much the same effect as explaining the Nun's Priest's Tale. It is a lovely concept as explored by E. T. Donaldson in his famous essay "Chaucer the Pilgrim," for his was the insight of a great humanist and witty nominalist, presented with tentativeness and subtlety. But academics have turned the notion into a formalist bauble. It puzzles students, already schooled in the inflated mystiques of the academy, because they assume it must be arcane and unnatural. The notion of a role-playing Chaucer doing a put-on does not puzzle them at all.

My other crotchet is spelling. For undergraduates there is so much to be learned about life from *The Canterbury Tales* that Middle English scribal spelling must rank low among priorities. It is only useful to editors. Few would argue—and those who do sound like Chanticleer—that we should spell Shakespeare's works in the spelling of his day. It would make the page look more quaintly Elizabethan, but this quaintness would put one more barrier between the student and the text. Yet it is conventional to spell Chaucer in this "authentic" way, and in his case the spelling is not even the authentic spelling of his day but that of the fifteenth-century manuscripts. Normalized spelling makes the language *and* pronunciation more accessible to students, and I believe it is what Chaucer would have wanted editors to use. His last word addressed to his text in *Troilus and Criseyde* was that he wished it to be understood. I cannot imagine him saying that he wished it to look medieval.

I don't know if any of these suggestions will be of use to anyone. What I know is that teaching is an art: no one can teach anyone how to teach anything except by encouraging him to find ways suitable to his own temperament and personal style. But while there can never be agreement on methods, there can be agreement on goals, and on this point I will risk being dogmatic.

The goal and idea of teaching *The Canterbury Tales* is to put the student in touch with the mind of Geoffrey Chaucer. Chaucer had a certain frame of mind, a way of looking at the world, which in our time we could use to our own great benefit if we could but grasp it. Chaucer teaches us how it is possible to take life and the world and one's self very seriously while at the same time seeing the transiency of life, the triviality of the world, and the ballooning potential for roosterhood in almost any self. This frame of mind in its full complexity is to be possessed only by reading Chaucer's works, but it comes out clearly at certain moments in *The Canterbury Tales*, certain peculiarly Chaucerian moments. These seem to me to come at the end of the Nun's Priest's Tale, at the end of the Pardoner's Tale, and probably at the end of the Franklin's Tale (to me the hardest tale to understand); at the end of the Manciple's Tale; and perhaps here and there *within* some of the tales. If I am right, then these Chaucerian moments come most dramatically in the last tales of the three interior groups and in the last tale before the Parson's Prologue. They are moments when we grasp with special clarity Chaucer's unique sanity—his impatience with cant and hypocrisy and with the posturings of seriousness, his sad tolerance for human orneriness, his humorous view of the world and of himself, his tragic and comic sense of life. This sanity is what we have it in our power to offer students. In his writings, Chaucer was able to furbish up a way of looking at life that, it may be, he himself was not able to achieve from day to day any better than we; but he glimpsed how one *should* look at life—in an age, like ours, when all the valued institutions of his culture and his nation seemed failed and falling in ruins.

DIVERSE FOLK DIVERSELY THEY TEACH

Emerson Brown, Jr.

If you have only one semester for your Chaucer course, which of his works will you teach? I know that many instructors teach "selected" tales or "the best" tales and then get on to *Troilus and Criseyde*, and I have tried that. But the many parts of *The Canterbury Tales* are related to one another in such complex and fascinating ways that I find it difficult to decide, arbitrarily, that some parts can be set aside. Not that I would give up the Nun's Priest's Tale for a thousand Physician's Tales, but the tales of less intrinsic value are still essential, and exciting, parts of the whole. They are part of the artistic and spiritual process that writing and assembling *The Canterbury Tales* recorded and, in a way, made possible. And they deepen and enrich the meaning of the great tales against which Chaucer plays them. If we omit the Physician's Tale, for example, the least part of our loss may be that tale itself, for omitting it at the same time diminishes two of Chaucer's masterpieces, the Franklin's Tale and the Pardoner's Tale. So in my semester course we read all of *The Canterbury Tales*, including the prose tales, in Middle English. Weekly translation and identification quizzes count half of the final grade and encourage the students to do their reading carefully throughout the semester. A long take-home essay on the final exam helps tie the semester together.

Emphasizing thorough familiarity with the whole Middle English text requires certain sacrifices. I no longer assign a long research paper of the usual sort, nor do I assign extensive outside reading. My students write papers in their other English courses, and hence reducing somewhat their end-of-semester trauma may not greatly impede their intellectual development. Also, given that apparently inevitable trauma, any great emphasis on a big paper at the end of the semester means that whatever you say about fragments VIII, IX, and X you end up saying, pretty much, to yourself. Up until this year I had regularly assigned a report or two on outside reading in three areas: major works of thought and literature having some bearing on Chaucer (e.g., parts of the Bible, the *Aeneid*, Dante's *Commedia*); sources and analogues of one tale; and interpretations of one tale. The good students get a lot out of an assignment like this, and I may well go back to it. This semester, however, I wanted to see how much we could accomplish by reading the entire *Canterbury Tales* and reading it well, while reading little else except Boethius' *Consolatio*, the introductory and explanatory material in our text, and several handouts of different sorts distributed as the semester went along.

But even if all we teach is *The Canterbury Tales*, it quickly becomes apparent that few of our students have the necessary background to read Chaucer well. We mean several things by "background," and I'll say a bit about three of them.

First of all, there is shared and wide reading in the important books of the Western world. Students may have read an astonishing amount by the time they get to Chaucer, but unless your college or university requires them to do so, you cannot be certain that all the students in a Chaucer class will have read any single book—not Genesis, not Matthew, not the *Aeneid*, not even *Julius Caesar* or *Silas Marner*. At the University of Puerto Rico, where all undergraduates took a two-year humanities course, the students in my Chaucer class had studied the *Iliad*, a bit of Plato and Aristotle, three plays of Sophocles, some books of the Bible, some Cicero, Augustine's *Confessions*, and so on. I understand that there are also colleges and universities among the fifty states with enough confidence in the great books of the Western tradition to require their students to study some of these masterpieces, but I have had no direct experience with such institutions. It would be wonderful, needless to say, if our students knew something of Plato and Aristotle, Vergil, Augustine, and Dante before they reached Chaucer, but it would be absurd to suggest doing much about filling such gaps during the Chaucer course itself. Furthermore, the most important "background" is Latin, and teaching Latin is even more beyond our capacities than teaching the great books. There is a limit to what one course can do to redress the errors of a whole society, and teaching "backgrounds" in this most important sense is something we might as well acknowledge to be beyond our powers.

Another kind of background, however, is more within range. Students need to know about the Middle Ages in general and about late fourteenth-century England and France in particular. I used to assign some readings and devote an opening lecture or two to a glib survey of such matters as medieval Christianity, the Black Death and the Peasants' Revolt, the Great Schism and the Hundred Years' War, Edward III, the Black Prince, Richard II, medieval Latin, French, and Italian literature, the emergence of English language and literature, and late medieval ideas about chivalry, money, and romantic love. But I have found it better to get going on the General Prologue immediately and let such things fall into place casually, as they are needed to understand the poetry. By spending three or four weeks on the General Prologue, students learn how to read Middle English pretty well before attempting longer assignments, and they also pick up useful background information of this second sort. One cannot say much about the portraits of the Knight, Squire, and Yeoman and the complex relations among them, for example, without talking about such things as the later Crusades, England's fortunes in the Hundred Years' War, changing attitudes toward knighthood and chivalry, and changes in military tactics and technology. And so it goes throughout the General Prologue. The richness of allusion, diversity in descriptive technique, and variation of satirical intensity that we so admire in Chaucer force us to inform our students about a vast range of things: about what really happened in the Knight's campaigns; about the Flemish Crusade, the long bow, and the sort of women who became nuns; about romantic literature, Saint Francis of Assisi and William of St. Amour, the Cook's "mormal" and W. C. Curry's research on medieval science; about ancient and medieval antifeminism, the Peasants' Revolt, estates satire, and the role of fictional narrators in medieval literature. One must also say something about the idea of pilgrimage, about *homo viator* as a pattern for all of human life, and about the realities of pilgrimages as criticized by reformers and as embodied in the remarkable memoirs of Margery Kempe. The General Prologue, then, taught in detail and with ample attention to that fascinating world of information and attitude that is both "outside of the text" and inseparable from it, provides—just when we most need it—a fine introduction to some of those elusive backgrounds we want our students to know about.

Finally, our students need to know specific texts and lore if they are not to miss important aspects of Chaucer's art. Dull old philologists long ago saw through a glass darkly the phenomenon critical theorists now see face to face and call "intertextuality," and the labors of several scholarly generations have greatly enriched our awareness of Chaucer's constant play with literary tradition. How do we impart this sort of information— and the skills of subtle reading needed to make proper use of it? One could begin as early as the opening lines of the General Prologue, and I do mention their connection with literary tradition. But at that point in the course I am content to have students reading what Chaucer wrote, without prodding them to examine its connection with a passage in Guido delle Colonne. I first try to examine in detail the relationship between Chaucer's verse and literary traditions he shared with his audience with the portrait of the Prioress. Few would deny that the description of her table manners is so closely related to La Vielle's explanation of how a woman makes herself attractive to a man that it constitutes not simply a borrowing from the *Roman de la Rose* but an allusion to it. So I prepare a handout with lines from the *Roman* and a facing English translation. On the same sheet are some stanzas from the Middle English lyric "A Catalogue of Delights." With these two particular pieces of "background" in hand, students can begin to see what Chaucer the poet has Chaucer the pilgrim narrator do with his apparent high praise of Madame Eglentyne's table manners and with his truncated *effictio*. With the Prioress, as often in teaching the General Prologue, Jill Mann's *Chaucer and Medieval Estates Satire* (1973) is invaluable.

Other handouts provide further background information and help students read more productively. For example, concerning Chaucer's Friar and literary tradition, I supply a few illustrations of antifraternal satire; to augment the information the text provides concerning such matters as the sanguine Franklin, the choleric Reeve, and the Physician's use of astronomy, a chart with the main features of the humoral system; to help with the Knight's Tale, which seems to be the most demanding assignment of the term, a set of study questions prepared more to encourage thinking about the poem than to elicit specific factual answers, a sheet with more detailed information about medieval astronomy than the students' text provides, and a chart showing some of the changes Chaucer made in adapting his Italian source;[1] to illustrate the problems involved in determining the order of the tales and my own acceptance of the Bradshaw Shift, parallel columns showing the "A" group order and the Bradshaw order, and a list of some of the textual problems involved;[2] for the Clerk's Tale, a list of the passages Chaucer added to his sources and an admonition to consider why Chaucer added them; for the Merchant's Tale, an English translation of the *Novellino* tale "A Rich Man and His Wife" and a list of study questions; for the Physician's Tale, an English translation of the source of the Virginius story in the *Roman de la Rose*; and, since currently available editions of *The Canterbury Tales* reorder the concluding lines of the Parson's Prologue (a matter of some importance thematically), a handout with the lines as they appear in all the manuscripts, with some other passages needed to support restoring the text to its original form.[3]

More elaborate than these one-page handouts is the "Love, Sex, Women, and Marriage in the Middle Ages Kit." I usually distribute it just before we take up the "Marriage Group." This "kit" includes Genesis 2 and 3, 1 Corinthians 7 and Ephesians 5, a passage from the Third Vatican Mythographer illustrating the commonplace of Adam and Eve as figures of the two parts of the soul, Augustine's *City of God* 13.13 and 14.18, Aquinas on such questions as "Whether virginity is more excellent than marriage" and "Whether no veneral act can be without sin," selections from the marriage service in the Sarum Missal, Canto V of the *Inferno*, and the passage from the Parson's Tale discussing sexuality in marriage.

Had Robert P. Miller's *Chaucer: Sources and Backgrounds* been available ten years ago when I started preparing these and other handouts, I could have saved some time. Yet, at the end of one class when you are talking about the joys and challenges involved in reading for the next one, there may be some value in handing your students a sheet of paper with information and questions prepared specifically for them.

Several of these handouts contain not only factual information and guide questions but also lists of books and articles that have helped me better understand the tales. I include these titles to encourage students to read some critical and scholarly work on their own and also simply to acknowledge my debts. Whatever success I may have in teaching Chaucer I owe largely to people who taught me, to my fellow graduate students, to many late night conversations at professional meetings, and to the hundreds of scholars whose editions, books, and articles have enriched our understanding of Chaucer and his world. Further, in the same way that I refer in class to an article in the *Chaucer Review* or to comments at a meeting of the New Chaucer Society, I refer to work done by my own students in previous years. I want my students to know that there is a scholarly community beyond the confines of their university, a community I belong to and that they can belong to as well, whatever career they choose in life. This last point is especially important at a time when there are so few opportunities for employment in the colleges and universities. The notion that only university professors do useful scholarly work is rather recent, and it may well be that over the next several decades important scholarly work may come increasingly from "amateur" scholars employed outside the academy. I am not suggesting for a minute that we should attempt to enlist all of our students into the ranks of the New Chaucer Society, but I do think the future of Chaucer studies will be more secure if we tell our students—and remind ourselves—that there is a large community of men and women devoted to improving our understanding of Chaucer—a community open to anyone who wishes to join.

While acknowledging the help of others, I avoid using studies I disagree with as straw men. Graduate students tell me that some of their undergraduate teachers found it difficult to get a lecture going without referring derisively to some piece of folly perpetrated by "the critics." One particularly regrettable squabble in contemporary Chaucer teaching and criticism is the polemic that has been raging for some thirty years concerning "Robertsonianism." Some students arrive in graduate school so enraged over the danger of this approach that it is difficult to get them to respond reasonably to any critic who mentions charity or Augustine. If I understand at all well what D. W. Robertson himself has been doing for the last several years, I think it safe to say that he is no longer a "Robertsonian" in the sense that some students are being taught to use the term. Be that as it may, there are surely more important things to do with undergraduates than to persuade them of the evils of a single critical approach, especially when that approach is constantly evolving in the hands of its best practitioners and is often tempered with other approaches and with good old-fashioned common sense. Among the most heavily thumbed pages on my Chaucer shelves are those devoted to the Commentary in E. T. Donaldson's anthology and those of Robertson's *Preface to Chaucer*. Readers who are able to absorb the best in these two different approaches and work out their own synthesis may come close to the heart of Chaucer.

A less controversial challenge is helping our students acquire a feel for the sound of the verse. Everyone agrees that we should do this, but opinions vary about how much time we should devote to it and about how to go about it. If modern technology can help with anything, it ought to be able to help students become comfortable with the language. A good language laboratory program could enable students to proceed comfortably, step by step, as they acquire a feeling for the vowel and consonant sounds of Chaucer's English and then move from simple iambics to more complex rhythms. There must be someone who can combine philological knowledge, phonetic precision, and pedagogical expertise with critical sensitivity and a gift for the dramatic to produce such a program. With it, we could have all but pathologically tin-eared students speaking Chaucer's verse reasonably well after just a few hours in the lab. While we wait for that program, however, what do we do to help our students catch the sounds and rhythms of Chaucer's poetry?

Two preliminary matters need to be mentioned. First, unless you have more confidence than I in the capacity of twentieth-century scholars to ascertain the exact point of articulation of fourteenth-century sounds (not to mention such features as pitch, stress, and juncture), you need to face the fact that we do not know what Chaucer's English really sounded like. We may come close enough, but we should neither fool ourselves nor try to fool our students about the scientific precision of our knowledge. Second, whatever late fourteenth-century London English sounded like, we are far from agreement about the "rules" of Chaucer's prosody. Our texts alter the poetry to fit modern theories of what it should sound like. As I become accustomed to the rhythms recorded by Chaucer's earliest scribes, I find my ears offended by the more regular lines touched up for us in modern editions. But don't students have enough trouble learning to read the text at hand without facing the disturbing possibility that Chaucer might have written something else? At least we can make them aware of the problem. At the outset, with line eight of the General Prologue, and now and then thereafter, we can point out where the editor has stuck in a final -e or picked up a reading from one of the inferior manuscripts to eke out a line. Some attention to the meaning of the line and to the rhythmic patterns that emerge when the text is freed of editorial improvement is usually enough to show that the lines as they appear in the manuscripts are quite satisfactory, even superior. By refusing to cite doctored texts in our writing we can help bring about a more general awareness of the effectiveness of Chaucer's own lines. Further, to avoid creating another generation of Chaucerians brought up to think that a poet writing during a period of extraordinary tonal and rhythmic complexity in music will invariably produce lines that reveal their essence to anyone capable of counting to five, we can put the facsimile and transcription of the Hengwrt manuscript on reserve and direct our students to it.[4] Thus eventually we may learn to respond sensitively and sympathetically to what the earliest and most dependable evidence indicates that Chaucer wrote.

Yet, whatever we decide about Chaucer's prosody, students are not going to approximate the sound of his verse without practice, correction from us, and further practice. How much class time do we want to devote to that? I begin with the sound of the verse. When I walk into class the first day, I distribute a handout containing lines 1–46 of the General Prologue and a close modern English translation. My first words are "Whan that Aueryll" right through to "And at a Knyght thanne wol I first bigynne." By memorizing and rehearsing the lines I can repeat them with only inconsequential variation in sound and rhythm. With a gesture or two, I have the students repeating after me, until they are speaking Chaucer's lines in the way we like to think Chaucer might have wished them to sound. All this happens before anybody has said a word of modern English. That seems to get our priorities straight at the outset. After that, whenever I quote from the text I try to get the sound right, but I don't take much class time to drill students on pronunciation. For interested students, there is the Tuesday Afternoon Chaucer Society. We meet for an hour or so in a quiet corner of Vanderbilt's congenial pub, read Chaucer aloud, and chat informally about things that don't come up in class. Since these meetings are voluntary and have no bearing on the final grade, not all students bother to come. The ones who do show up care, however, and some of them make remarkable progress in reading Chaucer.

Memorizing passages also helps fix the sounds and rhythms in mind. Having long recommended memorizing, I now require it. The students memorize lines 1–18 and at least two lines from the sketch of each pilgrim in the General Prologue and at least one passage of four lines or more from almost all the tales. They decide which passages they want to memorize, and they have an opportunity to write out their passages from time to time on the quizzes. In addition, they prepare one longer passage (again of their choosing) of ten to twenty lines, which they type out, scan, memorize, and then repeat aloud to me after class or in my office. If their first performance is not satisfactory, I work on it with them right then so that with a little more practice they can hardly help doing well. On the syllabus I urge the students to persuade themselves that they are memorizing these lines for their own interest and enjoyment and not simply to meet an assignment.

I expected loud, if not violent, objection to such a display of pedagogical totalitarianism, but to my great joy I find that most of the students *like* to memorize lines from Chaucer. We may underestimate the pleasure that comes from learning something perfectly and having the opportunity to demonstrate that learning. At the very least, this memorizing equips students to respond spectacularly when asked over Thanksgiving dinner what they have learned so far during the semester.

The final exam provides our last opportunity to help students deepen their understanding of Chaucer. Passages to translate and identify encourage careful rereading, but we want more than that. We want them to get a sense of *The Canterbury Tales* as a whole and a sense of it that is their own, not just something they have taken down from us in class. I have stopped assigning the traditional research paper for reasons stated already. The essay of a few hundred words that you can expect from a discussion topic treated within the exam period itself is likely to be fairly superficial. So I pass out a list of "take-home" essay topics the last week of the semester. The students write on just one topic, and they can alter the topic in the interests of producing a better essay. Students eager to work on topics of their own may do so. The only limitations are that the essays should consider *The Canterbury Tales* as a whole and deal specifically with several different tales and that they should not depend on extensive research beyond the text and information already provided in class.

To turn from more or less mechanical matters of pedagogical technique to interpreting the literature itself, what emerges from my graduate seminar on critical approaches to *The Canterbury Tales* is that a smart critic writing from almost any point of view can improve our understanding of Chaucer's poetry. Always beginning with proper philological grounding and its respect for the literal level of the text, we can take the best from each approach as we work with students to develop our own interpretations. Indeed, the more firmly and clearly a critic writes from a specific point of view (or even unexamined bias), the more sharply he or she may illuminate one aspect of Chaucer's art. To reject an interpretation simply because of the critic's point of view, then, may be to reject something that Chaucer may not have taken so seriously, or may not have taken in exactly the same way, but that is, nonetheless, part of the poetry. It is not essential to calculate, for example, the exact quantity of charity that the Miller's Tale or the Merchant's Tale promotes in order to recognize that the Song of Songs and medieval interpretations of it are part of those tales and must be taken into consideration in formulating interpretations of them. Our only obligation is to refrain from confusing the conclusions of a single critic with a satisfactory, comprehensive interpretation of the poetry. Exercising such restraint should not be too difficult. Surely we all recognize that a truly comprehensive interpretation of a literary work is simply beyond the capacities of any critic or critical approach.

Also, we fool ourselves if we assume that our students' interests in literature are as narrow, self-indulgent, and amoral as ours sometimes must seem to them to be. Students want to know not only about "texts" but about poets. They want to know how people lived. They are fascinated by such things as mythography, beast lore, and astronomy, and they are often unable to restrain themselves from thinking about religion, politics, economics, and the meaning of life—not only in Chaucer's world but in their own. In all this, students strike me as showing admirable respect for the importance of literature, and my guess is that if we responded a little more sensitively to the range and depth of their interests we would be able to spend a little less time worrying about such things as "the future of the humanities."

Chaucer recognized diversity and for most of his journey rejoiced in it:

> Diverse folk diversely they seyde
> But for the moore part they lowe and pleyde.

The Parson might not wish to accept as a general principle of human thought the Squire's observation that "As many heuedes as many wittes ther been." Yet most of us are still a long way from the gates of the Holy City and from the need to transcend all activity except penitence—the need to transcend even great art—that reaching such a point in our journey may require. Indeed, I see no reason why we may not assume, if we wish, that Harry Bailly spoke not only for us but to us when he "hadde the wordes for us alle" and said, in those last words that art measures out and rhymes in *The Canterbury Tales*:

> Beth fructuous and that in litel space
> And do to wel god sende yow his grace.

In chronicling his journey, Chaucer combined a greater diversity of storytellers, genres, and poetic forms than any man had ever before fused into a single work. Confronting a work that so rejoices in its own diversity, we may perhaps be excused for rejoicing in the diversity of our response—at least until the sun begins to set in our world, too, as we draw up closely in silence to hear the good Parson speak.

Notes

[1] Prepared by Eren Hostetter Branch as a by-product of the research that led to her dissertation, "Man Alone and Man in Society: Chaucer's Knight's Tale and Boccaccio's *Teseida*," Stanford 1975.

[2] Concerning the order of the tales, see now George R. Keiser, "In Defense of the Bradshaw Shift," *Chaucer Review*, 12 (1978), 191–201.

[3] Argued in detail in Emerson Brown, Jr., "The Poet's Last Words: Text and Meaning at the End of the Parson's Prologue," *Chaucer Review*, 10 (1976), 236–42.

[4] Paul A. Ruggiers, ed., *A Variorum Edition of the Works of Geoffrey Chaucer*, 1, *The Canterbury Tales: A Facsimile and Transcription of the Hengwrt Manuscript, with Variants from the Ellesmere Manuscript* (Norman: Univ. of Oklahoma Press, 1979), a volume most teachers of Chaucer will want for their personal libraries.

Appendix

COURSE SYLLABUS

Chaucer

Required Reading: Chaucer's *Canterbury Tales*, complete in Middle English
Boethius, *Consolation of Philosophy*
Some other material available in photocopies or on reserve
Numerous handouts distributed as we go along

Scope and Objectives of the Course: Our primary objective is to read and understand Chaucer's *Canterbury Tales* in the language he wrote in. We will learn something about the Middle Ages in general, and we may learn that study of a great medieval poet can sharpen our thinking about our own lives. But our main goal is simply to read *The Canterbury Tales*.

Memorizing: As one way of becoming more familiar with the sound and rhythm of Chaucer's verse and of getting something beautiful and lasting out of the course, you are to memorize passages throughout the semester. You will be expected to know lines 1–18 and at least two lines from the sketch of each pilgrim in the General Prologue and at least one passage of four lines or more from each of the tales. You decide which passages you want to memorize.

Further, you are to prepare one longer passage (again of your choosing) of ten to twenty lines to be repeated aloud to me, from memory. For this you should try to get as close as you can to the sound and rhythm of Chaucer's verse. You may have two tries at this, and your performance will be graded.

Try to persuade yourself that you are memorizing these lines for your own interest and enjoyment and not simply to meet an assignment. This attitude will make it easier and more enjoyable to memorize the lines in the first place and more likely that they will stay in mind after the course is over.

Quizzes, Final Exam: There will be a short quiz at the beginning of the hour every Tuesday. On these quizzes you may be asked to identify, translate, or discuss passages from your reading and to summarize or discuss points made in previous lectures. That's the bad news. The good news is that there is no midterm exam and no research paper. If you quickly get into the habit of reading Chaucer carefully and if you do your reading steadily through the semester, you should find a pleasant relief from the usual crisis atmosphere at midterm and endterm time.

The final exam will be in two parts. The first will be much like the quizzes; indeed, it will include some questions that have appeared on the quizzes. It will be considerably longer, however, and will cover the work of the whole semester. It will include opportunities for you to demonstrate your care in memorizing. The second part will be a take-home essay designed to encourage you to look at *The Canterbury Tales* as a whole and develop some topic that you find interesting. You will be given a list of topics toward the end of the semester. You may substitute a topic of your own choosing, but if you do so please clear it with me first. Although you are free to use information and insights picked up in your outside reading (with proper acknowledgment, of course), the essay is *not* a research paper. It is due at the hour of the final examination, though you may (and probably should) complete it sooner.

Final Grades: Final grades will be determined by the following formula or something fairly close to it: quizzes, 50%; performance of memorized lines, 10%; take-home final essay, 20%; in-class final exam, 20%.

The Tuesday Afternoon Chaucer Society: For students who are interested, we can get together on Tuesday afternoons to read Chaucer aloud, talk about things that interest us, and lament communally the ravages wrought by the Great Vowel Shift. With a little encouragement, I'll read the Miller's Tale aloud at one of these sessions, and a group of you might like to divide up the lines, rehearse a bit and do a reading of one of the tales.

Assignments and Lecture Schedule:

1. General Prologue, 1–18; Introduction to Chaucer's language and to the course.
2. Read and reread the General Prologue. Read my short essay "Chaucer and the European Literary Tradition" (on reserve) as well as the introductory material in the textbook. Know the material in the footnotes to the General Prologue. Be able to translate any passage from the first two hundred lines or so. Memorize the first eighteen (or more) lines.
3. Continue reading the General Prologue. You should now be able to identify or translate any passage in the GP. Have lines memorized from the portraits of the first half (or more) of the GP.
4. Continue reading the GP. You now have lines memorized for all the pilgrims. Also read Boethius, *Consolation of Philosophy.* Begin the Knight's Tale.
5. Knight's Tale.
6. Miller's Tale, Reeve's Tale, Cook's Tale.
7. Man of Law's Tale, Shipman's Tale, Prioress' Tale.
8. *Thopas, Melibee,* Monk's Tale, and Knight's Interruption. Some thoughts on unity of Groups II and VII. Begin Nun's Priest's Tale.
9. Nun's Priest's Tale, Wife of Bath's Prologue.
10. Wife of Bath's Tale, Summoner's Tale, Friar's Tale.
11. Clerk's Tale, Merchant's Tale.
12. Merchant's Tale (concluded), Squire's Tale, Franklin's Tale.
13. Franklin's Tale (concluded). Some thoughts on the "Marriage Group."
14. Physician's Tale, Pardoner's Tale.
15. Second Nun's Tale, Canon's Yeoman's Tale, Manciple's Tale, Parson's Tale, Chaucer's Retraction. This is a lot of reading, with more than half of it given to the Parson's long prose treatise. Try to plan ahead.

Forsan et haec olim meminisse juvabit.
Vergil

ON MAKING STUDENTS RELEVANT TO CHAUCER

Mary J. Carruthers

My first concern in teaching *The Canterbury Tales* in an upper-division course for English majors is to assure my students that they can read Chaucer in the language Chaucer wrote, and that he is worth their effort. The reason that American students are uncomfortable with any language other than contemporary English is obvious and too basic for any single teacher to hope to remedy fully, but I don't believe that one should therefore simply give up in despair. Many of the students I teach have families, hold full-time jobs, are from inner-city high schools, and have poor language preparation (though their motivation is high). Each student also carries three courses in addition to Chaucer during the quarter.

I begin my course with assigned reading and lectures on Chaucer's pronunciation and language. In order to familiarize my students' ears with Middle English, I read the text of *The Canterbury Tales* aloud frequently during class discussion throughout the term. I never translate except in response to a specific question concerning a grammatically difficult passage. All students must individually recite the introductory lines of the General Prologue to me, having prepared by listening to a tape I recorded and placed in the language lab (at my university it is possible for students to dial and request that a tape be played over the phone—in a commuter university this is very helpful). My students enjoy reciting

Chaucer, often unexpectedly; it encourages them to try reading other parts of Chaucer aloud to their friends, and, excruciating as the results may sometimes be, it is the best way I have discovered to make them feel a degree of familiarity and ease with Chaucer's poetry. It is often the first time some students have read *any* poetry aloud.

Both examinations in the course are essentially translation exams in which students render into modern English prose passages of about a dozen lines apiece. These exams are designed to test their knowledge of Chaucer's common constructions; students are failed if they simply paraphrase the general sense. The benefit of all these exercises to writing analytical papers is great, I believe, because it forces the students to get used to paying minute attention to what Chaucer actually says. By the time the students write their second analytical paper and final examination essay, the results demonstrate a rewardingly thoughtful understanding of Chaucer. I don't think it is sensible to expect students to write an analytical paper on a work of literature whose language is frightening to them—hence, my object through all these various written and oral exercises is to break down the barrier presented by Middle English sufficiently for students to read Chaucer with pleasure and profit.

Chaucer's age presents less of a barrier than his language. The chief difficulty for students is their complete ignorance of any history whatsoever, or indeed of what history is. I believe that the students' fascination in reading an old book will come not from any simpleminded "relevance" that it may or may not have "for today" but from understanding how a great writer took the materials of his own time—the books he read, the people he met, the political, social, and intellectual world in which he lived—and transmuted them into a book. I therefore talk about the literary sources available to Chaucer and even more about the qualities of life and thought in his time. I talk about knights, clerks, monks, and peasants, about the cloth trade, about the war in France, about intellectual concerns of the time. Students read Huizinga's *The Waning of the Middle Ages* as much to get an idea of how cultural history has been done successfully as to learn what the book says specifically about fifteenth-century Flanders. I recommend a readable history of England—Myers' *England in the Late Middle Ages* has replaced the too expensive Trevelyan on my list.

I have also recently made a series of slides (eighty is the maximum number of slides I can get through in a fifty-minute period) to illustrate daily life in the Middle Ages. I have copied the reproductions of manuscript illuminations that I have collected from books and on postcards over the years; with a copy stand and a flat-field corrected micro lens on my SLR camera, I am able to make excellent slides even of details from these reproductions. I have also purchased from the Huntington Library their set of slides of the Ellesmere portraits. I usually give the slide presentation early in the course. For the many students who are able to retain and comprehend visual material more easily than verbal, the "Chaucer slide show" is a valuable introduction. By selecting my own material, I can emphasize exactly what I want as well as answer questions as they arise. This, I think, is a decisive advantage of slides over the films, which are, of course, also available.

The task for my students is to make themselves relevant to Chaucer, because only then will Chaucer be truly relevant to them. Using this guiding principle, I have taught with equal success students in an elite Eastern women's college and in a new urban state university. I teach the Wife of Bath, for example, in the historical context of not only the literary writings of the time but also the economic realities of her own class and show how she uses the experience of the one to undercut the authority of the other. I do not present her as a proto-liberated woman, nor do I try to make her easier for modern students by supplying fake modern analogies for her statements. But I don't teach her as though she were a dusty antique, interesting in her own time but quite incompatible in a modern living room. I present her as one of the great creations of a great medieval poet, and my students are perfectly able to make for themselves the contemporary connections that they find interesting. Similarly, I teach the Pardoner's Prologue and Tale wholly within the context of an Augustinian analysis of the psychology of sin and redemption, the habits of medieval pardoners, and the universal games of confidence-men; I make no effort to Freudianize or allegorize him.[1]

My pedagogical style is that of neither formal lecture nor Socratic dialogue. I present Chaucer's tales in sequence, commenting on what I believe to be the major themes, their development, and the major critical issues and reading aloud liberal amounts of the text. My students interrupt with questions and comments of their own as they are moved to do so. I ask them questions, usually concerning details of the text, although I also solicit opinions on particular issues raised in a tale. Of the two kinds of questions, the former has consistently proved to be more useful and profitable for the class. I do not pretend to know less about Chaucer than my students know, nor do I pretend that my knowledge isn't important. My students learn to think about and appreciate Chaucer by thinking along with me, and I try to strike a proper balance between their intelligence and their ignorance. My students seem to respond well to this method. The typical comment that I get from them on course evaluations is that they expected to be bored and preached at by Chaucer but that they have been gratefully delighted and educated by him instead.

Note

[1] See Alfred Kellogg, "An Augustinian Interpretation of Chaucer's Pardoner," *Speculum*, 26 (1951), 465–81; A. Kellogg and L. A. Haselmayer, "Chaucer's Satire of the Pardoner," *PMLA*, 66 (1951), 251–77; E. T. Donaldson, "Chaucer's Three 'P's': Pandarus, Pardoner, and Poet," *Michigan Quarterly Review*, 14 (1975), 282–301; Donald R. Howard, *The Idea of the* Canterbury Tales (Berkeley: Univ. of California Press, 1976), pp. 333–71. My approach to the Wife of Bath is detailed in my essay, "The Wife of Bath and the Painting of Lions," *PMLA* 94 (1979), 209–22.

Appendix

COURSE SYLLABUS

Chaucer, *The Canterbury Tales*

Required Texts: E. T. Donaldson, *Chaucer's Poetry*, 2nd ed.
———, *Speaking of Chaucer*
R. Schoeck and J. Taylor, eds., *Chaucer Criticism*, Vol. I

Recommended Reading: J. Huizinga, *The Waning of the Middle Ages*
A. R. Myers, *England in the Late Middle Ages*

Written work: There will be a midterm exam and a final exam. There will also be two short critical papers (five to six pages each) on topics suggested or approved by the instructor. In addition, since all students are expected to demonstrate familiarity with Chaucer's English, each student must read individually to the instructor the first eighteen lines of the General Prologue in Middle English before the end of classes.

Assignments and Lecture Schedule:

WEEKS

1. Introduction to Chaucer's language and time
2. The General Prologue
3. Knight's Tale
4. Miller's Tale; slides shown
5. Wife of Bath's Tale, Friar's Tale, Summoner's Tale
6. Midterm exam; Clerk's Tale
7. Merchant's Tale, Franklin's Tale
8. Pardoner's Tale, Shipman's Tale
9. Prioress' Tale, *Sir Thopas*, Nun's Priest's Tale
10. Canon's Yeoman's Tale, Parson's Prologue and Tale, Chaucer's Retraction

THE CHAUCER COURSE: SPECIFIC APPROACHES

A RHETORICAL AND STRUCTURAL EMPHASIS

Robert M. Jordan

Once students overcome the imagined obstacles of Chaucer's era (medieval!) and his language, they invariably find that Chaucer speaks to them with remarkable directness and immediacy. Nevertheless, the language does present problems, and to prevent students from developing careless reading habits I spend two or three weeks concentrating on Chaucerian syntax and vocabulary. I do this in a poetic context, usually *The Parlement of Foules*, which is a good introduction to Chaucer for other reasons as well, including its coverage of most of the encyclopedic range of Chaucer's interests. At the same time, as part of the preliminaries, I try to provide an orientation to Chaucer's literary, social, philosophical, and theological milieu. Having done my best to demystify Middle English and my briefest to arouse a sympathetic interest in the late Middle Ages, I move quickly to the Chaucerian text, which, as I try to persuade my students, tells us more about Chaucer's era than any secondhand generalizations could and tells it better.

I generally spend some time with the easy questions, not necessarily only at the beginning of the course. I enjoy with my students some lively discussion and dispute about such engaging Chaucerian matters as the feminist vagaries of the Wife of Bath, the disarming villainy of the Pardoner, the flawed piety of the Prioress, and the problematic patience of

81

Griselda, to name a few. Beyond these ready delights I move toward a more rigorous critical scrutiny of the poetry in pursuit of certain theoretical questions that I think are of primary importance to a proper understanding of Chaucer and finally to a fuller appreciation of the pleasure and satisfaction Chaucer holds for us.

In my teaching of *The Canterbury Tales*, I look especially hard at that critical juncture and interplay between the fictional worlds peopled by Chaucerian characters—the pilgrims as well as their putative creations— and the verbal forms that create and contain those fictions. This emphasis is not arbitrary, and it is not merely a modish modernism, despite a similar emphasis in much contemporary fiction and structuralist theory. The determining fact is that Chaucer is an author keenly conscious of his role as a maker of fictions and a practitioner of verbal art. Despite the wonderful ease and fluency of his language and his ready store of stories and characters, Chaucer evidences throughout his work a fascination with the art of poetry, the process itself of using the flat, impalpable medium of language to make persuasive illusions of worldly reality. And he does this in palpable ways, by overt references to the act of writing or telling and by actually inscribing the viewpoint of the maker into the poetic structure.

A second emphasis in my teaching of Chaucer arises from the highly rhetorical character of Chaucer's art, its affinity for certain principles of structure and disposition of parts that are inherent in the rhetoricians' approach to composition. Here, too, I direct consideration to demonstrable characteristics of the text, and necessarily so, since hard evidence is required to persuade students that many of their assumptions and expectations, bred from their familiarity with naturalistic narrative, Romantic poetry, and movies and television, simply do not correlate with the realities of Chaucerian narrative. Because unexamined presuppositions exert considerable force, some effort is required to make students believe what they see. But dispassionate study of the text reveals quite clearly that narrative fiction as Chaucer composed it displays in abundance characteristics that popular culture, still largely under the sway of Romantic biases, regards as inimical to art.

We do Chaucer's art scant justice if we fail to discern and appreciate its definitive attributes. Despite the Romantic legacy of bias against rhetoric and all that term implies about constraints upon the artistic imagination, we have lately begun to see that Chaucer's rhetorical orientation imparts to his poetry traits whose esthetic possibilities are considerable and worthy of acknowledgment. For example, lengthy digressions, or "amplifications," to use a pertinent rhetorical term, are everywhere apparent in Chaucerian narrative, and although they are antithetical to widely cherished esthetic criteria of continuity and organic cohesion they nonetheless produce an energy and variety that are characteristically Chaucerian.

The rhetorical poet regards his task as the proper shaping and disposition of verbal forms. Certainly such was the message of rhetorical treatises well known to Chaucer and his contemporaries. Accordingly, junctures are often abrupt and outlines prominent; like the piers and buttresses of a Gothic cathedral, the framework and supporting articulations are themselves esthetically significant. Such structures do not disguise their "made" quality, unlike works constructed on an organic model, an important aim of which is to conceal the seams and devices of construction.

Fascinating and absorbing as they are, Chaucer's fictional world and its people cannot claim our exclusive attention, because Chaucer won't let them. He gives palpable as well as audible form to the narrating voice, the authenticator, which mediates between that world and ourselves. This voice, which in variously engaging and often ingenuous ways calls our attention to itself and thereby to the problematic issues of verbal representations of reality, constitutes a dimension of literary form that the untutored student would happily ignore as a digressive diversion from the story. Of course it is just such a faulty reader whom Chaucer has in mind when his narrating voice disclaims responsibility for the tales told by uncouth pilgrims and urges genteel readers to skip those tales (Miller's Prologue, 3171–85). Irony is one way of explaining this multivalence, but I find that trying to explain Chaucerian irony is as unrewarding as trying to explain a good joke.

I prefer a structural explanation because the stratified levels of Chaucerian narrative, constituted by the fiction, the narrating voice, and the audience, are easily differentiated and because such an explanation is applicable to varying Chaucerian situations. I would stress the fact that none of the levels of the text, though each is largely autonomous, is as important as the relationships among them—relationships that Chaucer constructs and manipulates in varying ways to form the full literary experience. Moreover, these structural relationships are repeated at different levels. The function of the voice narrating the Canterbury framework is analogically repeated in the voices of the narrators of individual tales, though Chaucer varies the circumstances considerably in individual instances. Sometimes the narrating voice approaches the status of a consistently recognizable personality; at other times, it splits into differing and often contradictory viewpoints, attitudes, and styles. But it is almost always clearly present, in one form or another, adding a supertextual dimension to the fictive text.

Skillfully and attractively drawn though it is, the illusion of a Canterbury journey exists within a larger literary structure, the apprehension of which can be obscured or missed entirely by the unschooled reader. In the belief that distance and closeness are equally indispensable to under-standing—a belief that Chaucer manifestly shared—I encourage students to stand back from the illusion, as Chaucer frequently does, and to see *The Canterbury Tales* as a synchrony, a constructed composition. To this end, I usually teach the work in nonsequential order. After the General Prologue I move directly to the ending and later fill in parts of the middle. This procedure is, of course, only a device, a means of highlight-ing the verbal form, whose synchrony can be perceived only after one has completed the temporal process of reading. From this perspective, it is easier to recognize the fictive limitations of the diachronic illusion of a pilgrimage. Such a procedure is especially appropriate for *The Canter-bury Tales* because the beginning and the ending are so decisively struc-tured and the inner parts so clearly articulated and separable. It is also useful as a means of highlighting Chaucer's own fascination with the magic of illusion. If we remain as fully absorbed in the illusion as the "roadside drama" theory requires, we miss the larger dimensions of the work, which are signaled in many ways but most overtly by Chaucer's manipulations of his self-designated role as pilgrim and reporter. (Note especially General Prologue, 725–46; Miller's Prologue, 3170–81; *Sir Thopas*; Parson's Prologue, 55–60; Chaucer's Retraction.)

The leap from the General Prologue to the Parson's Prologue and Tale presents some hazards since the Parson's Tale rarely appeals directly to even the most eager students. (A less rigorous approach serving the same purpose might treat the rest of Fragment I, including the Knight's and Miller's Tales, before moving to the ending.) The sheer mass of the Parson's Tale effectively balances the General Prologue as a structural pillar of *The Canterbury Tales*. The two parts balance each other meta-phorically as well, each being an encyclopedic rendering of the human condition, one in a sequence of poetic characterizations, the other in a prose exposition. My approach to the content of the Parson's treatise emphasizes its comprehensive mastery of human emotions, its contain-ment of the myriad guilts and anxieties of this life within the overwhelm-ing potential for salvation and eternal fulfillment. Although the prose does not approach the expressive power of Chaucerian verse, it nonetheless displays a trenchant and vigorous quality, most notably in the excursus on the Seven Deadly Sins, but elsewhere as well. Interesting as its content can be discovered to be, the Parson's Tale also serves a powerful symbolic purpose in thrusting the entire Canterbury enterprise upward toward salvation. Here, too, of course, Chaucer displays his indifference to the realistic strictures of the roadside plan, which prescribed two tales for each pilgrim on the outward journey and two during the return to London.

It takes some work to redeem the content of the Parson's Tale for the modern student, but even less readily apparent to the student is the significance of the formal organization of this strategically placed treatise. The overt and punctilious division of the work into parts and parts of parts betokens a habit of mind, scholastic in its analytical style, that is congenial to Chaucer and that manifests itself, in variously modified ways, as the esthetic principle underlying the structure of The Canterbury Tales and its parts and parts of parts. The General Prologue, for example, is a virtually self-sufficient whole, framed by the voice and perspective of the narrating pilgrim, and within it are independently wrought portraits of the individual figures. The succeeding tales are independent structures whose autonomy can be deemphasized but cannot be denied by psychological or dramatic interpretations. The Canterbury framework, which enjoys an autonomy of its own, encloses the tales and provides them with designated tellers but does not permeate them in ways that impair their autonomy or decisively determine their nature.

Such are the general critical bases of my approach to The Canterbury Tales. If I lack sufficient space here to argue these tendentious propositions effectively, perhaps I can at least suggest the direction they give to classroom discussion of a few particularly problematic tales. The Manciple's Tale, for example, has been widely neglected in Chaucerian scholarship, and the reasons are not difficult to surmise. Fully one-half of the tale is embroidery, the other half narrative, which is to say the tale is digressive in the extreme. Moreover, the digressions, most of which are spoken by the Manciple-narrator, offer very little in the way of characterization of the speaker. For a variety of reasons they are nevertheless very interesting in their own right, more so, perhaps, than the putative subject of the tale, the story of Phoebus and the crow. The digressions illustrate above all a rhetorical virtuosity, as in the sequence of examples, freely multiplied, of the proposition that despite outer refinements beings will revert to their essentially irrational nature: birds, cats, she-wolves, men (but not women, who will always be rational). Wit, verbal irony, and humor are here in abundance. Then there are the trenchant observations on language and linguistic connotation, which would be close to the heart of a practitioner like Chaucer, and finally the lengthy disquisition on speech and silence, interesting in itself for its rhetorical patterning as well as for its message, and a fittingly provocative conclusion to the last of the Canterbury "speeches" before the Parson's concluding treatise.

The Nun's Priest's Tale's bipartite form resembles the Manciple's Tale's structural differentiation between text and supertext. In this case, too, the supertext does not "dramatize" the nominal teller with any particularity.

Even more so here than in the Manciple's Tale, the "irrelevant" digressions of the supertext—on dreams, on marriage, on the fates of pagan heroes, on the certainty that murder will out, on methods of rhetorical apostrophe, and so on—so fully divert our attention that we cannot easily determine where the true center of this narrative lies. Hence, the humorously enigmatic character of the narrator's parting advice that we should take the fruit and let the chaff go. This and other comments about the tale he is telling, including especially his appeal for help to the rhetorician Geoffrey of Vinsauf, relate this speaker, designated the Nun's Priest, to the pseudo-Chaucer of the General Prologue as well as to other voices, nominally identified in various ways but all speaking in much the same voice about the activity of making fictions or recording the tales of others. Consistency of characterization is a distinct casualty in these recurring allusions (often mischievous and ingenuous) to the art of narrative.

At the other extreme, the Pardoner's Tale demonstrates the closest Chaucer comes to "dramatizing" a teller through a tale or, to put it the other way around, the closest he comes to "unifying" a tale through the personality of its teller. The critical literature resounds with disputation over the motives and the personality of this striking figure, and students are quick to contribute their own psychological analyses and speculations. They are less quick, however, to recognize the limits the text imposes on such psychologizing. I would first differentiate between the modes of literary discourse evident in the Prologue and the Tale. The former, a Chaucerian elaboration of the Faux-Semblant figure in the *Roman de la Rose*, is a personalized personification, hypocrisy with human name (or occupation) expounding his nature in the form of a confession. This is the conceptual framework—essentially expository and descriptive—that Chaucer embellishes with the kind of lively and subtle human touches we admire as "dramatic." The Tale itself has been celebrated as a superbly concentrated narrative, but it is that only in part. The whole of the tale, which includes supertext as well as the narrative of the three covetous young men, is a highly disjunct mixture of verbal modes. The somber and relentless narrative is abruptly interrupted, twenty lines after it begins, by high-pitched expostulations from the teller constituting approximately two hundred lines of digression. The expostulations are carried on in the vein of pulpit oratory established in the Prologue. The relationship between this voice and the controlled, underspoken voice of the narrative proper is problematic in the extreme. The Pardoner's own proposition that an immoral man can tell a moral tale hardly resolves the critical problem. I would argue that Chaucer has employed two distinct literary forms and interwoven them, or superimposed one upon the other, to produce a masterpiece of mixed forms.

The kind of "multiple unity" displayed by the Pardoner's Tale—to borrow a term coined by the art historian Heinrich Wölfflin to distinguish the style of a head by Dürer from the "unified unity" of a head by Rembrandt —is extended to its limits in the Merchant's Tale. The reason critical consensus about this tale is so elusive is that the tale offers no conclusive evidence to substantiate the hypothesis of "unified unity" that so many critics have brought to it. Despite the Prologue's enticing indications of a Merchant embittered by two months of wedlock, scrutiny of the ensuing narrative is very hard put to discern a pervasive voice of anguish unifying this long tale. On the contrary, the parts are unusually distinct in style and even in generic affiliation, and each part generates its own characteristic voice. Within the frail framework of the *senex amans* plot the tale contains four distinct segments, each amplifying an aspect of the January–May theme. The result is a mixture of autonomous forms: a rhetorical debate on marriage, composed of extended set speeches; a courtly romance in a conventional love-garden setting; a fantasy of pagan gods; a raucous and vulgar fabliau. To sort out the diverse voices that come and go in this turbulent narrative is a challenging critical task, and it raises innumerable questions about attitude and morality as well as about formal structure. Such questions, arising from an assumption of "multiple unity," are sufficiently provocative in themselves and leave behind the theory that this complex and dazzling tale finds a "unified unity" in the personality of its nominal teller.

What I have sketched here is not a master plan or a blueprint for teaching *The Canterbury Tales* but a critical approach that I think is appropriate both to the poetics Chaucer knew and to the text we have. Chaucer was not only a virtuoso rhetorical poet, a master of forms and styles; he was also an extremely self-conscious artist, fascinated with his power to make illusions and at the same time awed and even fearful of it. He built into his work the polar perspectives of immersion and withdrawal as he displayed the processes of making and breaking fictional illusions. His humility in the face of God's creation imparted a humor and a skepticism about his own capacities, which are in turn reflected in the character of his work. The signs of the maker are always there, in the shaping and articulating of structural parts as well as in overt references to the verbal art. Regularity and symmetry are not to be found, and narrative movement is spasmodic and digressive as Chaucer moves freely, in an often improvisatory fashion, to dilate, in the rhetoricians' way, on the subject of the moment. Nor do we find the kind of unity that is understood according to certain postmedieval critical canons to be based in theme or character. All things in Chaucer, pace Brooks and Warren, do not cohere neatly and organically. As the French theorist Gérard Genette has noted in a more general context, it seems foolish to search for "unity" at any price and in this way to force the coherence of the work. Our task as teachers is not to force *The Canterbury Tales* into a preconceived notion of unity or to deplore the absence of such a unity but to help our students appreciate the Chaucerian plenitude. If *The Canterbury Tales* is less the "organism" that the New Critics admired and more the "wall" they disdained, we can help our students to understand that this "inorganic" form is Chaucer's very human and very artful way of extending consciousness into words.

THE BOETHIAN UNITY OF THE TALES

William Provost

Chaucer's masterpiece is *The Canterbury Tales*. It is the poem in which he most fully and beautifully constructs an image of his own sane, human, clear understanding of man and his relation to God and the universe. Accordingly, this poem is the logical (and I think most common) culmination of a Chaucer course. The problem I will discuss in this essay is that of teaching as a logical end point, as a culmination, as an artistic masterpiece, a work as fragmented as *The Canterbury Tales*. This problem is aggravated by the exigencies of time so sharply felt in most quarter and semester Chaucer courses. The teacher who wants to begin with one or more of the early poems, perhaps glance at a few of the lyrics, give to *Troilus and Criseyde* anything like the time it so richly deserves, and sigh even briefly at having to skip *The Legend of Good Women* will, when it is time for *The Canterbury Tales*, be able to cover at most about half of an already fragmented work. How, despite its many brilliant, delightful passages, can such a work, thus presented, be honestly and effectively taught as the masterpiece of one of the two greatest poets in our language?

The solution to this pedagogical problem depends on an understanding of what the poem is, of how its structure, meaning, doctrine, and technique work together to make Chaucer's "book of the Tales of Canterbury" his finest and most powerful poem. The ideas I will use in developing this point derive from my own attempts to read, comprehend, and teach *The Canterbury Tales*. Many of these ideas have been corroborated, clarified, and corrected by the work of fine Chaucer scholars, past and present, including several whose essays are in this volume. (According to the guidelines of this series, these debts will not be specifically documented, though they will no doubt be recognized and are here gratefully acknowledged.)

Stated most simply, the solution is that *The Canterbury Tales* is a complete poem, even though Chaucer did not finish it in the same way he finished, say, *Troilus and Criseyde*. Moreover, its fragmentary nature is an essential part of what it is as a poem. The impression so strongly given that we have a radically incomplete work depends on a number of apparent inconsistencies between what the text promises and what it delivers. The most obvious and important of these is the difference between the ten dozen tales that seem to be planned and the two dozen (several of them unfinished) that we have. Actually, the four-tales-per-pilgrim plan is the Host's original, enthusiastic expectation, and even he apparently finds it necessary to cut back as the pilgrimage proceeds. Nowhere does Chaucer—as either poet or narrator, if we care to make that distinction in this particular context—even imply how extensive his poem (or his recounting of an experience from memory) will be. In those places where such an authorial intention has been descried—for instance, in the Miller's Prologue, where Chaucer says, "I moot reherce / Hir tales alle"—there is never any actual reference to the number of tales planned. The passage just quoted, for example, is simply part of the sly come-on to the Miller's Tale: "I'm even going to have to use some dirty words to retell all their tales." The other discrepancies that have seemed to many readers to indicate radical incompleteness—particularly inconsistencies in the order of some of the geographical references found in the links, uncertainties about some tale-teller relationships and/or assignments, and the absence of links for many tales—are all rather minor, even taken collectively. They can most simply and convincingly be accounted for by assuming, as I have said, that Chaucer never finished his revising and correcting of the poem. I will go one step further and say that a deliberate open-endedness was part of the poet's plan, and that such an open-endedness, with its accompanying inconsistencies, constitutes an important element in the very nature of the poem.

Turning to the positive, the evidence of completeness is clear. The beginning and ending of the poem, Fragments I and X, are obviously in place and complete, even finished (the barely started Cook's Tale might seem a problem, but by the time we get to it, as I will suggest, even so blatant a hiatus should come as no great surprise. This sort of structurally unambiguous marking of beginning and ending is a typically Chaucerian indication of completeness; compare, for example, the almost self-consciously fashioned beginnings and endings of such obviously complete poems as *The Book of the Duchess, The Parliament of Fowls,* or *Troilus and Criseyde* with such incomplete ones as *The House of Fame* or *The Legend of Good Women.* Furthermore, there are numerous echoes, balances, and other relationships throughout the poem that tie it firmly together. Various physiognomical details in the General Prologue that only become important much later on; such clear thematic linkings as those of the "Marriage Group," the Knight's-Miller's-Reeve's Tales, or the Monk's-Nun's Priest's Tales; and the many dramatically developed character relationships among pilgrims: such elements argue convincingly for accepting the poem as a unit, as a whole poem. Having thus accepted it, we are compelled, as readers and teachers, to comprehend it in such a way that both its wholeness and inconsistencies are subsumed in an interpretive approach. Such an approach exists, and it turns a pedagogical problem into a key to enlightenment and delight.

Chaucer crafted his greatest poem when he had fully come to grips with the core of Boethian philosophy. He may, of course, have reached a full understanding of Boethius before this, but it does not show up clearly in the earlier poetry. In *Troilus and Criseyde,* for example, the main Boethian elements derive from Books I, II, and V of the *Consolation of Philosophy,* material dealing with Fortune's Wheel and the problem of free will. It is in *The Canterbury Tales* that the central philosophic principle of the *Consolation,* deriving especially from Books III and IV, becomes the informing principle of Chaucer's poetry. The Boethian principle by which the unity and harmony of Providence are seen in relation to the apparently random, even disparate fates of the discrete units of creation—men, elements, planets, and so forth—becomes, in Chaucer's distinctively sane, human, confident rendering, the model on which the poem is constructed. Structure, meaning, doctrine, technique; General Prologue, dramatic frame, tales, and retraction; wholeness, open-endedness, and inconsistencies: all are subsumed within Chaucer's model, adding to it and at the same time drawing significance, power, clarity, and beauty from it.

How does an awareness of this model translate, practically and specifically, into a plan for classroom presentation? In the remainder of this essay I would like to sketch briefly a reading of the *Tales,* with particular emphasis on the first Fragment, that I have found useful in structuring such a presentation. Clearly, this is only a cursory outline of an actual course plan; many additional applications of the model occur, and many other features of the poem not directly or simply relatable to it must be dealt with by the teacher. I hope, however, that something of the comprehensiveness and usefulness of a presentation built essentially around this interpretive model may come across even in such a limited version as the one that follows.

The poem begins with those wonderfully mellifluous lines, the best known, I suppose, in all English poetry: "Whan that Aprill with his shoures soote / The droghte of March hath perced to the roote, / And bathed every veyne in swich licour / Of which vertu engendred is the flour. . . ." These lines and the fifteen or so that follow actually say very little, but they establish an ideal, harmonious, well-ordered scene; they are at least mildly suggestive of a *locus amoenus* description. And most important, they sound lovely. We hear sensuously as well as recognize rationally the typical medieval analogy between musical harmony and the greater harmony of God's well-wrought universe. The narrowing of the focus to England and a springtime journey to Canterbury does nothing to change our perception of this sort of universe or even of this particular, discrete part of it. Nor does our first encounter with the "sondry folk" who have gathered "by aventure" at the Tabard. This is an ideal, a well-ordered, a providential pilgrimage, the one we would want to join if we had the choice of the many that must have come together here in the waning years of the fourteenth century. It is, indeed, the one the Host and our own narrator choose to join. As we meet the individuals who constitute this group we feel an occasional, perhaps even a frequent, uneasiness about some of the disparities that seem to exist between the ideal of the estates the pilgrims represent and the reality of the particular characters we see as representatives of the various estates. But maybe our uneasiness simply points out our own small-minded churlishness. What could go wrong on a day like this, in a universe like this?

Man, of course, is the only creature that can go wrong, and of course he does so constantly, using his free will perversely, selfishly, destructively— opting for the part, for the moment, rather than accepting and embracing the harmony of the whole. Thankfully, the God of this universe is a loving God whose love is such that the misuse of free will does not destroy the harmony of the whole. (In most instances, we must all fervently hope, even the individual misuser is not destroyed.) But the propensity to go wrong certainly does make for many tragic or, depending on your outlook, comic situations. And it certainly provides an enticing plan for a long comic poem—particularly to a poet with a belief, deep and firm in his heart, in the complete harmony of the universe and with a vivid, amused, and perhaps occasionally tragic perception, clear in his mind, of the human tendency (including his own) to muck things up.

Such is the plan in Chaucer's masterpiece, and we continue to see its

effects. Early the next day (another lovely one, I feel certain), the journey begins, still orderly, still ideal, still following the grand, harmonious
plan whose "prime mover" now seems to be the Host. Surely we should
not take too seriously the hint of animallike disorder (chickens, after all,
don't have free will, so they cannot muck things up) in the description of
the start: ". . . oure Hoost . . . was oure aller cok, / And gadrede us
togidre alle in a flok." So what if human beings do look momentarily like
chickens! The harmony is affirmed even by chance itself when the cut
falls to the Knight to tell the first tale. What could be more appropriate,
more right? Should we worry about the statistical improbability of such
appropriateness? Not in such a universe, or such a poem, were it not that
we are told it is by "aventure, or sort, or cas" that such a providential
event occurs. I think anyone who reads much Chaucer learns that any one
of these words arouses suspicion. It is not just "aventure," for example, that
has brought these particular pilgrims together, any more than it is "upon
cas" that Troilus' eye lights on Criseyde in the temple. These are, it seems
to me, code words in Chaucer that invariably and ironically suggest some
form of mundane, human scheme—be it that of a poet, a Pandarus, or
maybe a Harry Bailly—more immediately and directly than they suggest
the grand unfolding of a providential plan.

But never mind even that. Let us turn to the Knight's Tale itself, the
"philosophic cornerstone" of the entire poem, as it has been called. The
informing principle that I have defined and that I have been tracing is
discernible here also. The tale is, on the surface, a well-ordered, smoothly
structured Boethian romance that seems to affirm harmony even in human
affairs. This stately, classical, well-proportioned tale is undercut throughout, however, by clever, often very funny evidences of human disorder
(or to put it in a different way, by Chaucerian irony), so that in itself the
tale becomes a paradigm for the whole of the poem. Theseus, the wise,
mature order-bringer of the tale, is tinged subtly but clearly time and
again with less than ideal human qualities: pride, political scheming, and
vacillation. His final, grave Prime Mover speech is undercut by his real
motive in bringing the two lovers together, the need for a docile Thebes,
and by his gestures—the staged silence and the little sigh that precede his
speech, for example, too obviously resemble Diomede's feigned gestures
when he speaks with Criseyde on the tenth day. The balanced, symmetri-
cal descriptions of the three temple scenes are similarly undercut, for
example, by the four occurrences in five lines of the word "queinte" just at
the point where the goddess of chastity is responding to Emelye's prayer.
The Knight himself, good man, even ideal type, that he is, is simply not
an apt story teller. His own structural breaks belie the organizational
precision the tale seems to have, as when he says, "Up to the ancle foghte

they in hir blood. / And in this wise I lete hem fightyng dwelle, / And forth I wole of Theseus yow telle." The Knight repeatedly gets himself involved in descriptions that make him distinctly uneasy: the naked Venus, or Emelye's bathing, or her hair, which was "a yerde long, I gesse." He tries to color his tale with rhetoric, as all the books recommend, but he gets involved in such matters as the impossibly long *preteritio* in the description of Arcite's funeral. And, of course, more generally we must have some suspicions about the true orderliness of a tale in which love, the binding force of God's universe, causes two loving cousins to fight over a girl each has caught a mere glimpse of, "as dide the houndes for the boon," or one in which human passion and disorder infect the very heavens, causing strife among the gods themselves until old Saturn goes against his accustomed path and smooths things over. Nor does it seem at all farfetched to imagine the effect of the tale on the other pilgrims. They all approve of it, we are told, but as we see in the Miller's response to it, that approval may itself be undercut in some very human ways. And I suspect that the Wife of Bath is not completely drawn into the grand, harmonious plan of things by the Knight's closing description of the natural course a human marriage will take.

One of Chaucer's most characteristic qualities is his unwillingness to make anything too pat, too formulaic. If his overall plan for the poem can encompass the Knight's Tale, in which we have surface harmony, order, and balance undercut by human frailties of various sorts, it can also encompass a tale in which we have, on the surface and very evident, a story of human frailty, disorder, and sin, just beneath the surface of which is a marvelously and precisely wrought work of art. The drunken Miller, himself a fine image of the human condition and the character who leads the pilgrimage at its start, breaks into the Host's well-ordered plan and proceeds to tell a coarse, barnyard tale with disturbing analogies to the Knight's courtly romance. Nowhere in his poetry more than in the Miller's Tale, though, does Chaucer exercise such careful, planned, truly harmonious control. The plot elements, the characterizations, the descriptive details, the biblical allusions, the dialogue: all are brought together into the sort of precise arrangement and balance that only great art can achieve, the sort of art that is one of man's closest approximations to the precision (perhaps even the incipient humor?) of God's craftsmanship. This quality is most pervasively seen in the poet's wonderfully skillful welding together of two common, comic story lines, yielding with old John's response to handy Nicholas' cry for "Water!" the finest comic moment I know of in literature. (Whether the two story lines were found together in Chaucer's immediate source is of no consequence; they could not have been put together like this in the source.)

And so the craftsmanship continues. The Reeve's Tale works another switch on the core plot of its two predecessors, and the Cook's Tale just stops after fifty-eight lines. The "Marriage Group," with the Wife of Bath temporarily taking over the role of earthly prime mover, sets up its own system of analogies, responses, and structure-theme reversals. The tragic, or at least near tragic, side of individual human disjointedness is dramatized in the Pardoner's Tale, where the pilgrimage actually stops for a while and comes perilously close to being destroyed. In the awed hush that, I believe, follows the Pardoner's offer to the Host, everything hangs in the balance. Harry Bailly's "hogges toord" and the Knight's truly gentle gesture set things going again, but we sense that neither of these leaders is consciously acting out his own plan; rather, each is an agent for a larger plan—Chaucer's and perhaps even that of Providence Itself. At any rate, at least a human semblance of harmony is restored, and the pilgrims continue on their flawed, funny way.

We glimpse this larger plan in the Nun's Priest's Tale, where an almost disembodied but still very Chaucerian-sounding narrator comments obviously on the general tendency of individual human beings to look like chickens and only a little less obviously on the members of the particular flock he is a part of. The unexpected intrusion of a Canon and his Yeoman into the flock and the quite unplanned-for Canon's Yeoman's Tale (perhaps the other side of the coin to the apparently unplanned-for breaking off of the Cook's Tale) are further elements that are readily subsumed within the poem's governing principle and that can be taught effectively in relation to it. Finally, when the pilgrims collectively turn to the Parson, and even Harry Bailly willingly gives over his appearance of authority to that worthy man, we sense the approaching completion of the overall plan. The poet's own leave-taking of his worldly craft is the only possible way of completing a poem that, like the human situation it images forth so remarkably, can never be finished. The completing of that greater work, which the poem images, will also involve a final statement by its Author, a statement that is at once beyond and startlingly different from, and yet also a necessary and clear part of, all that precedes it.

The interpretive advantage of the model I have defined and outlined is that it accounts for more features of *The Canterbury Tales* than any other I know of. The curious blend of order and disorder, so palpable at so many different levels of the poem, is seen to be a typically Chaucerian rendering of the consoling message of Boethius: there is a plan and a true harmony after all, even if we can get but glimpses of it here. For the avid student of love and of human nature that Geoffrey Chaucer was, this message must have provided a genuine philosophic consolation and a compelling artistic challenge. For the exceptionally busy man of affairs that he also was, so often unable to finish tasks as he would have liked to, it must have provided a very human sense of relief and the challenge of a great, high comic joke. For us, ordinary readers and teachers, an awareness of the plan Chaucer derived from Boethius and from his own knowledge of the way things are offers a valuable pedagogical tool for presenting to our classes, even when we can cover only parts of the fragmented whole, an accurate and satisfying reading of a masterpiece of literature.

THE CULTURAL CONTEXT

Terrie Curran

Both the recent proliferation of publications about Chaucer in relation to his age and the flourishing Medieval Studies programs across the nation are indicative of a healthy appetite for integrated perspectives on the Middle Ages; so, too, is the ambitious undertaking of the Chaucer Library and the University of Georgia Press in publishing virtually all the texts that constituted Chaucer's intellectual world. Although most of us who teach Chaucer function without benefit of supporting colleagues in Medieval Studies and with only modest library budgets, we can take advantage of the excellent work that has been done to integrate literature and its cultural milieu.

Certainly, integrated studies and cultural contexts in the literature classroom have not always been applauded, nor has the theory behind such teaching gone unchallenged. During the 1950s, the wave of New Criticism threatened to make many of us feel guilty for depending on footnotes, introductions, glossaries, and (God help us) cultural background studies. But we who took our fourteenth-century texts into the twentieth-century classroom were forced to reckon with our students' historical ignorance concerning summoners, pardoners, franklins, prioresses, and pilgrimages to shrines. It was (and remains) evident that, for a modern audience, fourteenth-century "common knowledge" is scarcely common; it is sometimes gleaned from the text, but it remains *history*, which needs selective but deliberate retrieval. Our function as teachers, therefore, has had to include making Chaucer's works accessible and comprehensible in order that they might be compelling as poetry. To accomplish even the least of these goals necessitates teaching cultural background.

The teaching of Chaucer and things medieval was again challenged in the tumultuous years of the 1960s, when "relevance" was the keynote of the classroom. There was a demand to justify not only teaching six-hundred-year-old poetry but also Chaucer's refusing to mention, much less comment on, the major cataclysmic events of his day: the Black Death, the Hundred Years' War, Papal Schism, and Peasants' Revolt. Perhaps the recent surge of scholarly interest in contexts is partially a response to a greater social consciousness that has developed since the 1960s, and perhaps the challenge has encouraged an enlightened assessment of the Chaucerian posture. I believe that as we gain perspective on Chaucer's age and on our own recent past, we are increasingly glad that Chaucer was not preoccupied with politics and that, rather than man the barricades or interview victims, he chose to sit "also domb as any stoon" with his books. We can now see more clearly that the particular sort of reporting the fictive Geffrey engaged in was appropriate for Chaucer's circumstances and that Chaucer's poetry remains perennially relevant because it embodies the fundamental texture of (fourteenth-century) life with all its ideals and corruptions, harmonies and contradictions. Indeed, I would not attempt to resurrect what appears to others to be antiquated philosophies and curious conceptions if such lore did not contribute to an understanding of Chaucer's essential humanity, the humanity that constitutes the common ground between his world and ours. Understanding this common humanity, it seems to me, is the point of studying the literature of the past.

Although emphasis on Chaucer's modernity can be misleading, the study of his poetry in relation to his times provides a balance of the strange and the familiar, each reinforcing the other. But when the novice sees "Whan that Aprill . . ." for the first time, Chaucer's foreignness leaps out immediately. Some teachers address the language barrier by eliminating it, and, indeed, Chaucer can be taught effectively in modern English. Nevertheless, rather than postpone what I see as necessary engagement in the Chaucerian world, I face the difficulties and attempt to render them intelligible (and therefore surmountable for students) by setting Chaucer's English in his world.

Initially, to my students' professed dismay, I ask that they memorize, for oral recitation, the first eighteen lines of the General Prologue. This frankly old-fashioned demand yields several class periods of fruitful entertainment and psychological solidarity: students are forced to cope with language, pronunciation, and versification in a compact and practical manner so that in the future they can read Chaucer as comprehensible poetry. Each day as I pull a few names out of a paper bag for the recitation (democratic potluck, not divine order, reigns), the students in the class listen over and over to the sounds that they must correct and to the lines that they must render in turn. Particular attention to phonology and vocabulary becomes more meaningful as the enormous cultural influence of French on English is recognized—and this influence extends from language to literary models, ideals, and conventions. Because I insist that the recitation be made to the class, my students also sense the need for dramatic articulation in oral delivery; they can perceive the importance of memory and the pleasures that recognition held for the audience in the days before printing made book ownership (and widespread literacy) feasible.

The substance of these eighteen lines opens still more avenues of investigation. Using the reliable maxim that few things are obvious or self-evident to an undergraduate, I deal with the obvious: the plot of *The Canterbury Tales*. No matter how fine the introduction in the text, the facts need reiteration: the reason for pilgrimages and the nature of travel in the Middle Ages; road conditions and highway robbers, which necessitated group travel, which in turn encouraged socializing rather than religious solemnity; and hence the tales. So, too, the destination, Saint Thomas à Becket's shrine at Canterbury Cathedral, provides a basis for discussing the turmoils of church-state rivalry as well as the credulity and faith that made shrines and magnificent cathedrals flourish.

Once the literal implications of the Canterbury journey are grasped, the more sophisticated underpinnings may be explored. Again, the opening lines of the General Prologue provide abundant opportunity to discuss the basically foreign frame of reference of the Middle Ages and to reveal the Chaucerian transformation of it. On the surface, we see traditional poetic subjects—spring, flowers, birds—and a simple enough narrative of characters and circumstances. But Chaucer shapes the ordinary material so that it reveals—to those with eyes to see—the cosmic hierarchy and (mirabile dictu!) the poet's purposeful inversion of it.

The concept of hierarchical order is a medieval commonplace that illuminates all medieval (poetic) sensibility. Without the knowledge that the cosmic order was thought to be mirrored in the mundane order and was to be consciously imitated in art, a modern audience would miss much of the vitality of medieval poetry. Not only would Geffrey's attempt to report of the pilgrims "ech of hem . . . and of what degree" be meaningless, but the subtleties of Harry Bailly's leadership and each pilgrim's individual accommodation to the divinely ordered schema would be lost. As important as recognizing Chaucer's reliance on the distinctly medieval ideal, however, is the subsequent recognition of his deviations from it. It is up to us to recapture for our students the ideal against which to measure the urbane artistic distortion. Only then can they appreciate fully the artistry and significance of Chaucer's poetic topsy-turvy world populated with the all-too-human pilgrims. Such is the narrative skill that separates the Chaucers from the Gowers and the Lydgates.

The implications of even this single concept—medieval order—can enlighten modern understanding of a host of factors that Chaucer's world took for granted. For instance, acceptance of a hierarchical world view implies reverence for authority and tradition, a reverence that not only signals theocentrism but also in more secular terms explains Chaucer's proud reliance on "olde bokes." It explains, given his social status and the circumstances of poetic delivery, his use of Geffrey the persona; it also serves as a key to understanding the attitudes and rivalries among many of the pilgrims. And the same cosmic perspective that underlies Chaucer's art underlies his life as well. Given the medieval view of *sub specie aeternitis*, we might begin to perceive, if not always agree with, the reasons for his posture of silence with regard to the devastating events of his day.

That contemporary ideals and circumstances helped shape the artist and the man is scarcely news, but it is a lesson in human understanding worth repeating (as Chaucer himself does with each Canterbury pilgrim). So, too, the obvious but jarring recognition that ideals such as democracy, individuality, and originality have not been historically and universally applauded is, in itself, valuable knowledge gleaned from examining different cultural contexts. That cheap paper, movable type, and all sorts of technological wizardry stand ready to replace the human memory; that cars and planes have altered our sense of distance as well as our girth; that eyeglasses, anesthesia, and the "Pill" have irrevocably changed the quality of our lives: all and more are cultural facets, the roots of which are the stuff of *The Canterbury Tales*.

Too much background information too soon, however, may well bury an audience rather than fill a chasm or build a bridge. Each cultural concept needs to await its appropriate literary context if both concept and context are to profit from and demonstrate the integrity of Chaucer's world and art. For instance, the only aspect of the medieval world view that is important for the first eighteen lines of the Prologue is the concept of the chain of being. The rest of the pieces of the cosmic story can wait for more demanding circumstances. Photocopied charts of the medieval cosmos, the chain of being, astrological associations, and so on are easy enough to carry around for distribution as the need arises. With more scheduled planning, films and slides may be used. For example, a thirty-minute, inexpensive film produced by Encyclopaedia Britannica entitled *The Medieval Mind* does a fine job of illustrating the tensions of the age (the world of the tavern versus the cloister, the city of man versus the City of God) using contemporary texts, artifacts, and scenes.

Though charts, films, slides, and background readings are helpful to illustrate the various aspects of the medieval world, immersion in the literature itself is the real purpose for the course. For, ultimately, *The Canterbury Tales* is not a philosophical, a scientific, or even a theological treatise. It is a celebration of imperfect pilgrims journeying through this uncertain world adopting various means for coping with their finitude: the portraits and the tales offer the full spectrum.

To particularize Chaucer's tolerance, if not always love, for these flawed creatures, I ask that each student "adopt" one pilgrim and his or her tale for investigation in a ten-page paper. Everything about the pilgrim should be scrutinized, beginning with vocation and status (Muriel Bowden's *A Commentary on the General Prologue to the* Canterbury Tales is a good first step) and moving into aspects such as the background and morals of the individual (sifting whatever clues Geffrey gives, as well as Chaucer's allowance for self-revelation in the links and tale). In addition, I ask that each student investigate, as a separate project, some aspect of cultural background that helps place his or her adopted pilgrim in the medieval world. For instance, those who choose the Prioress might research the status of women in the Middle Ages, or women and religion, or even the topic of food and table manners; those who choose the Knight may investigate the issue of courtly love or the role of knighthood in the fourteenth century; the Physician's vocation offers topics such as the Plague, disease and its treatment, or astrology; choice of the burly Miller might lead to research on the manor as an economic unit, taverns, or even music or games of the Middle Ages; and choosing the Clerk might lead one to investigate the manufacture of books or medieval knowledge of classical authors. And so on. Many of the topics are feasible for several different pilgrims (astrology, disease, and heresy have widespread applicability), and the possibilities are limited only by the student's imagination.

Clearly, many of these topics are tangential to literary concerns, but if they are investigated well, a sense of the theocentric unity of the age almost invariably comes through. For example, the justification for the status of women goes back, in medieval eyes, to Eve and to Mary and to the divinely ordained natural hierarchy; astrology and alchemy evidence the cosmic physical forces working on the earth and/or persons but also contain spiritual bases; and even a study of courtly love or book manufacture offers clues illuminating the medieval world view. Such investigations, therefore, serve to reinforce what Chaucer as an artist-creator and his creation, *The Canterbury Tales*, are about.

In order to spread the wealth of student research, I offer the students an individual choice of presenting their background reports orally to the class or allowing them to be duplicated for distribution. I schedule the reports to be due when they will be most relevant to the text assignment and try to avoid repetition by having students with similar interests divide the topic.

Finally, by way of encouraging a sense of the Middle Ages in all their glory and depravity, I offer a Hobson's choice between a stodgy midterm exam or a do-it-yourself project of crafting something medieval in the medieval manner. The project requires research and must be accompanied by a one- or two-page account of the methods, substitutions, and accommodations that had to be made. Examples include sewing a small portion of a medieval tapestry or embroidery, doing a manuscript illumination (a copy, or an original of the adopted pilgrim), or constructing a medieval book. Students with little dexterity can give a slide lecture on art or a musical lecture with records or an instrument; some may pool talents and dramatically reenact one of the tales. To foster student enthusiasm and pride in the work, I encourage the class to plan and prepare a medieval banquet, which serves as the occasion for presentation of the projects. Students frequently dress for the event (at Providence College, it is easy enough to secure a friar's robe or a nun's habit). One project may lead us to dance; another may attempt medieval ditties played with a lute or guitar. Usually everyone brings some semiedible medieval food (garbage pye is a favorite), and I supply the mead, wine, and ale. The banquet has turned into something of a departmental, if not a campus, event and, I trust, a learning experience. Not infrequently when I see former students from the class, they greet me with a "Whan that Aprill . . ." or recall the toil and accomplishment of their projects.

It is this kind of spirit, a sense of memorable individual and communal effort, that is at the core of Chaucer's *Canterbury Tales*.

Appendix

COURSE DESCRIPTION

In lieu of a syllabus providing the daily reading assignments, I here present the course requirements for my undergraduate Chaucer course.

Course requirements

1. Reading. In addition to the assigned text for *The Canterbury Tales* (*Chaucer's Major Poetry*, ed. Albert Baugh), I assign Boethius' *Consolation of Philosophy* (trans. Richard Green) as general background and with specific application to the Knight's Tale. An account of the medieval cosmos is provided by reading one of the C. S. Lewis works: "Imagination and Thought in the Middle Ages" (in Helaine Newstead, ed., *Chaucer and His Contemporaries*) or "Heavens" (Chapter V of the *Discarded Image*).

2. Memorization of the first eighteen lines of the General Prologue (spelling, pronunciation, vocabulary). Recordings (in a tape library) and guides such as D. Knapp and N. K. Snortum's *The Sounds of Chaucer's English* (pamphlet and record distributed by NCTE). Helge Kökeritz' *Guide to Chaucer's Pronunciation* and my own improvisation of the lines are helpful.

3. I ask that students know how to read dramatically (with as much talent as they can muster individually in my office) any twenty-five or so lines that make sense together (justification may be asked), excluding the General Prologue. Questions on vocabulary and translation should be expected.

4. Translation quizzes: unannounced and sprung when I feel there is a slackening off in attention to language (or I notice that all the translations are checked out from the library).

5. Written report on an "adopted" pilgrim (about 10 pages): the vocation, status, personality of any substantial pilgrim (21 "substantial" pilgrims, plus the 5 members of the guild who can be treated in a single report, the Host Harry Bailly, and the pilgrim Geffrey—for a total of 24 topics). The report should include consideration of internal evidence (portrait, links, tale) as well as external evidence (research on vocation, etc.)

6. An oral or written report on any aspect of the cultural background

(10–15 minutes or 5–6 pages) with special effort made to connect the topic to one of the pilgrims (preferably the "adopted" one). If the report is not presented orally, it will be photocopied for class benefit. The reports are scheduled as the topics pertain to the assigned reading for the day. Topics may include: alchemy/science; courtly love; astrology; the classical writers in the Middle Ages; disease and its treatment; status of women; book manufacture; the role of the artist; heresy; Jews in the Middle Ages; craft guilds; knighthood.

7. Choice of either a stodgy midterm exam or a do-it-yourself hand-crafted something using the methods/materials/knowledge of medieval industry. This requires research and must be accompanied by a short report (1–2 pages) describing the research, methods, substitutions, and difficulties arising. Though I warn students to attempt the project only if they have perseverance, steady nerves, and excess sanity, few ever ask for a midterm. Sample suggestions include:

    —2 or 3 students plan and prepare a medieval banquet including (enlisting) food preparation (finding recipes and ingredients, and cooking); (enlisting) entertainment (song, dance, live or, if no talent is available, recorded music); encouraging costuming and decorative skills (using other students' projects)

    —sew a sample portion of a medieval tapestry/embroidery

    —paint or ink a page manuscript page

    —paint, sew, or glue a doll-size medieval costume or make a life-size one

    —give a slide lecture on art or a musical lecture using records or talent

    —construct a medieval book

    —2, 3, 4 students get together and dramatically reenact one of the Tales (either with persons or puppets).

8. A short "term" paper of a literary nature either on some theme or aspect running through the *CT* or extending some idea/theme/image/convention from the *CT* to another of Chaucer's works. The topic is highly negotiable, but must be kept within the 10-page range.

9. A final exam. One week before the exam I distribute 6 to 8 "study" questions covering the range of material in the course. The students are told that two of those study questions will constitute the bulk of the exam, but they do not know which two until the time of the exam.

10. Course evaluation: anonymous and designed to ascertain the value of the above assignments to the students' appreciation of *The Canterbury Tales*.

AN APPROACH TO TEACHING CHAUCER'S LANGUAGE

Thomas W. Ross

Learning Middle English is pleasurable in itself: good undergraduate students with a curiosity about language and the history of language enjoy it simply as an exercise. There are, of course, more compelling reasons why students should learn the phonology, grammar, and prosody. It is an educational experience to realize that six centuries separate us from Chaucer's language and verse. One must learn the facts for oneself from the empirical experience of doing close analyses of a respectable number of lines of Middle English poetry.

I would acknowledge at once that not all undergraduates, English majors or generalists, are interested in, or capable of, learning the sounds of Middle English. If one draws from a qualified student body and if the Chaucer courses are elective rather than required, however, the self-selecting process operates to produce a class that will be capable of becoming acquainted with (if not mastering) Middle English phonology, syntax, and grammar in a brief time. With a one-semester course (thirteen weeks, let us say), a week to ten days of concentrated language study is enough for most students, with continuing reinforcement. After all, introductory Chaucer courses should be devoted primarily to literary rather than to philological matters: the less time spent on the sounds and prosody, the better.

I assume, then, that one has a "selected" class—students who know what a verb and a noun are though their concepts of gerund and present participle may be wobbly. The instructor should admit to them at once that scholarship has not achieved any certainty about Middle English sounds though we have pretty fair general ideas. We are not sure, for instance, how far [æ:] had moved in the general directions of raising and fronting. Was it [ɛ:] as some historians believe? And was the interdental fricative voiced in unstressed situations—was *that* [θɑt] or [ðɑt]? It is perhaps best to assume a conservative posture and transcribe [æ:] and [θ] while admitting that such pronunciations might have sounded old-fashioned to Chaucer himself.

On the first day of class I read a passage in Middle English. To learn the Middle English sounds, one must acquire a method of representing them with some measure of accuracy and consistency. The International Phonetic Alphabet (IPA) suggests itself because it is used in other disciplines (e.g., in courses in French language and literature) and because it is employed, with some modification, by Albert H. Marckwardt in his revision of Samuel Moore's *Historical Outlines of English Sounds and Inflections* and by Helge Kökeritz in *A Guide to Chaucer's Pronunciation* —both of which offer numerous transcriptions of Chaucer's poetry. Some instructors might prefer the phonemic notational system since today it is probably more widely used by linguists.

At any rate, students are given photocopied sheets presenting the IPA. Key words representing IPA sounds are chosen from Modern English, though the final column to the right indicates the Middle English sources of these sounds. Students are told that they will not have to memorize the IPA—that their charts will always be at hand, for class and for exams, but that most of the symbols will soon become as familiar as those in the Roman alphabet.

There are always problems: some students do not have an [ɔ] in their dialects or idiolects, especially if their speech is North-Central General American. These people will simply have to learn how to produce the sound, even though it is unfamiliar, with examples like [kɑt], [kɔt] and [dɑn], [dɔn] to help them. Then there are those who have been told that the diphthong [ɑɪ] is a "long *i*," a misconception that will, for a while, confuse the idea of phonetic length. Once students can recognize that the Modern English and Middle English diphthongs are true combinations of two sounds, they can discard the confusing nomenclature they have been carrying about with them since grade school.

Then there are students with some French who are inclined to pronounce -*ence* as it would be pronounced in Paris today. I have had little luck changing their Gallic habits, but this has not worried me much:

perhaps Chaucer and his circle actually used such pronunciations themselves.

Naturally, the vowels cause the most difficulty because the consonants have not changed much during the years since Chaucer wrote his poetry. Here, some acquaintance with a modern foreign language helps the student if you indicate that, in general, Chaucer's English had a "continental" vowel system—that the *ABC* was not [e, bi, si] but [ɑ, be, se] as it is in contemporary languages spoken across the Channel.

New readers of Chaucer can also be reassured that the alphabet in the fourteenth century was a more nearly phonetic instrument than it is today —that it approached the ideal of one sound/one symbol, one symbol/one sound. Middle English *a* usually represented [ɑ] or [ɑ:], sounds differing in quantity but not in quality. At this point the concept of vowel length, which is significant in determining the later history of some Middle English sounds, may be introduced. I find it useful to say that [ɑ] may be compared to a quarter note or to one centimeter of recording tape, while [ɑ:] is like a half note or two centimeters on a tape. And here students learn that Middle English [ɑ] becomes Modern English [æ] while Middle English [ɑ:] turns into Modern English [e]. This pure vowel [e] will not satisfy the student with sophisticated ears, who will observe that the modern sound is actually a half-developed diphthong [eⁱ]—and the student who wants to transcribe it this way should, of course, not be discouraged. The same applies to the unstressed sound, spelled -*y*, and the ends of words: should the transcription be [ɪ], [i], or [ɪ]? Let the students represent whatever they hear, so long as each student shows some degree of consistency.

The class now has a sheaf of photocopies marked with esoteric symbols. Some students are invited to the blackboard to write out their names in the IPA; others are given short phrases, still in Modern English, such as "I think I know how to pronounce Chaucer's English." Somebody will surely transcribe the last sounds in *pronounce* as [ns], which gives you the chance to explain the almost inevitable presence of the intrusive [t], resulting in [nts], in Middle as well as Modern English. The students are encouraged to use their ears, to listen and to transcribe honestly. If they hear *think* as [θɪŋk], that is what they should transcribe. And if the students are curious and receptive, you might introduce them to the concept of assimilation that helps explain the occurrence of this phenomenon.

The first acquaintance with English sounds is, then, keyed to the students' own Modern English pronunciation. If some pronounce *log* as [lɑg], fine—so long as they recognize that others have a right to their [lɔg], and so long as they can produce an [ɔ] even though it may not be part of their dialect habits.

All the linguistic material—for the first day and for subsequent days—is recorded on cassettes so that, after class, students can listen to the instructor's version and try to imitate it—again and again if need be. Some beginning Chaucerians find the cassettes useful; others think the whole business of machines is intolerable and thus would rather proceed at their own pace, moving faster than the slow rate at which, inevitably, the tapes run.

The second day of class is devoted to student practice and correction by fellow learners. The transition from Modern to Middle English is accelerated by reading together from a photocopied transcription of a Chaucerian passage, perhaps ten lines of a portrait from the General Prologue. The passage should illustrate how the sound effects—rhyme, alliteration, assonance—can be understood only with a knowledge of fourteenth-century phonology: how [kn] in *knyght* alliterates with the [k] in *can*, for instance. Chaucer is primarily a writer of narrative, but he *is* a poet and he depends on the organizational and emphatic techniques available to the writer of verse. These provide his major patterns, the forms and discipline of his art. On reserve in the English departmental lounge or in the library are copies of Kökeritz and Marckwardt, which students may consult in order to sharpen their acquaintance with the IPA as it is used to transcribe Chaucer's poetry (though one must at this point make it clear that Marckwardt and Kökeritz do not agree about some Middle English sounds and that each uses his own slight modification of the IPA).

For the third day of class, students are asked to bring in transcriptions of at least five consecutive lines of Chaucer's poetry. They are also assigned photocopied materials outlining Middle English syntax, stress, and grammar—sketches of the pronoun system, for instance, with the observation that for formal situations Chaucer generally uses *ye/you*; for familiar ones, *thee/thou*. (At which point you can ask why the vowel sound in *you* has remained the same as it was in Middle English while that in *thou* has undergone "normal" diphthongization: frequency of use, which tends to conserve archaic linguistic features, is the probable reason.) Students' transcriptions are handed to other students for comment—for example, "isn't it more likely that Chaucer's *maken* was pronounced with a long stressed vowel?" There are more handouts to work with, including diagrams of the pattern of raising and fronting of vowels and charts showing in detail what sounds are usually represented by groups of letters in Middle English spelling. There are, then, several ways for the students to check the accuracy of what they have transcribed.

In the following days and weeks, each student presents a critical analysis of problems in *The Canterbury Tales* or the *Troilus*, each presentation involving the reading aloud of a passage in Middle English. For instance, one student might deal with the function of the rhyme in the portrait of the Squire (I [A] 89–90 is a rhyme that can be understood only if one knows what the Middle English sounds were). Another might evaluate the possibility of irony in the alliteration in "bathed in a bath of blisse" at the end of the Wife of Bath's Tale (III [D] 1253).

Not every critical problem is tied to phonological phenomena, of course, but reading passages aloud keeps alive the idea that Chaucer's poetry was probably recited. Quizzes and examinations (open-book) also involve the transcription of the poetry and the evaluation of relevant grammatical and syntactic phenomena—though, again, the major emphasis is literary. The students' critical ability is sharpened if they recognize that they must develop some acquaintance with the history of the language in order to have a sound basis for their judgment.

In all of this attention to language, there is something of the delight of solving a puzzle. Throughout the semester, neither instructor nor student should lose sight of the pleasure in learning about the language as it was probably spoken six hundred years ago by one of the most ingenious poets who has written in English.

SURVEY COURSES FOR NONMAJORS

TEACHING CHAUCER IN A HISTORICAL SURVEY OF BRITISH LITERATURE

Michael West

The third edition of the *Norton Anthology of English Literature,* published in 1974, unhappily abridged the excellent summaries of historical periods that made the second edition a fine teaching tool. Since the editors acted in response to a broad survey of the profession, the implications of their revisions deserve attention, for the *Norton Anthology* dominates the competition and often determines the shape of the introductory course in English studies. For the third edition, apparently many members of the profession wanted more complete texts. To make room for works like *Sir Orfeo* and a second Shakespearean play, historical introductions shrank and many brief selections from minor authors illustrating the intellectual background were eliminated. Without Hoby's translation of Castiglione's *Courtier,* for example, the Renaissance love poetry in the third edition had to be taught in an intellectually deracinated fashion. Although "in accordance with the suggestions of numerous users" the recent fourth edition of the *Norton Anthology of English Literature* (1979) has restored the Castiglione-Hoby *Courtier*, thus returning somewhat to the sensible approach of the second edition, its introductions are still "succinct," and it drops almost all the topical selections. The net effect of these revisions has been to shift attention to literary works as presumably self-contained esthetic wholes. This premise is especially destructive to medieval literature and undermines perhaps the most important lesson that students might be expected to draw from an encounter with Chaucer in a survey course. How can Chaucer's works be presented as embodying medieval culture unless that culture is also illustrated?

How ironic it is that the profession should have chosen to revise its basic introductory text in this manner at the same time that many members of the Modern Language Association tend increasingly to highminded exhortations about the social and political relevance of literature. Will any number of modish topical courses in subjects like literature and the environment compensate in the long run for the intellectual impoverishment of the one course above all others where English studies might hope to convince students that literature is not just a collection of pretty poems and fun stories but the product of a cultural matrix, a product with historical consequences? To teach a survey of British literature successfully, one must not fight the basic historical structure imposed on the course by chronology. Instead of focusing on isolated individual works, the teacher should constantly try to show how the particular author being studied is part of a larger pattern of development. The true subject of a *historical* survey is not so much major works or major authors as the connections between major and minor authors. To maintain this approach I dropped the *Norton Anthology* in its third avatar. Despite a slightly more limited selection, the *Oxford Anthology of English Literature*, with its copious supporting material and splendid illustrations, seemed preferable for a historical survey of English literature, in which Chaucer figures preeminently as the *fons et origo*.

The opening classes on the Middle Ages invite students to speculate about the relation between literature and culture, and this theme is stressed throughout our survey of the entire medieval period. Students are ready enough to see how Old English literature reflects Anglo-Saxon society, but oddly enough they must be prodded into realizing how distorted that reflection sometimes is. They need reminding that none of the first English epic is set in England, that dragons were not a major environmental problem for the audience, and that women may well have enjoyed more importance in Anglo-Saxon society than in Old English literature. But with prompting students can grasp that *The Battle of Maldon* reflects outdated poetic conventions perhaps even more vividly than it reflects historical facts. Likewise, they can imagine that the literary hiatus brought about by the Norman Conquest does not necessarily indicate that a social vacuum then prevailed in England. Conversely, the artistic power of "Sir Patrick Spens" may derive from a compositional process that purged away details suggesting a petty historical intrigue in the Scottish court. How sophisticated was "provincial" English culture? Does what we know of the West Midlands in the fourteenth century help us to understand the *Gawain* poet? Does an apparently complex poem like *Sir Gawain* force one to hypothesize a complex culture to account for it, or was its author simply one of the most notable fantasts and eccentrics of English literature? By the time the survey reaches Chaucer, students can appreciate both the necessity of asking such questions and the difficulty of answering them.

The Prologue to *The Canterbury Tales* affords a further opportunity to enlarge students' naive ideas concerning literature, history, and "realism." The opening reference to "the droghte of March" indicates that Chaucer's manipulation of literary convention does not result in a meteorologically accurate representation of the English climate. To what extent, then, does his manipulation of characters result in a sociologically accurate representation of medieval English society? Presiding over "this gentil hostelrye/ That highte the Tabard, faste by the Belle," Harry Bailly—travel agent, caterer, and emcee—is, of course, a historically recognizable citizen of Southwerk, and his combination of commercial enterprise and bonhomie is rendered plausibly enough. By contrast, despite the painstaking agglomeration of specific historical campaigns, the Knight remains a faintly unsubstantial figure who invites us to wonder just how vital a role chivalric idealism played in Chaucer's England. No homely details like the father's rusty tunic even try to humanize the son, and students can see that the charming portrait of the Squire derives directly from the world of literary romance that they encountered in *Sir Gawain*. But if the Yeoman seems essentially as stylized as a figure on a recruiting poster, the portrait of the Prioress is so complexly multidimensional as to appear almost fully individualized. Though a historic individual like Thomas Pynchbek may be discerned lurking behind the Sergeant of Law, students at my university are understandably skeptical that medieval Oxford ever harbored a teacher so disinterested financially as the Clerk.

Such scrutiny encourages students to distinguish realistic but faceless occupational types like the Merchant and Doctor, whose brethren might be encountered in medieval London or postmodern Pittsburgh, from more eccentric and fully individualized characters like the Friar and the Wife of Bath, who impress us as unique human beings. Representing various styles, the reproductions of medieval art in the *Oxford Anthology* (all quite "unrealistic" to an eye accustomed to Renaissance pictorial conventions like perspective) are useful in suggesting how a literary artist also creates a recognizable reflection of the world through highly formalized conventions that refract it rather than mirroring it directly. This visual analogy particularly helps students see the need for formally distinguishing literature from life yet relating literature to life mimetically and categorizing the various modes of that relationship. Differentiating various styles of realism in graphic art makes students readier to see the Plowman as a highly idealized, faintly allegorical figure who scarcely seems to move on the same plane of being as the other pilgrims—even though the very concept "pilgrim" incorporates all the characters, however tenuously, in an overarching symbolic world view. Class discussion of the Plowman emphasizes that in other figures naturalistic representationalism is a limiting convention; by no means does such representation completely reproduce Chaucer's comprehension of reality. This insight prepares the students to appreciate Langland's achievement in dealing with aspects of medieval experience that tend to lie beyond Chaucer's range.

Tracing the shifting levels of realism in *The Canterbury Tales* sensitizes students to literary values at the same time that it stresses the interaction of literature with culture. Chaucer's dramatization of himself as naive— deliberately distorted for satiric purposes, of course—invites speculation about how much authorial irony attaches to his claim to "ful devout corage." The negatives and adversatives sprinkled so plentifully throughout the portrait of the Parson suggest that this ideal figure is perhaps less important as a representative specimen of the medieval English clergy than as a satiric criticism of priests who too often fell short of the ideal. Likewise, the distortions and exaggerations that make the Summoner seem not so much a realistic figure as a sort of demonic "grotesque" point to the prevalence of ecclesiastical corruption in Chaucer's England and foreshadow the Reformation. In studying Chaucer's satire on religious themes, students thus confront with peculiar force fundamental questions about literature: does the literary artist seek primarily to reflect the real world? to create an alternative world? or to re-create historical reality in the hope of transforming it?

"Realism" thus becomes a pedagogical leitmotif that also leads students fruitfully through the narrative conventions of the tales themselves. With coaching, they can see that both the Miller's Tale and the Franklin's Tale involve highly conventionalized treatments of human sexuality. The orgy of renunciation in the Franklin's Tale suggests how much the Western tradition of romantic love is rooted in artificial self-denial; students find especially stimulating the notion that our modern concept of romantic love is in its origins essentially a medieval literary invention. But they need more prodding to admit that despite its air of barnyard realism the Miller's Tale is also a highly artificial literary construction in which the conventions of the fabliau are pitted against those of courtly love. As the elaborate concatenations of its plot suggest, we are still miles away from a frank and natural treatment of sexuality, which must be foreshortened as much for the purposes of a dirty story as for literary romance. So taught, both tales illustrate how much our ideas about sexual love tend to derive from literary models—so much so that it is ultimately difficult to decide whether literature imitates life or life literature.

In its transparent wish fulfillment, the Wife of Bath's Tale is another example of the transforming power of literature. Though her Prologue suggests that she owes her incredible vitality to frank acceptance of life as it is, the tale goes one step further to imply that the capacity for such acceptance may be grounded in creative imaginative illusion. Likewise, in reading the Nun's Priest's Tale students must decide whether Chaunticleer is treated as a satiric butt or a comic hero. Do the touches of high style inflate or create this remarkable rooster? Is his pride morally rebuked by the fox's incursion? Or is Chaunticleer's sense of self-importance as the fitting recipient of a prophetic *somnium celeste*, previously jeopardized by Pertelote's blithe unconcern, actually confirmed by Reynard's momentary triumph and by the cacophonous outcry raised over his abduction? Perhaps Chaunticleer should be compared to Sir Gawain as a character struggling comically to live up to a lofty literary reputation and largely, if not entirely, succeeding. Similarly, we can ask whether the conclusion of the Pardoner's Tale may not dramatize a character transported momentarily beyond himself by his own fictions.

Surveyed in this manner, selected tales can teach students that literature often not only reflects historical change but also helps bring it about. Approached from this angle, Chaucer's Middle English becomes a little less of a sticking point. Given the shape of our departmental major (I blush to confess that even our course devoted exclusively to Chaucer has sometimes been taught in translation) and my university's sad but all too typical lack of a language requirement, the students I encounter are often not very adventuresome linguistically. But thanks to the largesse of the *Oxford Anthology*'s editors, when we slog through the forbidding text of *Caedmon's Hymn* word by word, most can realize that Anglo-Saxon is not so much a foreign tongue as the oldest form of English. (One wishes the editors would also reproduce a passage from *Sir Gawain* in the original so that students could see how much closer to modern standard English is the dialect of *The Canterbury Tales*.) Since one can argue that Chaucer's literary achievements may have played their minuscule part in helping to establish the dialect of the East Midlands as standard, it is even possible to persuade a few students that they are particularly indebted to the poet for not having to speak Anglo-Saxon today. Watching the gratitude flower on their faces has not been the least of my pedagogical rewards while teaching Chaucer in a course surveying British literature from *Beowulf* halfway to Virginia Woolf.

Appendix

COURSE SYLLABUS

Early British Literature

Required Texts: F. Kermode, et al., eds. *Oxford Anthology of English Literature*, Vol. I
Selected paperbacks

Assignments and Lecture Schedule:

MEETINGS

1.	Orientation
2.	Anglo-Saxon literature
3.	Medieval lyrics and ballads
4.	*Sir Gawain and the Green Knight*
5–7.	Chaucer
8.	Medieval satire and drama
9.	Tudor prose and poetry
10.	Sidney, Spenser
11.	Spenser
12.	Spenser, Shakespeare
13.	Shakespeare, Marlowe
14.	Midterm examination

. . .

28.   Final examination

A NEW ROUTE DOWN PILGRIMS' WAY: TEACHING CHAUCER TO NONMAJORS

Stephen R. Portch

Masterpieces of literature belong to us all. No longer can—or should—they be regarded as the hallowed domain of that endangered species, the English major. Indeed, lower-division non–English majors now dominate literature survey courses in many colleges. Their presence requires particular effort by the teacher to involve students who regard a master such as Chaucer with amorphous distrust, determined apathy, or active dread. A teaching approach that crosses disciplines and passes beyond the formal lecture can help nonmajors better understand and enjoy Chaucer's "foreign" language in a discipline different from their own and can inject a vitality often absent from the classrooms of their majors.

Such an approach can be achieved without making any concessions to the content or the demands of the survey course. Like many survey courses, the one I teach at a two-year college follows a two-semester sequence with an artificial boundary; in this instance, that line has been drawn at 1798. The course covers a number of masterpieces in British literature but inevitably gives many others only an honorable mention. To study all worthwhile works written in Britain since pen first touched parchment up until the last blot of ink has barely dried is to ask too much. Selectivity, then, is one key to a good course. But this selectivity should

116

not lead to reading fragments of great works. Complete works take longer to read and discuss, but fragments often prove unsatisfactory. Consequently, the first half of the course usually includes the complete *Beowulf* in translation, the Prologue to *The Canterbury Tales, Sir Gawain and the Green Knight, Hamlet, Dr. Faustus, Samson Agonistes, The Rape of the Lock, Gulliver's Travels,* and a number of shorter works. Conveniently, such a syllabus provides for the discussion of all major genres.

To teach these works in isolation, however, would be to teach a "great books" course and not a true survey course. The survey course deals not only with the literary context but also with the biographical, historical, cultural, geographical, and textual contexts as well. Brief oral biographies (wild Marlowe's, stern Milton's, deformed Pope's) fascinate students. And—to a surprising extent—so does geography. Students seem to respond when they realize that real people living in real places wrote what at first reading appeared strange and distant words. These distant words also come closer when the essential history and evolving culture of the country are studied: the history and culture serve as the bridge that leads the way to literature; they link words to a way of life.

No amount of background material, however, can substitute for careful attention to the text itself. To demand careful and critical reading is to encourage development of an important intellectual skill in every student. In the beginning of the course, detailed reading guide questions may be used both to help develop critical reading skills and to serve as a framework for class discussion and greater student involvement. Short formal lectures, student presentations, and the use of slides and recordings also enhance class involvement. The unit on Chaucer follows a pattern of varied teaching approaches, active student participation, and creative critical writing. Time limitations allow only three seventy-five-minute classes on Chaucer; therefore, we can work with only the General Prologue in detail. The objectives of these classes are to present to the students a fundamental understanding of Chaucer's England and English and to ask from them—in oral presentation and in writing—perceptive portrayals of Chaucer's pilgrims. Since above all else Chaucer wrote with exceptional vitality, much of his accessibility to students depends on how much of his vitality a teacher can bring to the classroom.

Before Chaucer's vitality can be re-created, however, his place in literary and cultural history has to be examined. Since *Beowulf* precedes and Middle English lyrics follow this unit, Chaucer's contribution to literary history stands as a landmark and a signal. Chaucer's genius blossomed in a fallow literary field and sowed the seed for later literary achievements. After this point has been underscored at the beginning of the first class in the Chaucer unit, Chaucer's England must then be explored.

This exploration focuses on three historical events and illuminates a feudal system on the decline. Three events that resonated within the fourteenth century and beyond—the Hundred Years' War, the Black Death, and the Peasants' Revolt—invite the teacher to discuss the lingering remnants of a warrior society, the decimating effects of an epidemic, and the far-reaching consequences of social revolution. The cause of social revolution may be highlighted by explaining feudal hierarchy, a concept that I represent graphically with a simple, two-column chart (either mimeographed or developed on the blackboard) depicting ideal secular and religious order. The word "God" stands above both columns. The first column—the secular hierarchy—starts with the king and ends with the serf, and the second—the religious hierarchy—begins with the pope and ends with the parson. Later, when all the pilgrims have been discussed, pilgrim names can be filled in on the chart next to the appropriate slot. Since the name slotting really cannot be done until the end of the last class in the unit, the exercise provides a circular framework for the unit. To those students who are eager for more historical and cultural information, I usually recommend Derek Brewer's *Chaucer in His Time* (1963).

Since this literary and cultural history segment must be condensed into approximately an hour of the first class in the unit, much of the hour must be devoted to formal lecture. Therefore, the last fifteen minutes or so of the class require a change of pace—particularly important in a class of nonmajors. For this segment of the class, I rely on the visual. Slides depicting portraits of Chaucer, tapestries of his pilgrims, and pictures of his places provide a pictorial focus for an abbreviated discussion of Chaucer's life and geography. Students expressing further interest in the visual can look at Maurice Hussey's *Chaucer's World: A Pictorial Companion* (1967).

After a look at some of Chaucer's world, the class listens to some of his words. Chaucer's English, which intimidates students at first, eventually fascinates many of them. A good recorded reading can make all the difference. To open the second class, we read along in our texts as we listen to a recording of the vibrant voices of Nevill Coghill and Norman Davis reading selections from *The Canterbury Tales* on Spoken Arts Records. The recording also includes a discussion of the characteristics of Chaucer's English. Students are encouraged to listen to more of the record on their own (since we can only listen for about fifteen minutes in class). A number of students even learn—by imitation—to pronounce short passages of *The Canterbury Tales*.

Listening to the record leads to a discussion of some of the characteristics of Chaucer's English (such as the pronunciation of his final -*e*), discussion that can be illustrated by specific sections of the text as they are considered in class. The opening lines of the General Prologue present a perfect opportunity for talking about both language—syntax, grammar, pronunciation—and pilgrimages. Geography helps with the latter. A mimeographed map of the London-Canterbury Pilgrims' Way makes discussion of the distance and time of the journey more concrete. From the logistics of the trip, we move to various reasons why people embarked on these dusty roads. For some pilgrims, the answer is simply frequent pubs; for others, spiritual needs.

At this point in the second class, detailed examination of two portraits fixes attention on the pilgrims as real and representative figures. The Knight provides a good starting point. We can discuss his physical characteristics, his achievements in battles, and his moral traits. We can relate his place in the General Prologue and the tale-telling to his place on the hierarchical scale. To balance this positive secular portrait, we look at a negative religious portrait: the Friar. After examining this particular avaricious Friar, we discuss the clergy in general and Chaucer's—and many of his contemporaries'—attitudes toward them.

The students now have some feel for reading and interpreting Chaucer's portraits. Between the second and third class, they prepare a presentation of one portrait for the class. This preparation varies from background reading in such books as Muriel Bowden's *A Commentary on the General Prologue to the* Canterbury Tales (2nd ed., 1967) to creative script writing. Some students even team up to present an appropriate dialogue between their chosen pilgrims. Whatever their manner of preparation, the students, by nature of the assignment, must study the text of their chosen portrait with great care.

The third class belongs to the students. The vitality that we all hope to develop in our survey courses becomes a reality. In the ideal class of fifteen students, the atmosphere encourages creativity and the time allows for five-minute presentations. Shy students often model their presentations on the portraits of the Knight and the Friar presented in the previous class. More outgoing students come in costume, complete with props (e.g., relics and bagpipes). In short, the students re-create and reveal the pilgrims—and their own grasp of Chaucer as well.

Although this last class devoted to Chaucer passes all too quickly, its staying power becomes evident in the creative critical papers required at the end of the unit. The out-of-class paper assignment builds on the in-class oral presentation. Students are asked to retain their pilgrim persona for the paper, but now—using evidence from the text and their own intuition and interpretation—they must also introduce two of their traveling companions among the various rogues and assorted angels on the pilgrimage. This two-part requirement (description of "self" and description of "companions") leads to some novel approaches and significant insights.

Some "pilgrims" write letters home; others keep diaries. One Wife of Bath's diary revealed, for example, that early on she fantasized over the many-talented, much-touted Squire; later, she more realistically aimed her attentions at the Merchant. In addition to insights, many "pilgrims" exhibit refreshing attention to details from the text in both their papers and their presentations—from the April weather they experienced to the clothes they wore to the horses they rode. The language, too, often shows sensitivity—the Knight's courtly courtesy, the Pardoner's cringing calls, the Miller's caustic crudities.

In three classes and one paper, then, nonmajor students can travel from indifference and ignorance to an involvement in, and commitment to, Chaucer's excellence. Perhaps no other unit in any survey course has so much to offer the nonmajors. After all, how many English majors does Chaucer include in his pilgrimage? And the variety of classroom techniques available to those who would "gladly . . . lerne and gladly teche" *The Canterbury Tales* is no less than the variety of pilgrims within the tales. From this variety comes vitality—off the page and into the classroom. I think Chaucer would have been pleased.

THE CROOKED RIB: WOMEN IN MEDIEVAL LITERATURE

Susan Schibanoff

I designed The Crooked Rib, a course on images of women in medieval literature, for students whose interests in—or curiosity about—feminist criticism, pre-1500 literature, and Chaucer coincided. Beyond this mutual concern, the group of thirty-five undergraduate students who enrolled in the class had little in common. There were botany, business, English, history, premedical, political science, women's studies, and other majors; traditional and nontraditional students; men and women; sophomores, juniors, and seniors. And the group ranged from one who later confessed to wondering why the English department was offering a course in anatomy to another who, on the first day of class, translated for us the medieval phrase, "crooked rib," into what she saw as its modern equivalent, "spare rib." Partly because of this diversity, the scope of the course was wide. We read and discussed literature written over a seven-century span by authors from five countries and in as many different languages (all, though, translated into modern English). My aim here was to include some famous authors and literary masterpieces familiar to everyone, even if by name only (e.g., Dante, Chaucer, *The Decameron*), and to introduce students to less familiar or completely unknown medieval writers and works (e.g., Chrétien de Troyes, *The Romance of the Rose*).

The scope and the organization of course readings were determined, however, by pedagogical reasons other than the desire to expand students' knowledge of medieval literature from known to unknown masterpieces. I wanted students both to have the experience of drawing connections between and among different historical periods and cultures, authors, genres, and, to a limited extent, disciplines and to consider the value of this comparative methodology as a principal concern of feminist criticism. At the same time, I saw the first major goal of the course to be a valid assessment of Chaucer's literary treatment of women, and I felt this goal could be best accomplished if we began by viewing his works in their contemporary context rather than in the inevitable alternative, the context of modern life and literature. For a number of class members, "modern life" meant the decades in which they had lived, the 1960s and 1970s, a period relatively tolerant of women's self-expression; for them to look backward to Chaucer from this perspective would, I feared, obstruct their vision of his works. Accordingly, during the first part of the semester, we familiarized ourselves as broadly as time allowed with literary images of women in the several centuries preceding Chaucer's. For the next part, we focused almost exclusively on Chaucer himself. And, finally, we set to work on the second major goal of the course—connecting our classroom materials and experiences with our own lives and literature.

The principle of organization in the readings for the first part of the semester was generic, which, as it happened, was also roughly chronological, beginning with *Beowulf* and ending with Chaucer's contemporary, Boccaccio. We sampled the major medieval genres, such as epic and heroic literature (*Beowulf, Waldhere, Finnesburgh*); hagiography (the Latin life of St. Anthony and the Anglo-Saxon lives of Sts. Guthlac, Juliana, and Elene, as well as Jacobus de Voragine's life of St. Cecilia) and related didactic legends of "good women" (the Anglo-Saxon *Judith*, Boccaccio's and Petrarch's tales of Griselda); courtly romance and allegory (Guillaume de Lorris's *Romance of the Rose*, Chrétien's *Lancelot*, Dante's *Vita Nuova*, and sections of Boccaccio's *Teseide*); lyric ("women's songs" and selections from male and female troubadours, Dante, Petrarch, and others); and satire and fabliau (sections of Jean de Meun's *Romance of the Rose*, fabliaux by Jean Bodel and others, Book VII of Boccaccio's *Decameron*, and selections from his *Corbaccio*). This first part of the course culminated in our reading of a generically complex work, *The Nibelungenlied*, and, throughout, our primary readings were supplemented by philosophical, religious, and social comment on the nature of woman, love, and marriage in the works of writers as diverse as Plato, Aristotle, Plutarch, Ovid, Paul, Augustine, Jerome, Theophrastus, Thomas

Aquinas, Walter Map, Andreas Capellanus, and Peter Abelard. (For texts, see the bibliographical note at the end of this essay.)

There were several reasons for organizing the first part of the course by genre rather than by author. Principally, I wanted to focus on the issues of convention and tradition in medieval literary images of women as well as on the nature of literature itself. In terms of the latter, the generic approach helped us to address a difficult question, one that seems particularly important both to newer readers of medieval literature and to feminist critics: what relationships exist between the roles women play in literature and the lives they actually led? To clarify this question, we regularly used a "game theory" of literature modeled along the lines of John Leyerle's "The Game and Play of Hero" (in Norman T. Burns and Christopher J. Reagan, eds., *Concepts of the Hero in the Middle Ages and the Renaissance*, 1975). That is, we viewed a literary genre as a game (such as Monopoly, chess, or tennis) in which there is a tacit contract between players (author and audience) to abide by certain rules (for the author, literary conventions; for the audience, suspension of certain disbeliefs). And for each of our genres, we attempted to identify the series of rules operative for men and women in that particular literary game. In the game of secular epic, for instance, we identified one of its central rules as the requirement that the warrior be male, the "peace-weaver" female; in the game of courtly romance, we found a central rule to be that the male lover must experience alternating emotions of fear and hope and that the female lover must induce this amatory psychology through her successive encouragement and discouragement of his suit. Once we had established our taxonomy of rules for different medieval literary games, we were then able to compare the games and to inquire about their origins and effects.

For hagiography and didactic legends—games that modern readers often play with great reluctance—a comparative approach proved quite successful. We discussed, for instance, the discrepancies in the circumstances and consequences of the obligatory worldly renunciation in male and female saints' lives: usually, the female must be sexually inexperienced, her renunciation must take the form of the decision to remain chaste or not to marry, and she must encounter opposition to her resolve from a father, would-be spouse, or lover; the male, however, may be sexually experienced (in fact, he often may have led a profligate youth) and his renunciation of the world may involve a literal retreat to desert or mountain, an action for which he encounters neither opposition nor antagonism. We considered the medieval religious emphasis on female purity as a source for the hagiographical rule of female innocence; we wondered whether the more significant act of asceticism for a medieval woman was to refuse sex and marriage or to refuse companionship and community; and we were curious about why we heard so little of the early history of a female saint when we heard so much more about the early life of a male saint. For "good women" tales, such as the Anglo-Saxon *Judith,* we noted that the audience was required to suspend its disbelief in the existence of a female warrior and protagonist or, in other words, to put aside the rule by which *Beowulf,* for instance, is played.

Throughout these discussions of genre and images of women, we kept in mind the paradigm that our controlling game metaphor offered for defining the relationships between life and literature: a game may mirror the current values and beliefs of the society that invents it (as does Monopoly's central value of acquiring real estate); at the same time, it may include outmoded or unfeasible values and beliefs (Monopoly's valuation of the Boardwalk as a more expensive and desirable property than the Electric Company); and, again simultaneously, it may incorporate elements of sheer fantasy and unreality, some of which exist in contradiction to its other values (Monopoly's welfare system of distributing cash to each player who survives another turn around "Go"). Using this paradigm, we considered whether, in female hagiography, the significance accorded to the renunciation of sex and marriage was a true reflection of medieval women's values and experiences, an anachronistic value inherited from earlier times, and/or a fantasy based on the antifeminist notion that what woman desires most is erotic involvement (and hence her greatest sacrifice is to live chastely). We also discussed the Janus-faced relationship literature may have to life. The rule of female "fickleness" (alternating Fair Welcome and Dangier) in courtly romance, for instance, may in fact reflect one writer's experience with women and, in turn, prescribe female behavior, just as Monopoly may both echo and teach to its players one version of twentieth-century values.

Our final exercise for this first section of the course was an analysis of *The Nibelungenlied.* I put this work last partly because it defies easy attempts to classify it as one genre or another, and hence would anticipate for us the generic elusiveness of some of Chaucer's writing, and partly because its eclecticism provided a chance to review much that we had covered thus far. Students were asked to compose an essay on the "art of reading well" one of several set passages from *The Nibelungenlied;* it required them to discuss the analogues with which a modern reader should be familiar in order to appreciate best the generic complexity of the work and, ultimately, the effects of this generic mix. Concerning Kriemhild, one writer concluded that the mixed roles she plays make her a complicated and lifelike woman, a "game" rare in medieval literature; another writer, in contrast, argued that the author of *The Nibelungenlied* plays a version of "paradise lost," a *reductio ad absurdum* in which Kriemhild sequentially degenerates from the independent and self-assured woman of hagiography into the "bartered bride" of epic, the "battered bride" of satire and fabliau, and finally the avenging fury who persists in her spitefulness until, like Satan or Eve, her irrational malice threatens basic order and cosmic harmony.

During the second part of the course, we focused almost exclusively on Chaucer's *Canterbury Tales* but still utilized the generic framework established earlier. Our first effort was to examine a series of tales, many of which were no doubt written during the earlier period of the composition of the overall work, which allowed us to consider Chaucer's use of the literary conventions and traditions we had previously surveyed. Thus, we viewed the Knight's Tale in relationship to the epic and romance traditions; the tales of the Miller, Reeve, and Shipman, to the fabliau tradition; the Nun's Priest's Tale, to antifeminist satire; the Second Nun's Tale, to female hagiography; and the Man of Law's and Physician's Tales, to legends of "good women." Sometimes, we had already read specific sources for, or close analogues of, these Chaucerian selections (e.g., *Teseide* for the Knight's Tale; *Romance of the Rose* for the Physician's Tale; *Decameron* IX.6 for the Reeve's Tale; and so forth). On these occasions, we were able to base our discussions of Chaucer's artistry and literary treatment of women on fairly close comparisons with the earlier material. The remaining tales we discussed more generally in the context of their genres.

In these early discussions of Chaucer, students were easily able to place individual tales in their generic context as well as to isolate elements in them that appeared atypical. In the Knight's Tale, for instance, they saw Emily in the context of her romance sisters: the female lover of Guillaume's *Romance*, Chrétien's Guinevere, even Dante's Beatrice. But they noted that, in contrast to these earlier women, Emily remains remarkably oblivious to the amorous interest she invokes in her two suitors. In other words, she breaks what we had found to be a cardinal rule of courtly literature—the female's obligation to encourage her lover with Fair Welcome, underlined in Emily's case by her later prayer to Diana (reminiscent of hagiography) that she be spared participation in the love game altogether. Women's roles in Chaucer's fabliaux likewise present both traditional echoes and some surprises. Conventionally, the women in Chaucer's fabliaux pursue sex, money, or both in as clever and raucous a fashion as do their literary antecedents. But unlike them, on occasion they break the fabliau rule requiring women, as well as men, to be stock characters, interchangeable parts in the comic mechanism. Alisoun of the Miller's Tale, for instance, achieves some individual identity through her lavish depiction as a "child of nature"; Malyn some substance as she pursues her own plot of rebellion within and around the male games of the Reeve's Tale. As a piece of antifeminist satire, the Nun's Priest's Tale rings with familiar echoes of misogynic concepts of woman, but we also encounter some unusual and complementary attitudes toward men in the tale's comments on male vanity and susceptibility to flattery.

At the close of this introductory section on Chaucer, we found ourselves in a dilemma concerning his literary treatment of women in these earlier tales. For sure, and for whatever reason—individual genius, late medieval fatigue with traditional genres, sympathy for women—Chaucer had made innovations in women's literary roles and images. But many class members felt that these individual innovations did not amount to a significantly new view of woman. Emily may protest, but she submits wordlessly; Malyn may rebel, but she remains under paternal control. At this point, Arlyn Diamond's statement that ". . . we want more from [Chaucer], perhaps because he has already given us so much" summarized our sentiments well (see "Chaucer's Women and Women's Chaucer," in *The Authority of Experience: Essays in Feminist Criticism*, ed. Arlyn Diamond and Lee R. Edwards, 1977). To see whether Chaucer did give us more, we turned our attention to what for us was the centerpiece of *The Canterbury Tales*, the so-called "Marriage Group," comprising tales by the Wife of Bath, the Clerk, the Merchant, and the Franklin. We approached this set of tales as a mature section of the work (written or assembled during the last decade of the composition of *The Canterbury Tales*, the 1390s), and we asked one major question of it: does it show evidence of Chaucer's earlier interest in redefining women's literary roles, and, if so, what form does that interest take?

The Wife of Bath's Prologue and Tale immediately provided us the beginnings of an answer. We first observed that while the Wife's story of the loathly lady can generally be classified as romance, it is more difficult to name the literary game the Wife plays in her Prologue. We found in it the familiar elements of the first-person voice of lyric and autobiography, but we also saw in it motifs traditional to fabliau, epic, satire, art of matrimony, and sermon. None of us felt secure enough to pigeonhole it in one generic niche or another; nor did we feel that Ovid's Dipsas and Jean de Meun's La Vieille fully anticipate Chaucer's character. With this observation, we noted another discrepancy between the Wife's Prologue and Tale: while the Wife is impressive for her complex, often contradictory, nature, the protagonist of her tale is disappointing in her willingness to assume a one dimensional role, that of "beautiful young thing," so typical for romance women. These related observations led us to suspect that the Wife achieves her unique status among medieval literary women not so much because of her outspokenness, a trait typical enough of women in the fabliau and hagiography, but because of her refusal to limit her life story to one particular genre, her life to one particular role. While the Wife may attack clerics for the literary misfortunes of women, more precisely it is the either/or (single-role) images of women in traditional medieval genres that she challenges. Furthermore, the extent of the Wife's achievement in her Prologue is underscored by her later failure to create anything other than a conventional ending to her tale; in other words, she falls under the spell of traditional romance and rules that her protagonist must display Fair Welcome in a fashion acceptable to her man. The Wife's Tale thus emblemized for us Chaucer's earlier attempt to redefine women's literary images by changing only a few rules in the game, while her Prologue suggested Chaucer's new direction of changing the game altogether.

We viewed the remainder of the "Marriage Group" not as a simple battle between the sexes but as a complex battle among the genres. In response to the Wife's generic autonomy in her Prologue, the Clerk attempts to reassert the value of traditional genres in his tale of the "good woman" Griselda, but the Merchant and the Franklin follow the Wife's cue and perform generic experiments on, respectively, the fabliau and the romance. Our opinions on what these latter two pilgrims accomplish differed widely: some held that the Merchant's attempt to elevate fabliau into romance ironically backfires into antimatrimonial satire, others that it represents the Merchant's desire that his protagonist, January, escape stereotyping; some felt that the Franklin pretends to compose romance but forces his characters to play by fabliau rules, while others saw in the end of the tale a different game, that of one player, the author, challenging another, the audience, to identify the name of the literary game in which they have just participated. Whatever our conclusions, I believe that we all came away from *The Canterbury Tales* with a healthy respect both for Chaucer's artistry and for his comments on the power of literature over our lives and the centrality of literature in our lives.

On this note, we proceeded to the final segment of the course, in which we drew connections between classroom materials and our own literature and lives. For some, this took the form of exploring literature written by women in the Middle Ages (e.g., Marie of France, Christine de Pisan, the women troubadours) to see if or how they played the literary games we had been considering all semester. For others, it took the form of re-examining, in the light of what our study had suggested to them, later literature that they had read for other courses or on their own. These analyses ranged from comparisons of the Wife of Bath and Moll Flanders or of the types of generic experiments in *Tristram Shandy* and *The Can-*

terbury Tales to comparisons of Doris Lessing and Chaucer on the subject of women and rationalism. One student decided to reread *The Adventures of Tom Sawyer*, a former favorite that had nevertheless always disturbed her, and to try to explain in literary terms why the book had always vaguely upset her. Using a generic approach, she saw that the boys in *Tom Sawyer*, versions of the epic hero and courtly lover, are "given a wider scope of acceptable behavior and, therefore, the leeway to become active participants and plot-shapers." But the females conform to the ideals of "courtly beloved or epic hero's girl friend" and thus "remain passive and consequently suffer a *de facto* exclusion from adventure and action." The value of the connection this student was able to make between medieval and modern literature is, I think, best expressed in her own words:

> Re-reading a childhood classic like *Tom Sawyer*, in the light of what this course has offered, for me has the ultimate pragmatic value of reducing the heretofore awesome imperative of traditional sex-roles from a mystique to simply a man-made misconception. This reduction from mystique to misconception subsequently validates my reaction—then and now—to the subtle role-playing in *Tom Sawyer*. The book, despite its humor and excitement, upset me then and it still does, but now I know why it does. And, what's more significant, I can see, finally, that I was right all the time. (Janet Eagleson, "A Childhood Classic Revisited: *The Adventures of Tom Sawyer*," unpub. paper, 1979)

Bibliographical note: The readings for this course are available in R. K. Gordon, trans., *Anglo-Saxon Poetry* (New York: Dutton, 1926); Charles W. Jones, ed., *Medieval Literature in Translation* (New York: McKay, 1950); Robert P. Miller, ed., *Chaucer: Sources and Backgrounds* (New York: Oxford Univ. Press, 1977); Larry D. Benson and Theodore M. Andersson, *The Literary Context of Chaucer's Fabliaux* (Indianapolis: Bobbs-Merrill, 1971); Guillaume de Lorris and Jean de Meun, *The Romance of the Rose*, trans. Harry W. Robbins (New York: Dutton, 1962); Chrétien de Troyes, *Arthurian Romances*, trans. W. W. Comfort (1914; rpt. New York: Dutton, 1975); Giovanni Boccaccio, *The Decameron*, trans. J. M. Rigg (1930; rpt. New York: Dutton, 1973); A. T. Hatto, trans., *The Nibelungenlied* (1965; rpt. New York: Penguin, 1976); *The Portable Dante*, ed. Paolo Milano (New York: Viking, 1961); Boccaccio, *Corbaccio*, ed. and trans. Anthony K. Cassell (Urbana: Univ. of Illinois Press, 1975); and Rosemary Agonito, ed., *History of Ideas on Women: A Source Book* (New York: Putnam, 1977).

TEACHING THE BACKGROUNDS

THE INTELLECTUAL, ARTISTIC, AND HISTORICAL CONTEXT

D. W. Robertson, Jr.

I believe that an advanced or graduate course including Chaucer's *Canterbury Tales* should introduce students to a variety of primary materials useful to an understanding of that text, should recommend only such secondary materials as are based firmly on primary research or that help to control the use of primary materials, should place Chaucer's work in a cultural tradition that extends from classical antiquity through the early decades of the eighteenth century, and should lead finally to an appreciation of Chaucer's techniques for making what he had to say vivid, attractive, and meaningful to his own special audience. The tendency to read Chaucer from a "modern" point of view, a point of view, incidentally, that has changed considerably during my lifetime, results in distortions, leads to cultural deprivation which should not be an educational goal, and makes the *Tales* less attractive to students, who can supply this point of view spontaneously and need no instruction in its application. Students, both graduate and undergraduate, do enjoy learning something about a different and now remote culture with its own ideals, spontaneous attitudes, and, not least, sense of humor. With reference to the last, much of what is now frequently taught about the *Tales* reduces some of the most witty and humorous passages to solemn nonsense. Humor results from departures from reason, and unless we have clear ideas about what Chaucer and most of his contemporaries thought to be true and reasonable, we cannot perceive his humor.

During the last thirty years, it has become possible to develop a number of new approaches to the *Tales*, partly as a result of scholarly progress in other fields. It is now possible to offer students significant insights into the principal intellectual traditions that underlie the attitudes in Chaucer's writings as well as insights into the application of those attitudes to the rapidly changing social and economic conditions of the later fourteenth century—conditions that affected persons in all walks of life. Basic to any reasonable grasp of these attitudes, both traditional and contemporary, is some knowledge of the Bible, its exegesis, and the principles derived from exegetical study in what is loosely called "theology," although the more technical ramifications and speculations of academic theology are probably of small relevance to the study of Chaucer. As a preliminary grounding in these traditions, a knowledge of the Latin Fathers, especially Augustine, whose works found a prominent place in almost all fourteenth-century libraries of any consequence, is essential. A familiarity with standard medieval works like the commentaries of Peter the Lombard on the Psalms and the Pauline Epistles, known together as the *Major glossatura*, and the *Glossa ordinaria* is necessary as an approach to the later exegetical tradition, while these works were themselves standard references throughout the later Middle Ages. In the late fourteenth century there was also a revival of interest in the spiritual writings of the twelfth century, in part stimulated by the Franciscans. Ancillary material is available in letter collections, in treatises, and in a variety of miscellaneous writings on special subjects, as well as in sermons. These last often afford insights into popular attitudes, figurative conventions, conventional thought structures, and, where fourteenth-century English sermons are concerned, into the application of traditional attitudes to contemporary problems.

It has been said that early Christian writers embraced "the best traditions of Classical philosophy." The classical influence was maintained in medieval schools, where Cicero, Seneca, Vergil, Ovid, Horace, Statius, Lucan, and other Latin authors were carefully studied with special attention both to their eloquence or literary technique and to their wisdom, chiefly moral. In considering the relevance of these authors, especially the poets, to the study of Chaucer, however, it is necessary to become familiar with the attitudes developed toward them in the Middle Ages and to study the works of medieval mythographers and commentators. We are now fortunate to have available both reprints of earlier editions of such works and new editions of others, as well as some valuable secondary guides and studies. One work that illustrates vividly the adaptation of classical thought for Christian purposes is *The Consolation of Philosophy* of Boethius, which exerted a profound influence on English writers from the Old English period to the mid-eighteenth century. It is not strange that the *Consolation* and Saint Gregory's *Moralia* on Job were two of John of Salisbury's favorite works and that both were often found in fourteenth-century English collections. The influence of Boethius was especially powerful in Europe during the years following the Black Death, when themes from it appeared frequently in English wall painting. All serious students of English literature should, if only in a detached way, accord the *Consolation* a sympathetic understanding without quarreling with its metaphysical principles, which are developed for a moral purpose, or suggesting that it is somehow "pagan." It would also be especially helpful if students could have access to the standard medieval commentaries of William of Conches and Nicholas Trivet. Meanwhile, we now have available in English translations two of the most useful guides to medieval educational practice, the *Didascalion* of Hugh of Saint Victor and the *Metalogicon* of John of Salisbury, as well as a good recent book by Nicholas Orme (1973) on educational practice in English schools in the Middle Ages.

Scriptural and classical texts, together with their medieval interpretations, provided fruitful sources of imagery, conventional descriptions, and patterns of action in medieval literary texts. Thus, knowledge of the Bible and the classics provides not only a philosophical basis for understanding the *Tales* but also a background for studying Chaucer's literary techniques. Sometimes a series of scriptural passages acquired special medieval connotations. For example, a series of them, first used by William of Saint Amour, became associated with attacks on the fraternal orders, and these are reflected in unmistakable fashion in Chaucer's portrayals of friars. Chaucer was neither the first nor the last poet to make use of these materials, some of which he undoubtedly found in earlier works like the *Roman de la rose*, now available in a good English prose translation by Charles Dahlberg (1971) and well treated in a number of secondary studies, although it is still systematically abused by advocates of "courtly love" or "sensualistic naturalism." It is extremely important to seek to understand not only literary works, like the *Roman*, that Chaucer knew and used extensively but also the literary traditions that such works represent. There is a close connection, for example, between the *Roman* and the Latin literature that developed in the monasteries and cathedral schools of the twelfth century and provided both the *Roman's* authors with ironic and satiric techniques. Again, the "form" of this poem, the Dream Vision, represents a fusion of classical and Scriptural traditions that took place in the twelfth century, a fusion that gave the poem and others like it special connotation and helped to assure their widespread appeal. Where medieval commentaries on medieval authors are available, like those on Dante, for example, they should be treated with respect and not dismissed as irrelevant in the light of our own supposedly superior knowledge.

Much the same sort of influences that shaped both the techniques and the general content of literary works is also evident in the visual arts of the Middle Ages. Emile Mâle's great study of religious art in France, the first volume of which has recently appeared in a new translation with supplementary notes (Princeton Univ. Press, 1978), is, in spite of certain limitations, a basic guide to the meaning of medieval religious art. Since Raimond van Marle's *Iconographie de l'art profane au Moyen Age et la Renaissance* (1931–32) other special studies have provided similar analyses of "nonreligious" art that now enable the student of Chaucer often to find significant imagery common to the visual arts and to Chaucer. In addition, changes in style during the course of the Middle Ages, which were sometimes fairly rapid, are more clearly evident visually than they are textually.

Research in the other arts is frequently rewarding, both in the illumination of details in Chaucer's text and in leading to an understanding of his general outlook. Thus, some knowledge of medieval music, both in its basic theory—as illustrated in the treatises of Augustine and Boethius and in a series of subsequent medieval treatises—and in its actual practice, can be very rewarding. The usefulness of a knowledge of medieval astrology, cosmology, medicine, and logic has been amply demonstrated.

Chaucer lived among clerks and administrators familiar with the law. A distinguished legal historian has recently observed that the actual structure of a society, the nexus of commonplace relationships that is frequently taken for granted and not much discussed, is most readily discernible in its laws and their application. Thus, students of *The Canterbury Tales* should find a study of law useful in evaluating the behavior of Chaucer's characters. There are now available good editions of some of the relevant Year Books, an excellent selection by G. O. Sayles of cases from the King's Bench, some fine editions of rolls of the Justices of the Peace, coroners' rolls, borough court records, records of courts with the View of Frankpledge, and manorial court records. The Civil Law has been less thoroughly studied, but there are studies that offer good introductions to the work of the ecclesiastical courts, like R. H. Helmholz, *Marriage Litigation in Medieval England* (1974). Meanwhile, a new edition of the synodal decrees of English bishops is under way. Finally, there is a good study of the laws of war by M. H. Keen. More generally, we now have a good brief history of English law in J. H. Baker, *An*

Introduction to English Legal History (2nd ed., 1979), and some special studies that shed light on the development of law during the fourteenth century.

Among the changes that took place during Chaucer's lifetime were those in the organization of the royal administration. Since Chaucer was closely associated with the Chamber and had frequent dealings with the Exchequer, we need to know something about administrative history to understand his daily concerns. In this connection, it is important that we study the characters of Chaucer's associates, some of whom probably made up the membership of the audience he usually addressed. The recent publication of the works of Sir John Clanvowe is especially welcome. Medieval political theory offers another field of fruitful inquiry although such theory in Chaucer's time represented a Christian modification of the ethical principles of Aristotle's *Politics* and was not in the modern sense "political." John of Salisbury's *Policraticus*, which Chaucer knew, forms a useful introduction, and the *De Regimine Principum* of Aegidius Romanus was popular in the later fourteenth century. Fourteenth-century court "politics" itself, which was partly a matter of rivalries among magnates domestically and friction between followers of reformers like Philippe de Mézières on the one hand and advocates of the recovery of English power on the Continent on the other, surely influenced Chaucer's attitudes. He was also undoubtedly cognizant of events in what has been called "the turbulent London of Richard II."

England in the fourteenth century was still basically an agrarian society. During recent years a great many manorial documents, in addition to the court rolls mentioned above, have become available, and there are some extremely useful regional histories, histories of estates, and studies of individual manors. These often shed a great deal of light on the significant changes in English society after the Black Death, some of which undoubtedly disturbed Chaucer and his associates and influenced his treatment of rural characters. In fact, it is probably impossible to understand what he was saying about them and why he was saying it without some understanding of contemporary developments. While rural society was changing, certain industries and trades were undergoing changes as well, and there have been good specialized studies of the cloth industry, the wool trade, and the wine trade, as well as general studies in social and economic history. Developments in rural society and in trade and industry affected towns, some of which were also deeply affected by relations with foreign powers. There is a good recent general *Introduction to the History of English Medieval Towns* by Susan Reynolds (1977), and there have been useful studies of individual towns.

In view of the presence of ecclesiastics in the *Tales*, students also need to know something about diocesan administration and the characters of English bishops. Further, the basic ideals and the actual conditions of cathedrals, regular and secular, of monasteries, of nunneries, and of friaries familiar to Chaucer's audience but no longer familiar today need further study on the part of Chaucerians. Ecclesiastics of all varieties were deeply affected by the same social changes that affected the rest of society, and Chaucer's attitude toward these religious figures, in the light of traditional ideals, has a great deal to do with their appearance in the *Tales*. For example, the persistence of certain of William of Saint Amour's accusations against the friars is explicable only in part as a result of literary tradition. Finally, ecclesiastical records often include wills, which afford excellent clues to the value placed on a variety of material possessions as well as indications of the nature of private devotion.

It should be emphasized, I think, that all the various areas of investigation suggested above are interdependent. Thus, one can learn a great deal about friars and monks, for example, from the study of towns, and since some towns had close connections with agricultural activity, the study of one sector of society can hardly be carried out without the study of the other. Similarly, statements by bishops and other ecclesiastical authorities sometimes reflect the figurative conventions discernible in both literature and the visual arts. There is a sense, indeed, in which the various "fields" of modern research may be misleading since society itself was an integrated whole.

In the above remarks, I may have omitted certain "fields," but I have sought to show that Chaucerians still have a great deal to learn and that those wishing to deepen their understanding and appreciation for Chaucer's writings still have a great deal to do. There is plenty of room left for hard work, for the excitement of discovery, and for the satisfactions of real accomplishment. Teachers of advanced and graduate Chaucer courses should, I think, offer their students every opportunity to enjoy the possibilities that lie before them.

Editor's Note: For another view of D. W. Robertson's "program" of reading in the Middle Ages, see his anthology, *The Literature of Medieval England* (New York: McGraw-Hill, 1970). Its introduction discusses medieval life and ideals, medieval astronomy and astrology, the medieval Bible, the character of medieval literature, and the literature of medieval England. Its twelve chapters are devoted to early Celtic literature in Britain, early Anglo-Latin literature (Gildas, Bede, Boniface, Alcuin, et al.), Old English literature, later Celtic literature in Britain, later Latin literature in Britain (John of Salisbury, Geoffrey of Monmouth, et al.), medieval literary theory (John of Salisbury, Dante, Boccaccio, Richard de

Bury, Bernard Silvestris, Nicholas Trivet, William of Conches, et al.), French literature in England (Marie de France, Jean Froissart, et al.), songs and short poems in Middle English, the English medieval romance (*Sir Gawain and the Green Knight* and Malory's *Morte d'Arthur*), *Piers the Ploughman*, Chaucer, and early English drama.

Hugh of St. Victor's *Didascalion* appeared in an English translation by Jerome Taylor (New York: Columbia Univ. Press) in 1961. John of Salisbury's *Metalogicon* is available in a translation by Daniel M. McGarry (1955; rpt. Gloucester, Mass.: Peter Smith, 1962). *The Statesman's Book* (trans. John Dickinson, New York: Knopf, 1927) includes Books 4, 5, and 6 and selections from Books 7 and 8 of John of Salisbury's *Policraticus*; the volume entitled *Frivolities of Courtiers and Footprints of Philosophers* (trans. Joseph B. Pike, Minneapolis: Univ. of Minnesota Press, 1938) also offers selections from Books 7 and 8 as well as the first three books of the *Policraticus*. For translations of other works mentioned in the essay, see the appropriate bibliographical listings for, among others, Vergil, Ovid, Boethius, Augustine, Dante, Guillaume de Lorris and Jean de Meun, and Emile Mâle.

THE CANTERBURY TALES IN THE TRADITION OF WESTERN LITERATURE: CHAUCER AS SCHOLIAST AND ETYMOLOGIZER

Ernest N. Kaulbach

Although it sounds as academic as pompous processions and intimidates as much as a quick peep into Tobler-Lommatzsch, the title of this essay does convey my approach to teaching *The Canterbury Tales*. Geoffrey Chaucer is only one exponent of a tradition that preceded him by at least fourteen hundred years. The "matter" of *The Canterbury Tales*, the narratives and the science and the schemes of imagery and even the languages, was an inheritance. When put in the mouths of divergent narrators, Chaucer's Middle English made brilliant "sense" of the ambiguous coherence of the inherited "matter" to a fourteenth-century audience. His Middle English now intimidates, however, and the "matter" of the tales involves slow process through sidenotes and footnotes. It is difficult to make contemporary sense out of Chaucer's "sense."

Rather than make contemporary sense out of Chaucer's "sense," my World Literature I course attempts to make historical sense out of Chaucer's "matter." Since the course introduces ancient and medieval world literature of the West, it deals with the matter of the tradition primarily, treating the authors simply as exponents of that tradition. We deal with the narratives, the schemes of imagery, the science, and even the languages; we use individual authors only to indicate the growth and ambiguous coherence of the matter. In other words, we let Chaucer's matter explain his sense.

In the course, we read selections from *The Canterbury Tales* as if Chaucer had been a fourteenth-century commentator on, and interpreter of, old language and schemes of imagery encapsulated in manuscripts or renditions of Homer, Moses, Vergil, Ovid, Catullus, Macrobius, and Augustine; as if all of these had been reinterpreted by the more recent goliards, troubadours, romancers, hagiographers, theologians, astrologers, alchemists, popularizers, and hacks; and as if Chaucer had inherited all the matter of the continuators. Since his language and patterns of imagery updated romancers and hagiographers, who overlaid goliards and troubadours, who in turn overlaid Caedmon and the vernacular English poets, who overlaid Carolingian scholiasts on Augustine and Macrobius, who overlaid Vergil and Cicero, Ovid and Catullus, who overlaid Plato, Moses, and Homer, Chaucer continued commentary on the meaning of an established tradition to his fourteenth-century audience. Since the *Tales* related the sense of ancient texts to his audience, Chaucer appears as a brilliant scholiast. Because the *Tales* adapt images, old words, and texts to suit the taste of a fourteenth-century audience, Chaucer appears as an etymologizer who added new connotations to a language already loaded with connotations from Greek, Latin, Anglo-Saxon, French, and the Scandinavian languages. As a scholiast, he made sense out of the older narratives, science, and images, much as screen writers interpret and reinterpret the matter of Cowboys and Indians to generations of moviegoers. As etymologizer, he rearranged the connotations of images and word roots to suit the "sense" of his audience. His language becomes accessible to students when they see the roots of it in Latin, French, and Anglo-Saxon and when the images under the word roots become familiar from the old narratives. We make sense out of *The Canterbury Tales* by relating the tales to the classics and the classical languages, as well as to Anglo-Saxon and French, not by relating them to contemporary sense.

This, then, is a World Literature I course taught on the principle of "overlay," that is, the interpretation of an earlier text in the terms and concepts of a later text. Overlay began, as we (the teaching assistant and I) teach it, when Alexandrian scholiasts began to interpret Homer in terms of the Bible or the Bible in terms of Homer. To meld Greek and Hebrew cultures for students who understood little of either, the scholiasts wrote extended commentaries on both of the texts, with heavy emphasis on etymologies and schemes of imagery. The coherence of Western literary tradition developed when the same scholiasts overlaid interpretations of Plato's *Timaeus* upon interpretations of the first two chapters of Genesis. Plato and Moses told a coherent narrative of beginnings for the West. Vergil, looked at from the scholiast point of view, merely overlaid Homer's Troy story. Solomon and his Song of Songs became attached to interpretations of Ovid, and Vergil's continuation of the Troy story metamorphosed into a "historical" basis for the *Brut* poems. Ovid reworked the epic hero into a lover and was himself rewritten by commentators on the Song of Songs or by troubadours. If you prefer generic terms, "history" became epic and epic became lyric and elegiac because of the scholiast tradition. Augustine and Macrobius, by way of Cicero, overlaid Vergil and Ovid to expand the *Aeneid* and the *Ars Amatoria* respectively into theological and scientific treatises on politics and the psychology of love. With Caedmon, gleemen, and the Alfredian schools came the necessity for translating languages and images of Roman-Greek-Judaeo-Christian civilization into the vernacular English and Germanic traditions. From vernacular scholiasts and etymologizers came romances and more hagiography, more science and political theory —and the tradition of the West became Teutonic-Roman-Greek-Judaeo-Christian. Chrétien de Troyes represented the tradition in France; Dante and Petrarch, in Italy; Chaucer, in England; Cervantes, in Spain. The quest for Canterbury, *mutatis mutandis*, somewhat resembles the quest for the Grail, Beatrice, Laura, or the remnants of chivalry.

In the classroom, we never use the expressions "principles of overlay" or "etymologies of words and images" or "scholiast commentary," just as we do not use the title of this essay. The students are able to see the method for themselves when they acquire interest in the languages and the construction of the images. We say rather that we are teaching a course in World Literature I and that the selections form a "Western Tradition," that is, a tradition separate from that of Vedic literature, Japanese or Chinese literature, African literature, or American Indian literature. We encourage students to read other, non-Western literatures as a contrast; and, at the end of the course, we use a work like the *Bhagavadgita* to compare and contrast differences of tradition. The point, of course, is that none of these non-Western literatures appears in the scholiast tradition from Alexandria. Chaucer might be saying the same things that the *Bhagavadgita* says about the human condition, but he says them in the manner taken from the Alexandrian scholiasts.

For the method of overlay to make sense to students, our lectures involve close reading of texts chosen by the scholiasts, as if we were the scholiasts commenting on the texts. We begin the course with Books IX-XI of the *Odyssey*, Odysseus' summary of all his travels. In the manner of Alexandrian commentators, we pick up the topography of Odysseus' journey and try to attach it to geographies of the ancient Mediterranean world. We try to locate the place where the storm drove Odysseus' ship off course, the land of the Lotus Eaters, the palace of the winds, the caves of the Cyclops near the water, Circe's palace, the place where Hermes warned Odysseus about Circe's power, the land without a setting sun, the location of the underworld. We attempt to make geographic sense out of Odysseus' matter to show, in the attempt, that Homer's sense doesn't work in terms of exterior geography. So then we do what the scholiasts did: we show how the exterior geography becomes interior geography. Odysseus journeys to grow as a man: he avoids shipwreck (an image of personal chaos, such as sin); he does not change into a beast (an image of vice); he avoids the snares of women (an image of woman as siren); he finds secret self-knowledge in dreams (an image of self-knowledge through dream visions); he journeys into the underworld (an image of memory); and so on. At the beginning of the course, we do more with the images than with etymologies because of the difficulty with the Greek alphabet. Besides, students have enough difficulty understanding how scholiast commentary makes "sense" out of Homer.

After looking at selections from the *Iliad* and more sources for Chaucer's matter, we begin selections from the Bible, limited in class to only the first two chapters of Genesis. Augustine is the scholiast, and *On the Literal Meaning of Genesis* the source for our lectures. Since Augustine's reading of Genesis is no more literal than are Alexandrian interpretations of Homer, we can show with Augustine the "scientific" origins of the world described by Moses. Out of the repetitions of "And God said," we can make comments on the importance of number theory, on the days of the week, on the elements, seasons, stars, planets, and the creation of man "in the image and likeness of God," that is, as a body composed of four elements and a mind of three powers, the body resembling the elements in the macrocosm and the mind resembling the Trinity of persons in God.

Because the Bible and Homer cohere in the *Timaeus* (1-42B), we again follow the examples of Macrobius (*Commentary on the Dream of Scipio*) and Augustine (*The City of God*, Bk. VIII, Ch. xi) and make Timaeus speak of the origins of the world as if he were a Hellenic Moses. We begin to lay the *Timaeus* over Genesis and Homer with the same concerns: number, God in Trinity (of persons or powers or attributes), man in the triune image of God, the seven planets in the cosmos and seven days of the week, the four elements and four humors of man, virtues and vices, and the destiny of heaven or reincarnation. The overlay is simple, and a coherence for the "Western Tradition" develops from it. Augustine's commentary makes the ambiguities of the matter of this tradition stand out. The origins of a duality in the motions of the "Same" and the "Different" in the *Timaeus* are translated by Augustine into the motion of the firmament to the right but of the planets to the left, translated again into the motion of reason to the right but of emotion to the left, and finally translated into images and nuances of "Right" (right reason, dextrous, skillful, Northern) as opposed to "Left" (sensuality, sinister, gauche, Southern). The ambiguities of these nuances, images, patterns, theories, and geocentricity underlie *The Canterbury Tales*. This dense material is Chaucer's legacy although it lacks a personal voice.

For the lyrical inheritance, we begin with Sappho, whose translator, Catullus, develops a personal voice that ties the dense material of Plato, Genesis, and Homeric commentary down to a speaker. After Plato, the personal voice of classical lyric poets seems a welcome relief to the students. As good Christian scholiasts, we convert Ovid and Catullus in order to speak about an alleged source of courtly love. Again we emphasize the personal voice, the ideas tied down to a speaker, the ambiguities of love relationships; and we skip ahead to Andreas Capellanus to show how the classics endure in times of French romance. After a pleasant interlude of lyrics, we return to the sobriety of Vergil.

By now students see for themselves that the *Aeneid* is the *Odyssey* translated into a Roman *imperium*. To bring the *translatio imperii* up to Chaucer's England, it remains for us to quote some of Layamon's *Brut* and the opening chapters of Geoffrey of Monmouth's *History of the Kings of Great Britain*. While some students read outside on Arthurian materials and others on Dido and Aeneas, we spend much class time on scholiast commentaries on Aeneas' descent into the underworld (VI. 792 ff.). Besides the Dido and Aeneas story (Bk. IV), this passage brings up to Chaucer's time summaries of *Timaeus*-Genesis commentaries and also brings into sharp focus questions about dream visions and the psychology and imagery of dreams. (Should there be more interest in the commentaries, we bring in Delphin editions of Vergil used in the United States in the nineteenth century. What was taught in Chaucer's time about Aeneas' descent into the underworld was still taught in nineteenth-century America. And, of course, the interest justifies our discussions of theories of memory in Freud and Jung as well as the students' acquaintance with commentaries on the *Aeneid*.)

Next comes the *translatio Teutonica*, the overlay of Anglo-Saxon, Scandinavian, and Germanic traditions upon the "classics." To make the overlay concrete, we sketch the cosmology of the *Elder Edda* on the blackboard beside a sketch of Plato's cosmos. Perfunctory bows are made to Hobbits and Middle Earth, but class time is spent reading "The Seafarer" in Anglo-Saxon in juxtaposition to Pound's translation. The idea is a simple one: to show the difficulties of translating the Homeric or Vergilian *gubernatio* with all its cultural connotations into an Anglo-Saxon kenning such as the one in the title, "sea-faring." Through a comparison of Pound and the original text, we can etymologically demonstrate that "metaphor" (Greek root) and *translatio* (Latin root) are one and the same thing, and that the Teutonic Weltanschauung overlays the Classic-Judaeo-Christian milieu in still another sense of "translation," that is, the movement of literature from Jerusalem to Athens to Rome and to the various vernaculars of the capitals of Europe. Latin etymologies and images are being translated into Old English: *fatum* into *wyrd;* *narratio* into *reccan; caelum* into *heofon; mens* into *mōd;* and so on. When we compare words and images in their respective *cosmoi,* the cosmos of the *Elder Edda* and Anglo-Saxon poetry compares well with that of the *Timaeus* and the Bible. If there is time, we try to read one of the shorter sagas to give Icelandic literature its deserved place in the Western tradition and in the development of Chaucer's language ("sake," "outlaw," "undertake," "rood").

Selections from the troubadours and goliards, in the original languages with facing translations, span the period from Old English to Dante and Chaucer. Again, the principle of overlay is discernible. Ovid, Catullus, and the Song of Songs live on in French, Italian, German, Latin, and Middle English. The personal voices of the poets, tying down abstract ideas into speakers and singers, again appeal to the students. (Their reaction encourages us to suggest that they learn some of the languages. We do not hesitate to point out appropriate courses, departments, requirements, and names of instructors in the catalog.) From this point, the sequence of Dante, Chaucer, and Petrarch, with Cervantes as conclusion seems to work well. Each poet in his own vernacular and time refers to the romance-troubadour tradition, overlaying the lyric poets who overlay the *Timaeus,* the Bible, and Homer.

Though lofty, the intricacies of Dante's imagery and his choice of words become somewhat accessible because of acquaintance with medieval cosmology. Vergil as guide, the search for the beloved, the number symbolism are familiar ideas to the students. Students still must wrestle with the intricacies of images and Dante's choice of words. In the search for Canterbury, the images become even more accessible, in spite of the Middle English. The personal voices of the Miller and the Wife of Bath make the matter from the goliards and romancers take on the qualities of vivid confessional literature, albeit jarring. Up to Chaucer, etymologies and patterns of imagery have been attached to ideas and not to speakers. The Miller and the Wife of Bath adapt the matter to their own, somewhat jarring sense. The Wife, for example, twists the theological expression "auctorite" to make herself the authority for the voice she adopts in her tale. The Miller subverts the classic sense of "hende" (Latin, "gracious") to introduce bawdy reinterpretations of the legend of Saint Nicholas. The images of "auctorite" and "hende" jar, of course, when compared to their original context; but they are appropriate to the personal voices of Chaucer's speakers. As I mentioned at the beginning of this essay, we let Chaucer's matter speak for itself so that we can concentrate on the rich connotations of Chaucer's language. We read the General Prologue to set the context for words and tone, and we read according to the "overlay" principle.

The course concludes with Petrarch and Cervantes by way of a look forward into the Renaissance, where the same matter is overlaid with yet another sensibility. Chaucer made one use of Petrarch; Sir Thomas Wyatt, another. Although the first part of *Don Quixote* laid *Amadis of Gaul* to rest, the second part revived him in the chronicles of the famous Don. The final exam is a three-hour oral review of all the matter of the course from Homer to Cervantes. In the latter part of the exam, we contrast all this "Western matter" with a literary representative of a "non-Western" literature.

Since "the lyf [is] so short, the craft so long to lerne," three months are too little an introduction to the material of the course. Yet, both the sophomores who are looking for an introduction into humanities and the seniors who are looking for a way to tie together four years' worth of seemingly unrelated courses find what they are seeking as we go about defining what might be called the "Western Tradition." Even if they do not personally believe a word of this tradition, it forms a basis for "Chapter One" of their physics, health sciences, psychology, and history texts, and it provides a sense of the coherence of a series of nonrelated but required courses. The "sense" is left to the students. We, the TA and myself, provide the "matter." The students keep journals of class notes, summaries of outside reading, and an occasional summary of reactions to class discussion. We harp on close readings of small selections of texts— but with a velvet harp. With English and humanities majors on the decline, we are teaching students who meld this matter into preprofessional programs: business, advertising, engineering, medicine, law, social work, computer technology, or radio astronomy. To them, this matter is frankly hoary, pompous, and intimidating. The "sense" they make of it smacks of a jarring and yet apt coherence for them. It is not unusual to have premed students studying Galen and Arabic medicine here. Psychology students tend to read further in humor psychology or dream analysis. Engineers tend to enjoy stress studies of medieval cathedrals; business majors, the origins of money and trade routes. We make "vertu of necessitee," hoping that someday necessity will be overlaid by virtue.

MEDIEVAL PILGRIMAGE

Julia Bolton Holloway

Ma noi siam peregrin come voi siete.

Dante, *Purgatorio* II.63

• for pylgrymes are we alle.

Langland, *Piers Plowman* B.XI.234

And pilgrimes were they alle.

Chaucer, *Canterbury Tales* I.26

The major poetry of the fourteenth century concerns pilgrimage. I proposed, then taught, a seminar on Pilgrimage in the Middle Ages in the Humanistic Studies Program at Princeton University in order to study these poems in relation to one another and to the background of pilgrimage in the Middle Ages. The interdisciplinary course centered on Dante's *Commedia*, Guillaume de Deguileville's *Pèlerinages*, Langland's *Piers Plowman*, and Chaucer's *Canterbury Tales* but also discussed the material that preceded these fourteenth-century poems, such as *Tristan and Ysolt*, the *Roman de la Rose*, and *Vita Nuova*, and the material that followed them, such as Elizabethan poetry that makes use of pilgrimage as a metaphor (Ralegh, Spenser, Shakespeare), Bunyan's *Pilgrim's Progress*, and James Joyce's *Ulysses*.

The introductory weeks of the seminar were dedicated to the study of pilgrimage in its own right, beginning with an investigation of Hellenic and Hebraic social practices related to the exiled traveler, seen as a democratic Everyman or a God-going-a-begging, then proceeding to a study of liturgical pilgrimage materials: the Hebrew pilgrimages to the Temple in Jerusalem, at Succoth the bearing of palms to lay on the horns of the altar; the Christian Pilgrim Blessing, the *Benedictio Peregrinorum*; and the liturgical drama of the Emmaus pilgrims from Luke 24, the *Officium*

Peregrinorum, acted each Easter Monday. This last generated rich icon-ographical and musicological materials of great value for studying fourteenth-century pilgrimage poems. (We had already produced the *Officium Peregrinorum* at Princeton University, making use of the Fleury manuscript rendition from the twelfth century, under the direction of Fr. Gerard Farrell, a Benedictine monk and chant master from St. John's Abbey.) Following this background material, we studied actual pilgrimage accounts that have survived from the Middle Ages and noted their formulaic quality—particularly evident in the publications of the Palestine Pilgrims' Text Society. One student discussed Egyptian and Irish monastic pilgrimages and reported on Arculf's account to Adamnan, when shipwrecked on Iona, of his pilgrimage to Jerusalem. Another reported on Icelandic accounts of pilgrimages to the Holy Places and showed an Icelandic map depicting the buildings of Jerusalem with high wooden gabled roofs rather than with stone and brick domes and flat roofs. Accounts by and of women on pilgrimage to the Holy Places were also noted (Paula, Egeria, Margery, Bridget), and the medieval pilgrimage to Compostela discussed, especially in relation to the Reconquista's Apocalypse imagery representing Saint James as *Matamoros* ("Moor Slayer").

By the fourth week, we were ready to study pilgrimage literature. Surprisingly, the early appearance of pilgrimage as a literary theme is satirical, "up-so-doun." 1 Peter 2.11 declared: "Dearly beloved, I beseech you as strangers and pilgrims, abstain from fleshly lusts, which war against the soul." Canon law required pilgrims to be chaste. But literary works such as *Tristan*, the *Roman de la Rose*, and the *Vita Nuova* show their heroes as "passionate pilgrims," pilgrims of lust. Much use was made during this week of iconographical materials from illuminated manuscripts and elsewhere, centering on Amant's rape of the rose by means of his scrip and staff.[1] The *Vita Nuova* was viewed as seeming to be about Dante as a foolish and uncomprehending passionate pilgrim, lusting for Beatrice as his idol and Golden Calf, who is converted by her death into a true Exodus and Emmaus pilgrim to God. The typologies of the Exodus and Emmaus pilgrimages were basic to the seminar.

The sixth week, we began our study of Dante's *Commedia*, discussing the meaning of exile and pilgrimage by juxtaposing this work with the antecedent Italian poem, *Il Tesoretto*, which begins with its poet, Brunetto Latini, returning from embassy in Spain and learning in the pilgrim Pass of Roncesvalles that he has been sentenced to exile and is not permitted to return to Florence. Sorrowing, he loses his way and wanders into the landscape of allegory in his vision poem.[2] Dante consciously echoes these lines in *Inferno* I and XV. During the week, we concentrated on the themes of Exile and Exodus in Dante's *Inferno*, noting that in these pages Hell is both Egypt and Florence, afflicted with nine of the ten plagues, including that of the frogs.

The seventh week was spent discussing the medieval pilgrim psalm, 113 in the Vulgate (114 and 115 in the King James Bible and sung in its entirety in *Purg.* II), "In exitu Israel de Aegypto," and its meaning in the *Purgatorio*, in which it is juxtaposed to Dante's own Golden Calf lyric of love. In the pages of the *Purgatorio*, Dante climbs Mount Sinai/Mount Purgatorio.[3] The psalm repeats the Exodus tale and speaks out harshly against Golden Calf idolatry. Its music in the Middle Ages was intact from the Hebraic tradition and sung to a unique *tonus peregrinus*. The eighth week was spent discussing the *Paradiso* and the Roman pilgrimage stations and pilgrimage landscapes in the Jubilee year of 1300, Rome in Dante's poem replacing Jerusalem; Italy, Israel.[4]

During the ninth week, we discussed Deguileville's *Pèlerinages* and Langland's *Piers Plowman*, both of which center on pilgrimage allegory and both of which were influenced by twelfth-century neo-Platonism. After the Council of Whitby monastic clergy were forbidden to be pilgrims, however, and this prohibition tended to make pilgrimage poetry a lay rather than a monastic genre. When lay poets such as Dante and Chaucer write of pilgrimage, they can incorporate its reality into their poetry. But both Deguileville, a Cistercian monk, and Lydgate, his Benedictine translator, forbidden in actual fact to be pilgrims, tended to make their poems allegorical. The poetry of Langland, who was married and in lower orders, mixes reality with allegory.

The tenth week centered on *The Canterbury Tales*, and almost all the antecedent material was found to be useful in analyzing Chaucer's masterpiece as a pilgrimage poem. It was paired with plague programs, the frescoes by Francesco Traini of the *Triumph of Death* in Pisa and by Andrea da Firenze of the *Via Veritatis* in Florence, and with literary works, such as Sercambi's *Novelle* and Boccaccio's *Decameron*, occasioned by the Black Death.[5] Iconographical materials had taught us to envision medieval pilgrims on foot and dressed in sober colors; often solitary and garbed in sheepskin with scrip, staff, and hat. It was a shock, therefore, to see the Ellesmere illuminations of the travelers in *The Canterbury Tales* dressed in bright clothing and on horses.[6] To ride horseback invalidated the medieval pilgrimage; only asses were permitted, and only to the weak and infirm. Suddenly Chaucer's joke became as clear to us as it would have been to his own audience. He was writing satire. His lecherous pilgrims—the Wife, and the odd couple, the Summoner and the Pardoner—are "passionate pilgrims" and as such are ironical depictions. The Monk and the Prioress have no business traveling beyond their cloisters (Lydgate in his continuation to *The Canterbury Tales, The Siege of Thebes*, goes to great lengths to rationalize his presence as a monk on that pilgrimage), and certainly the Monk and the Prioress ought not to be in each other's company. Though still on horseback, Chaucer's "ideal" pilgrims—the Knight, the Clerk, and the Parson—are noted for their sober clothing; the Parson, moreover, is described in the General Prologue as being like a Wyclifite priest, journeying about his parish on foot with only his pilgrim staff to support him and refusing to abandon his flock to run off to London.

There are, however, two false-seeming pilgrims, the Wife and the Pardoner, present on the pilgrimage, and much of the class discussion centered on them. They are the only two who are "professional" pilgrims—the one having journeyed to all the major pilgrimage sites of the Middle Ages, to Compostela, Jerusalem, and so forth; the other wearing the Roman vernicle, or replica of the Veronica veil, on his pilgrim hat. Both are garbed by the Ellesmere illuminator, however, not in pilgrim white but in scarlet. (Andrea da Firenze's *Via Veritatis* shows on God's right hand a pilgrim in sober clothes, fleeceskin, and hat with Compostela shell and Roman vernicle, while on God's left is a figure in scarlet wrenching pages from a book—as the Wife does.) In her Prologue, the Wife harps on Christ's speaking to the Samaritan woman at the well, which is identified more precisely in John 4 as Jacob's Well, a site that was visited by Jerusalem pilgrims and alluded to in the *Benedictio Peregrinorum*. It was at Jacob's Well that Rebekah was found as a bride for Isaac and that Rachel was encountered by Jacob, who also married her sister Leah. The Well was the site where Jacob's daughter Dinah, like the maiden in the Wife's Tale, was raped. Seminar students, familiar with pilgrim accounts, immediately caught these echoes. Moreover, the Wife of Bath, at the *Benedictio Peregrinorum*, the Pilgrim Blessing, would have lain on the church floor in the shape of the cross; the church at Jacob's Well was in the shape of a cross because Christ spoke to the Samaritan woman at the sixth hour, the hour of the Crucifixion. Yet, Samaritans refused to perform the Jerusalem pilgrimage, worshiping Golden Calves in the mountains instead. Both the Wife and the Well are fraught with ambiguities.

The Pardoner does not bring to mind the landscapes of medieval pilgrimages so much as he does such other false-seeming pilgrims in medieval literary texts as Faus Semblant of the *Roman de la Rose*, who disguises himself as a pilgrim along with Dame Abstinence in order to slit Male Bouche's throat while hearing his confession, and Renart of the *Roman de Renart*, who is disguised as a pilgrim when he nearly catches Chauntecler; which reflects in turn Chaucer's Nun's Priest's Tale, having this last serve as a warning to the pilgrims against their false Pardoner—and also their false Friar since Russell was both Renart the Fox's son and a friar. Manuscript illuminations and other examples in art were used in class to demonstrate Faus Semblant's and Renart's guises as "false-seeming," counterfeit pilgrims and to relate these to the Pardoner's stance to the pilgrims as that of Faus Semblant and the Preaching Fox—who would devour his congregation at his sermon's conclusion.

Saint Gregory had spoken of the inn and the pilgrim as an allegory of the flesh and the soul.[7] Christ had supped at the Emmaus Inn with the two foolish disciples, however, that being the paradoxical spiritual conclusion to their pilgrimage rather than their crossing the *limina* of the Jerusalem Temple. Similarly, *The Canterbury Tales* plays with the dichotomy of the Tabard Inn and the Canterbury Cathedral. The latter is deliberately not attained. Instead, the great feast and the matter are knit up by the Parson, who, while the sun sets (Luke 24, *quoniam advesperascit, et inclinata est iam dies*), tells a fable that is also a sermon (Luke 24, Christ and the disciples converse, *hi sermones*, and narrate, *dum fabularentur*). Thus, *The Canterbury Tales* parallels the Emmaus pilgrimage, a type made familiar to the medieval audience through its enactment as liturgical drama each Easter Monday. The medieval tradition considered that the two pilgrim disciples were the named Cleophas, usually depicted as elderly, and the unnamed authorial Luke, usually depicted as youthful. Moreover, the tradition held that Luke, carrying the book of his Gospel, did not comprehend Christ at his side and was chided by Christ as "Fool!" This tradition gave to all these pilgrimage poems their shared paradigm: their authors, like Luke the Gospel writer, present within their texts as foolish pilgrims who later wisely write of their pilgrimages.

The seminar ended with a discussion of sixteenth- and seventeenth-century English pilgrimage material—now only a metaphor, an allegory, because physical pilgrimages were forbidden at the Reformation—and with Joyce's *Ulysses*, in which Joyce plays with Hamlet-hatted Stephen as a Saint James figure, a *matamoros* who would free Ireland of the infidel English ("How shall I your true love know, / From another one? / By his cockle hat and staff, / And his sandal shoon"), and in which Bloom as Moses and Stephen as Aaron, in Exodus symbolism, together sing Psalm 113, *modus peregrinus*. In addition, the Emmaus typology is superimposed upon the Odyssey typology, Stephen representing the unrecognized Christ/Telemachus, Bloom the unrecognizing Cleophas/Odysseus.

The approach in the seminar was intensely interdisciplinary, making use of art, music, literature, theology, liturgy, and history in order to restore the texts to their pilgrimage contexts and to provide a sound understanding of the satire present in them. The seminar table became burdened with large Dante commentaries, art books, Icelandic and Latin pilgrim texts. Slides and microfilms were used extensively. Guest lecturers included an art historian speaking on idols and idolatry, seen in Psalm 113 and elsewhere to oppose true pilgrimage, and a musicologist discussing Psalm 113 and the Fleury *Officium Peregrinorum.* The course seemed to be very well liked by the students, who performed splendidly in it. I learned much that was new not only from the guest lecturers but also from the students' research.

Notes

[1] John V. Fleming, *The* Roman de la Rose: *A Study in Allegory and Iconography* (Princeton: Princeton Univ. Press, 1969), gives plates of manuscript illuminations to this poem. For Dante illuminations see Peter Brieger, Millard Meiss, Charles S. Singleton, *Illuminated Manuscripts of the* Divine Comedy, 2 vols. (Princeton: Princeton Univ. Press, 1969).

[2] I am currently preparing an edition and translation of this poem. I have recently completed *The Pilgrim and the Poet: A Study of Dante, Langland, and Chaucer.*

[3] John G. Demaray, *The Invention of Dante's* Commedia (New Haven: Yale Univ. Press, 1974), discusses the Mount Sinai–Mount Purgatorio parallel and its relationship to medieval pilgrimages—which patterned themselves on the Israelites' Exodus.

[4] Julia Bolton Holloway, "Dante's *Commedia*: Egyptian Spoils, Roman Jubilee, Florence's Patron," *Studies in Medieval Culture,* 12 (1978), 94–104.

[5] Millard Meiss, *Painting in Florence and Siena after the Black Death: The Arts, Religion, and Society in the Mid-Fourteenth Century* (New York: Harper and Row, 1964), discusses the plague context. Exodus typology related plague and pilgrimage.

[6] Theo Stemmler, *The Ellesmere Miniatures of the Canterbury Pilgrims* (Mannheim: Univ. of Mannheim, 1977).

[7] Gerhart B. Ladner, *"Homo Viator:* Medieval Ideas on Alienation and Order," *Speculum,* 42 (1967), 223–59.

PARTICIPANTS IN SURVEY OF CHAUCER INSTRUCTORS

The following scholars and teachers of Chaucer generously agreed to participate in the survey of approaches to teaching *The Canterbury Tales* that preceded preparation of this volume. Without their invaluable assistance and support, the volume simply would not have been possible.

John G. Allee
George Washington University

Margaret G. Amassian
Fordham University

Mark E. Amsler
University of Delaware

Christopher P. Baker
Lamar University

Nicholas P. Barker
Covenant College

Stephen A. Barney
University of Virginia

Peter G. Beidler
Lehigh University

Robert G. Benson
University of Georgia

Ellen Blais
Mansfield State College

Leger Brosnahan
Illinois State University

Emerson Brown, Jr.
Vanderbilt University

Mitzi M. Brunsdale
Mayville State College

John M. Bugge
Emory University

Ruth A. Cameron
Eastern Nazarene College

Mary J. Carruthers
University of Illinois, Chicago Circle

Robert L. Chapman
Drew University

Mili N. Clark
State University of New York, Buffalo

Edward I. Condren
University of California, Los Angeles

Georgia Ronan Crampton
Portland State University

Terrie Curran
Providence College

Susan Dannenbaum
St. Olaf College

Mary Clemente Davlin
Rosary College

A. Inskip Dickerson
University of Vermont

Julia Dietrich
University of Louisville

E. Talbot Donaldson
Indiana University

Victor A. Doyno
State University of New York, Buffalo

Kathleen E. Dubs
University of Oregon

Caroline D. Eckhardt
Pennsylvania State University

George D. Economou
Long Island University

Judith Ferster
Brandeis University

John H. Fisher
University of Tennessee

Robert Fleissner
Central State University

William Frost
University of California, Santa Barbara

Donald Fry
State University of New York,
Stony Brook

Thomas J. Garbáty
University of Michigan

Theodora R. Graham
Pennsylvania State University,
Capitol Campus

Eugene Green
Boston University

David Hamilton
University of Iowa

Harlan Hamilton
Jersey City State College

Dorrel T. Hanks, Jr.
Baylor University

Ralph Hanna
University of California,
Riverside

M. Labouré Harig
Notre Dame College

A. L. Harris
Georgia State University

Dabney Hart
Georgia State University

Vernon Harward
Smith College

T. J. A. Heffernan
University of Tennessee

Richard L. Hoffman
Virginia Polytechnic Institute
and State University

Linda Tarte Holley
North Carolina State University

Julia Bolton Holloway
Princeton University

Donald R. Howard
Stanford University

Kathryn L. S. Hutchinson
Georgia State University

Robert M. Jordan
University of British Columbia

James G. Juroe
Hillsdale College

Stewart Justman
University of Montana

Ernest N. Kaulbach
University of Texas

H. A. Kelly
University of California,
Los Angeles

Ben Kimpel
University of Arkansas

R. T. Lenaghan
University of Michigan

R. H. Llewellyn
Temple University

Jane Marie Luecke
Oklahoma State University

Judith Weise Marsh
New York State University College,
Potsdam

J. Bard McNulty
Trinity College

Elaine M. Miller
St. Olaf College

Robert P. Miller
Queens College

Patricia Moody
Syracuse University

Marguerite P. Murphy
Georgia State University

Charles Muscatine
University of California,
Berkeley

Jane Chance Nitzsche
Rice University

Glending Olson
Cleveland State University

Lee W. Patterson
University of Toronto,
Victoria College

F. Anne Payne
State University of New York,
Buffalo

Michael P. Peinovich
New York University

Henry H. Peyton, III
Memphis State University

Stephen R. Portch
University of Wisconsin,
Richland Center

William Provost
University of Georgia

Genevieve Quigley
Hillsdale College

Esther C. Quinn
Hunter College

Burton Raffel
University of Denver

Walter Reinsdorf
Columbia-Greene Community
College

Robert V. V. Rice, Jr.
Hillsdale College

Florence H. Ridley
University of California,
Los Angeles

D. W. Robertson, Jr.
Princeton University

Thomas W. Ross
Colorado College

Beryl Rowland
York University

E. L. Rudolph
University of Arkansas

Edgar T. Schell
University of California,
Irvine

Susan Schibanoff
University of New Hampshire

Herbert N. Schneider
University of California,
Santa Barbara

R. Allen Shoaf
Yale University

Susan Martha Shwartz
Ithaca College

Malinda Snow
Georgia State University

Ellen Spolsky
University of New Mexico

William A. Stephany
University of Vermont

Robert K. Stone
University of Wisconsin,
Milwaukee

Wesley D. Sweetser
New York State University College,
Oswego

Ann M. Taylor
Salem State College

R. Eugene Templeton
Hillsdale College

Derek Traversi
Swarthmore College

Raymond P. Tripp, Jr.
University of Denver

Huling E. Ussery
Tulane University

Martha S. Waller
Butler University

Barry Weller
Johns Hopkins University

Michael D. West
University of Pittsburgh

Philip West
Skidmore College

James I. Wimsatt
University of Texas

Joseph S. Wittig
University of North Carolina

Chauncey Wood
McMaster University

Frank T. Zbozny
Duquesne University

LIST OF WORKS CITED

Books and Articles

Abrams, M. H., gen. ed. *The Norton Anthology of English Literature.* 4th ed. 2 vols. New York: Norton, 1979.

Ackerman, Robert W. *Backgrounds to Medieval English Literature.* New York: Random House, 1966.

Agonito, Rosemary, ed. *History of Ideas on Women: A Source Book.* New York: Putnam, 1977.

Andreas Capellanus. *The Art of Courtly Love.* Trans. John H. Parry. New York: Ungar, 1957.

Arnold, Matthew. "The Study of Poetry" (1880). In *Essays in Criticism: Second Series.* Ed. S. R. Littlewood. London: Macmillan, 1956, pp. 1–33.

Augustine. *Confessions.* Trans. E. B. Pasey. New York: Dutton, 1953.

———. *On Christian Doctrine.* Trans. D. W. Robertson, Jr. Indianapolis: Bobbs-Merrill, 1958.

Baird, Lorrayne Y. *A Bibliography of Chaucer, 1964–1973.* Boston: Hall, 1977.

Baker, J. H. *An Introduction to English Legal History.* 2nd ed. London: Butterworths, 1979.

Baldwin, Ralph. *The Unity of the* Canterbury Tales. 1955; rpt. New York: AMS, 1971.

Baugh, Albert C., ed. *Chaucer's Major Poetry.* New York: Appleton-Century-Crofts, 1963.

———. *Chaucer.* 2nd ed. Arlington Heights, Ill.: AHM, 1977.

———, and Thomas Cable. *A History of the English Language.* 3rd ed. Englewood Cliffs, N.J.: Prentice-Hall, 1978.

Baum, Paull F. *Chaucer: A Critical Appreciation.* Durham, N.C.: Duke Univ. Press, 1958.

———. *Chaucer's Verse.* Durham, N.C.: Duke Univ. Press, 1961.

Bennett, H. S. *The Pastons and Their England.* 2nd ed. Cambridge: Cambridge Univ. Press, 1932.

———. *Chaucer and the Fifteenth Century.* New York: Oxford Univ. Press, 1947.

Bennett, J. A. W. The Parlement of Foules: *An Interpretation.* Oxford: Clarendon, 1957.

———. *Chaucer's* Book of Fame. Oxford: Clarendon, 1968.

Benson, Larry D., and Theodore M. Andersson. *The Literary Context of Chaucer's Fabliaux: Texts and Translations.* Indianapolis: Bobbs-Merrill, 1971.

Benson, Larry D., ed. *The Learned and the Lewd: Studies in Chaucer and Medieval Literature.* Cambridge, Mass.: Harvard Univ. Press, 1974.

Bergman, Ingmar. *The Seventh Seal.* Trans. Lars Malmström and David Kushner. New York: Simon and Schuster, 1960.

Bethurum, Dorothy, ed. *Critical Approaches to Medieval Literature: Selected Papers from the English Institute, 1958–59.* New York: Columbia Univ. Press, 1960.

Bloch, Marc. *Feudal Society.* Trans. L. A. Manyon. Chicago: Univ. of Chicago Press, 1961.

Bloomfield, Morton. *Essays and Explorations: Studies in Ideas, Language, and Literature.* Cambridge, Mass.: Harvard Univ. Press, 1970.

Boase, Roger. *The Origin and Meaning of Courtly Love: A Critical Study of European Scholarship.* Manchester: Manchester Univ. Press; Totowa, N.J.: Rowman and Littlefield, 1977.

Boccaccio, Giovanni. *Boccaccio on Poetry.* Trans. Charles G. Osgood. Indianapolis: Bobbs-Merrill, 1956.

———. *Corbaccio.* Trans. Anthony K. Cassell. Urbana: Univ. of Illinois Press, 1975.

———. *The Decameron.* Trans. J. M. Rigg. 1930; rpt. New York: Dutton, 1973.

———. *The Decameron.* Trans. Richard Aldington. New York: Dell, 1949.

Boethius. *The Consolation of Philosophy.* Trans. Richard H. Green. Indianapolis: Bobbs-Merrill, 1962.

Bowden, Muriel. *Reader's Guide to Geoffrey Chaucer.* New York: Farrar, Straus, and Giroux, 1964.

———. *A Commentary on the General Prologue to the* Canterbury Tales. 2nd ed. New York: Macmillan, 1967.

Boyd, Beverly. *Chaucer and the Liturgy.* Philadelphia: Dorrance, 1967.

Brewer, Derek. *Chaucer in His Time.* 1963; rpt. London: Longman, 1973.

———. *Chaucer.* 3rd ed. London: Longman, 1973.

———. *Chaucer and His World.* New York: Dodd, Mead, 1978.

———, ed. *Chaucer and Chaucerians: Critical Studies in Middle English Literature.* University: Univ. of Alabama Press, 1966.

———, ed. *Geoffrey Chaucer.* London: Bell, 1974; Athens: Ohio Univ. Press, 1975.

———, ed. *Chaucer: The Critical Heritage.* 2 vols. London: Routledge and Kegan Paul, 1978.

Brieger, Peter, Millard Meiss, and Charles Singleton. *Illuminated Manuscripts of the* Divine Comedy. 2 vols. Princeton: Princeton Univ. Press, 1969.

Brink, Bernhard ten. *The Language and Metre of Chaucer.* Trans. M. Bentinck Smith. 1901; rpt. New York: Greenwood, 1969.

Bronson, Bertrand H. *In Search of Chaucer.* Toronto: Univ. of Toronto Press, 1960.

Brooke, Christopher. *The Structure of Medieval Society*. New York: McGraw-Hill, 1971.

Brown, Emerson, Jr. "The Poet's Last Words: Text and Meaning at the End of the Parson's Prologue." *Chaucer Review*, 10 (1976), 236–42.

Bryan, William F., and Germaine Dempster, eds. *Sources and Analogues of Chaucer's* Canterbury Tales. 1941; rpt. New York: Humanities Press, 1958.

Burlin, Robert B. *Chaucerian Fiction*. Princeton: Princeton Univ. Press, 1977.

Burns, Norman T., and Christopher J. Reagan, eds. *Concepts of the Hero in the Middle Ages and the Renaissance*. Albany: State Univ. of New York Press, 1975.

Burrow, J. A. *Ricardian Poetry: Chaucer, Gower, Langland, and the* Gawain *Poet*. New Haven: Yale Univ. Press, 1971.

————, ed. *Geoffrey Chaucer: A Critical Anthology*. Middlesex, Eng.: Penguin, 1969.

Carruthers, Mary J. "The Wife of Bath and the Painting of Lions." *PMLA*, 94 (1979), 209–22.

Cawley, A. C., ed. *Chaucer's Mind and Art*. Edinburgh: Oliver and Boyd, 1969.

————, ed. *The Canterbury Tales*. Rev. ed. New York: Dutton, 1975.

Chaytor, H. J. *From Script to Print: An Introduction to Medieval Vernacular Literature*. Cambridge: Heffer, 1945.

Chrétien de Troyes. *Arthurian Romances*. Trans. W. W. Comfort. 1914; rpt. New York: Dutton, 1975.

Chute, Marchette. *Geoffrey Chaucer of England*. New York: Dutton, 1946.

Clements, Robert J., and Joseph Gibaldi. *Anatomy of the Novella: The European Tale Collection from Boccaccio and Chaucer to Cervantes*. New York: New York Univ. Press, 1977.

Coghill, Nevill. *The Poet Chaucer*. 2nd ed. New York: Oxford Univ. Press, 1968.

————. *Geoffrey Chaucer*. Rev. ed. London: Longmans, Green, 1969.

————, trans. *The Canterbury Tales*. 1952; rpt. Baltimore: Penguin, 1975.

Cook, Daniel, ed. The Canterbury Tales *of Geoffrey Chaucer*. Garden City, N.Y.: Anchor-Doubleday, 1961.

Cooke, Thomas D. *The Old French and Chaucerian Fabliaux: A Study of Their Comic Climax*. Columbia: Univ. of Missouri Press, 1978.

Corsa, Helen S. *Chaucer: Poet of Mirth and Morality*. Notre Dame, Ind.: Univ. of Notre Dame Press, 1964.

Cosman, Madeleine P. *Fabulous Feasts: Medieval Cookery and Ceremony*. New York: Braziller, 1977.

Coulton, G. G. *Chaucer and His England*. 5th ed. London: Methuen, 1930.

————. *Medieval Panorama: The English Scene from Conquest to Reformation*. 1949; rpt. New York: Norton, 1974.

Crawford, William R. *Bibliography of Chaucer, 1954–63.* Seattle: Univ. of Washington Press, 1967.

Crow, Martin M., and Clair C. Olson, eds. *Chaucer Life-Records.* Austin: Univ. of Texas Press, 1966.

Cummings, Hubertis M. *The Indebtedness of Chaucer's Works to the Italian Works of Boccaccio.* 1916; rpt. Folcroft, Pa.: Folcroft, 1973.

Cunningham, J. V. "The Literary Form of the Prologue to the *Canterbury Tales.*" *Modern Philology,* 49 (1952), 172–81. Rpt. "Convention as Structure: The Prologue to the *Canterbury Tales.*" In *Collected Essays of J. V. Cunningham.* Chicago: Swallow Press, 1976, pp. 180–95.

Curley, Michael, trans. *Physiologus.* Austin: Univ. of Texas Press, 1979.

Curry, W. C. *Chaucer and the Mediaeval Sciences.* 2nd ed. New York: Barnes and Noble, 1960.

Curtius, Ernst Robert. *European Literature and the Latin Middle Ages.* Trans. Willard R. Trask. Princeton: Princeton Univ. Press, 1953.

Danker, Frederick E. "Teaching Medieval English Literature: Texts, Recordings, and Techniques." *College English,* 32 (1970), 340–57.

Dante Alighieri. *The Divine Comedy.* Trans. John D. Sinclair. Rev. ed. 3 vols. New York: Oxford Univ. Press, 1961.

———. *The Portable Dante.* Ed. Paolo Milano. New York: Viking, 1961.

David, Alfred. *The Strumpet Muse: Art and Morals in Chaucer's Poetry.* Bloomington: Indiana Univ. Press, 1976.

Deaux, George. *The Black Death, 1347.* London: Hamilton, 1969.

Delany, Sheila. *Chaucer's House of Fame: The Poetics of Skeptical Fideism.* Chicago: Univ. of Chicago Press, 1972.

Demaray, John G. *The Invention of Dante's Commedia.* New Haven: Yale Univ. Press, 1974.

Dempster, Germaine. *Dramatic Irony in Chaucer.* 1932; rpt. New York: Humanities Press, 1959.

Diamond, Arlyn, and Lee R. Edwards, eds. *The Authority of Experience: Essays in Feminist Criticism.* Amherst: Univ. of Massachusetts Press, 1977.

Dillon, Bert. *A Chaucer Dictionary: Proper Names and Allusions, Excluding Place Names.* Boston: Hall, 1974.

Donaldson, E. Talbot. *Speaking of Chaucer.* New York: Norton, 1970.

———. "Chaucer's Three 'P's': Pandarus, Pardoner, and Poet." *Michigan Quarterly Review,* 14 (1975), 282–301.

———, ed. *Chaucer's Poetry: An Anthology for the Modern Reader.* 2nd ed. New York: Ronald, 1975.

Donovan, Mortimer J. *The Breton Lay: A Guide to Varieties.* Notre Dame, Ind.: Univ. of Notre Dame Press, 1969.

DuBoulay, F. R. H., and Caroline Barron, eds. *The Reign of Richard II: Essays in Honour of May McKisack.* London: Athlone; New York: Humanities Press, 1971.

Dunn, Charles W., ed. *A Chaucer Reader: Selections from* The Canterbury Tales. New York: Harcourt, 1952.

Economou, George D. *The Goddess Natura in Medieval Literature.* Cambridge, Mass.: Harvard Univ. Press, 1972.

―――, ed. *Geoffrey Chaucer: A Collection of Original Articles.* New York: McGraw-Hill, 1975.

Eliason, Norman E. *The Language of Chaucer's Poetry: An Appraisal of the Verse, Style, and Structure.* Copenhagen, 1972; rpt. Atlantic Highlands, N.J.: Humanities Press, 1973.

Elliott, Ralph W. *Chaucer's English.* London: Deutsch, 1974.

Esch, Arno, ed. *Chaucer und seine Zeit: Symposion für Walter F. Schirmer.* Tübingen: Niemeyer, 1968.

Fansler, Dean S. *Chaucer and the* Roman de la Rose. 1914; rpt. Gloucester, Mass.: Peter Smith, 1965.

Ferrante, Joan M., and George D. Economou, eds. *In Pursuit of Perfection: Courtly Love in Medieval Literature.* Port Washington, N.Y.: Kennikat Press, 1975.

Fisher, John H., ed. *The Complete Poetry and Prose of Geoffrey Chaucer.* New York: Holt, Rinehart, and Winston, 1977.

Fleming, John V. *The* Roman de la Rose: *A Study in Allegory and Iconography.* Princeton: Princeton Univ. Press, 1969.

―――. *An Introduction to the Franciscan Literature of the Middle Ages.* Chicago: Herald Press, 1977.

Ford, Boris, ed. *The Age of Chaucer.* Baltimore: Penguin, 1954.

French, Robert D. *A Chaucer Handbook.* 2nd ed. Englewood Cliffs, N.J.: Prentice-Hall, 1947.

Friedman, Albert. "The Prioress' Tale and Chaucer's Antisemitism." *Chaucer Review,* 9 (1974), 118–29.

Furnivall, Frederick J., ed. *The Ellesmere Manuscript of Chaucer's* Canterbury Tales. 8 vols. London: Chaucer Society, 1868–84.

―――, ed. *A Six-Text Print of Chaucer's* Canterbury Tales. 8 vols. London: Chaucer Society, 1869–77.

Fyler, John M. *Chaucer and Ovid.* New Haven: Yale Univ. Press, 1979.

Gardner, John. *The Life and Times of Chaucer.* New York: Knopf, 1977.

―――. *The Poetry of Chaucer.* Carbondale: Southern Illinois Univ. Press, 1977.

Gordon, Ida. *The Double Sorrow of Troilus: A Study of Ambiguities in* Troilus and Criseyde. Oxford: Oxford Univ. Press, 1970.

Gordon, R. K., trans. *Anglo-Saxon Poetry.* New York: Dutton, 1926.

Griffith, Dudley David. *Bibliography of Chaucer, 1908–1953.* Seattle: Univ. of Washington Press, 1955.

Grose, M. W. *Chaucer.* New York: Arco, 1969.

Guillaume de Lorris and Jean de Meun. *Romance of the Rose.* Trans. Harry W. Robbins. New York: Dutton, 1962.

————. *Romance of the Rose.* Trans. Charles Dahlberg. Princeton: Princeton Univ. Press, 1971.

Hall, D. J. *English Mediaeval Pilgrimage.* London: Routledge and Kegan Paul, 1965.

Hammond, Eleanor P. *Chaucer: A Bibliographical Manual.* 1908; rpt. New York: Peter Smith, 1933.

Harrison, G. B., gen. ed. *Major British Writers.* 2 vols. New York: Harcourt, 1959.

Haskell, Ann S. *Essays on Chaucer's Saints.* The Hague: Mouton, 1976.

Hatto, A. T., trans. *The Nibelungenlied.* 1965; rpt. New York: Penguin, 1976.

Helmholz, R. H. *Marriage Litigation in Medieval England.* New York: Cambridge Univ. Press, 1974.

Héraucourt, Will. *Die Wertwelt Chaucers.* Heidelberg: Winter, 1939.

Hieatt, A. Kent, and Constance Hieatt, eds. *Canterbury Tales/Tales of Canterbury.* New York: Bantam, 1964.

Highet, Gilbert. *The Art of Teaching.* New York: Knopf, 1950.

Hoffman, Richard L. *Ovid and the* Canterbury Tales. Philadelphia: Univ. of Pennsylvania Press, 1967.

Holloway, Julia Bolton. "Dante's *Commedia*: Egyptian Spoils, Roman Jubilee, Florence's Patron." *Studies in Medieval Culture*, 12 (1978), 94–104.

Hopper, Vincent F., ed. *Chaucer's* Canterbury Tales *(Selected): An Interlinear Translation.* 1948; rpt. Brooklyn, N.Y.: Barron's Educational Series, 1970.

Howard, Donald R. "Literature and Sexuality: Book III of Chaucer's *Troilus*." *Massachusetts Review*, 8 (1967), 442–56.

————. *The Idea of the* Canterbury Tales. Berkeley: Univ. of California Press, 1976.

————, ed. *The Canterbury Tales.* New York: Signet-New American Library, 1969.

Hugh of St. Victor. *Didascalion.* Trans. Jerome Taylor. New York: Columbia Univ. Press, 1961.

Huizinga, Johan. *The Waning of the Middle Ages: A Study of the Forms of Life, Thought, and Art in France and the Netherlands in the Fourteenth Century.* London: Arnold, 1924.

Huppé, Bernard. *A Reading of the* Canterbury Tales. Albany: State Univ. of New York Press, 1964.

————, and D. W. Robertson, Jr. *Fruyt and Chaf: Studies in Chaucer's Allegories.* Princeton: Princeton Univ. Press, 1963.

Hussey, Maurice. *Chaucer's World: A Pictorial Companion.* Cambridge: Cambridge Univ. Press, 1967.

————, A. C. Spearing, and James Winney. *An Introduction to Chaucer.* Cambridge: Cambridge Univ. Press, 1965.

Hussey, S. S. *Chaucer: An Introduction.* London: Methuen, 1971.

John of Salisbury. *Metalogicon.* Trans. Daniel M. McGarry. 1955; rpt. Gloucester, Mass.: Peter Smith, 1962.

————. *The Statesman's Book.* Trans. John Dickinson. New York: Knopf, 1927. (*Policraticus,* Books 4–6, complete; selections from 7 and 8.)

————. *Frivolities of Courtiers and Footprints of Philosophers.* Trans. Joseph B. Pike. Minneapolis: Univ. of Minnesota Press, 1938. (*Policraticus,* Books 1–3, complete; selections from 7 and 8.)

Johnson, William C., and Loren C. Gruber, eds. *New Views on Chaucer: Essays in Generative Criticism.* Denver: Society for New Language Study, 1973.

Jones, Charles W., ed. *Medieval Literature in Translation.* New York: McKay, 1950.

Jordan, Robert M. *Chaucer and the Shape of Creation: The Aesthetic Possibilities of Inorganic Structure.* Cambridge, Mass.: Harvard Univ. Press, 1967.

Jusserand, J. J. *English Wayfaring Life in the Middle Ages.* Trans. Lucy T. Smith. 4th ed. 1888; rpt. New York: Barnes and Noble, 1950.

Kean, P. M. *Chaucer and the Making of English Poetry.* 2 vols. London: Routledge and Kegan Paul, 1972.

Keen, M. H. *The Laws of War in the Late Middle Ages.* London: Routledge and Kegan Paul, 1965.

Keiser, George R. "In Defense of the Bradshaw Shift." *Chaucer Review,* 12 (1978), 191–201.

Kellogg, Alfred L. "An Augustinian Interpretation of Chaucer's Pardoner." *Speculum,* 26 (1951), 465–81.

————. *Chaucer, Langland, Arthur: Essays in Middle English Literature.* New Brunswick, N.J.: Rutgers Univ. Press, 1972.

————, and L. A. Haselmayer. "Chaucer's Satire of the Pardoner." *PMLA,* 66 (1951), 251–77.

Kelly, Henry A. *Love and Marriage in the Age of Chaucer.* Ithaca, N.Y.: Cornell Univ. Press, 1975.

Kennedy, George A. *Classical Rhetoric and Its Christian and Secular Traditions from Ancient to Modern Times.* Chapel Hill: Univ. of North Carolina Press, 1980.

Kermode, Frank, and John Hollander, gen. eds. *Oxford Anthology of English Literature.* 2 vols. New York: Oxford Univ. Press, 1973.

Kittredge, George Lyman. *Chaucer and His Poetry*. 1915; rpt. Cambridge, Mass.: Harvard Univ. Press, 1970.

Knowles, David. *The Evolution of Medieval Thought*. New York: Random House, 1964.

Koch, John. *A Detailed Comparison of the Eight Manuscripts of Chaucer's* Canterbury Tales. 1913; rpt. New York: International Publications Service, 1968.

Kökeritz, Helge. *A Guide to Chaucer's Pronunciation*. New York: Holt, 1961.

Kraus, Henry. *The Living Theatre of Medieval Art*. Bloomington: Indiana Univ. Press, 1967.

Kurath, Hans, Sherman M. Kuhn, et al. *Middle English Dictionary*. Ann Arbor: Univ. of Michigan Press, 1952–

Ladner, Gerhart. "*Homo Viator*: Medieval Ideas on Alienation and Order." *Speculum*, 42 (1967), 223–59.

Lawrence, W. W. *Chaucer and the* Canterbury Tales. New York: Columbia Univ. Press, 1950.

Leach, MacEdward, ed. *Studies in Medieval Literature*. Philadelphia: Univ. of Pennsylvania Press, 1961.

Leff, Gordon. *Medieval Thought: St. Augustine to Ockham*. Baltimore: Penguin, 1958.

Lewis, C. S. *The Allegory of Love*. 1936; rpt. New York: Oxford Univ. Press, 1958.

———. *The Discarded Image*. Cambridge: Cambridge Univ. Press, 1964.

Loomis, Roger S. *A Mirror of Chaucer's World*. Princeton: Princeton Univ. Press, 1965.

Lopez, Robert S. *The Commercial Revolution of the Middle Ages, 950–1350*. Englewood Cliffs, N.J.: Prentice-Hall, 1971.

Lounsbury, Thomas R. *Studies in Chaucer: His Life and Writings*. 1892; rpt. New York: Russell and Russell, 1962.

Lowes, John L. *Geoffrey Chaucer and the Development of His Genius*. Boston: Houghton Mifflin, 1934.

Lumiansky, Robert M. *Of Sondry Folk: The Dramatic Principles in the* Canterbury Tales. Austin: Univ. of Texas Press, 1955.

———, trans. *The Canterbury Tales*. 1948; rpt. New York: Pocket Books, 1971.

Mack, Maynard, gen. ed. *World Masterpieces*. 2 vols. 4th ed. New York: Norton, 1979.

Magoun, Francis P., Jr. *A Chaucer Gazetteer*. Chicago: Univ. of Chicago Press, 1961.

Mâle, Emile. *The Gothic Image: Religious Art in France of the Thirteenth Century*. Trans. Dora Nussey. 1913; rpt. New York: Harper and Row, 1958.

———. *Religious Art in France: The Twelfth Century*. Trans. Marthiel Mathews. Princeton: Princeton Univ. Press, 1978.

Malone, Kemp. *Chapters on Chaucer*. Baltimore: Johns Hopkins Univ. Press, 1951.

Manly, John M. *Some New Light on Chaucer*. New York: Holt, 1926.

———. *Chaucer and the Rhetoricians*. 1926; rpt. New York: Folcroft, 1972.

———, and Edith Rickert, eds. *The Text of the* Canterbury Tales. 8 vols. Chicago: Univ. of Chicago Press, 1940.

Mann, Jill. *Chaucer and Medieval Estates Satire: The Literature of Social Classes and the General Prologue of the* Canterbury Tales. Cambridge: Cambridge Univ. Press, 1973.

Marle, Raimond van. *Iconographie de l'art profane au Moyen Age et la Renaissance*. 2 vols. 1931–32; rpt. New York: Hacker, 1971.

Mathew, Gervase. *The Court of Richard II*. New York: Norton, 1968.

Maurer, Armand. *Medieval Philosophy*. New York: Random House, 1962.

McAlpine, Monica E. *The Genre of* Troilus and Criseyde. Ithaca, N.Y.: Cornell Univ. Press, 1978.

McKisack, May. *The Fourteenth Century, 1307–1399*. Oxford: Clarendon, 1959.

Mead, W. E. *The English Medieval Feast*. 2nd ed. London: Allen and Unwin, 1967.

Meiss, Millard. *Painting in Florence and Siena after the Black Death: The Arts, Religion, and Society in the Mid-Fourteenth Century*. New York: Harper and Row, 1964.

Milhaud, Darius. *Cantate sur des poèmes de Chaucer*. Paris: Menestral, 1963.

Miller, Robert P., ed. *Chaucer: Sources and Backgrounds*. New York: Oxford Univ. Press, 1977.

Miskimin, Alice S. *The Renaissance Chaucer*. New Haven: Yale Univ. Press, 1975.

Miskimin, Harry A. *The Economy of Early Renaissance Europe, 1300–1460*. Englewood Cliffs, N.J.: Prentice-Hall, 1969.

Mitchell, Jerome, and William Provost, eds. *Chaucer the Love Poet*. Athens: Univ. of Georgia Press, 1973.

Moore, Samuel, and Albert H. Marckwardt. *Historical Outlines of English Sounds and Inflections*. Ann Arbor, Mich.: Wahr, 1957.

Morrison, Theodore, ed. and trans. *The Portable Chaucer*. Rev. ed. New York: Viking, 1975.

Murphy, James J. *Rhetoric in the Middle Ages: A History of Rhetorical Theory from Saint Augustine to the Renaissance*. Berkeley: Univ. of California Press, 1974.

———, ed. *Medieval Eloquence: Studies in the Theory and Practice of Medieval Rhetoric*. Berkeley: Univ. of California Press, 1978.

Muscatine, Charles. *Chaucer and the French Tradition*. Berkeley: Univ. of California Press, 1957.

Myers, A. R. *England in the Late Middle Ages*. Baltimore: Penguin, 1966.

————. *London in the Age of Chaucer.* Norman: Univ. of Oklahoma Press, 1972.

Newman, F. X., ed. *The Meaning of Courtly Love.* Albany: State Univ. of New York Press, 1968.

Newstead, Helaine, ed. *Chaucer and His Contemporaries.* New York: Fawcett, 1968.

Nohl, Johannes, comp. *The Black Death: A Chronicle of the Plague.* Trans. C. H. Clarke. 1926; rpt. New York: Humanities Press, 1961.

Oberman, Heiko A. *The Harvest of Medieval Theology.* Rev. ed. Grand Rapids, Mich.: Eerdmans, 1967.

Ong, Walter J. "The Writer's Audience Is Always a Fiction." *PMLA,* 90 (1975), 9–21.

Orme, Nicholas. *English Schools in the Middle Ages.* New York: Barnes and Noble, 1973.

Ovid. *Art of Love.* Trans. Rolfe Humphries. Bloomington: Indiana Univ. Press, 1957.

————. *Metamorphoses.* Trans. Mary Innes. Baltimore: Penguin, 1955.

Owen, Charles A., Jr. *Pilgrimage and Storytelling in the* Canterbury Tales. Norman: Univ. of Oklahoma Press, 1977.

————, ed. *Discussions of the* Canterbury Tales. 1961; rpt. New York: Greenwood, 1978.

Owst, G. R. *Preaching in Medieval England: An Introduction to Sermon Manuscripts of the Period, c. 1350–1450.* 1926; rpt. New York: Russell and Russell, 1965.

————. *Literature and Pulpit in Medieval England.* Oxford: Blackwell, 1966.

Painter, Sidney. *French Chivalry: Chivalric Ideas and Practices in Mediaeval France.* Baltimore: Johns Hopkins Univ. Press, 1940.

Panofsky, Erwin. *Studies in Iconology: Humanistic Themes in the Art of the Renaissance.* 1939; rpt. New York: Harper and Row, 1962.

Patch, Howard R. *The Tradition of the Goddess Fortuna in Roman Literature and in the Transitional Period.* 1922; rpt. Folcroft, Pa.: Folcroft, 1976.

Payne, Robert O. *The Key of Remembrance: A Study of Chaucer's Poetics.* New Haven: Yale Univ. Press, 1963.

Pickering, Frederick. *Literature and Art in the Middle Ages.* Miami, Fla.: Univ. of Miami Press, 1970.

Poole, Austin L. *Medieval England.* Rev. ed. 2 vols. Oxford: Clarendon, 1958.

Postan, M. M. *Medieval Economy and Society: An Economic History of Britain in the Middle Ages.* Baltimore: Penguin, 1972.

Power, Eileen. *Medieval People.* 10th ed. New York: Barnes and Noble, 1963.

————. *Medieval Women.* Ed. M. M. Postan. Cambridge: Cambridge Univ. Press, 1975.

Pratt, Robert A. "The Order of *The Canterbury Tales*." *PMLA*, 66 (1951), 1141–67.

———, ed. *The Tales of Canterbury*. Boston: Houghton Mifflin, 1966.

Quennell, Marjorie, and C. H. B. Quennell. *A History of Everyday Things in England*. Vol. I. New York: Scribners, 1918.

Reynolds, Susan. *Introduction to the History of English Medieval Towns*. Oxford: Clarendon, 1977.

Richardson, Janette. *"Blameth nat me"*: *A Study of Imagery in Chaucer's Fabliaux*. The Hague: Mouton, 1970.

Rickert, Edith, comp. *Chaucer's World*. Ed. Clair C. Olson and Martin M. Crow. New York: Columbia Univ. Press, 1948.

Ridley, Florence H. "The State of Chaucer Studies: A Brief Survey." *Studies in the Age of Chaucer*, 1 (1979), 3–16.

Robertson, D. W., Jr. *A Preface to Chaucer: Studies in Medieval Perspectives*. Princeton: Princeton Univ. Press, 1962.

———. *Chaucer's London*. New York: Wiley, 1968.

———, ed. *The Literature of Medieval England*. New York: McGraw-Hill, 1970.

Robinson, F. N., ed. *The Works of Geoffrey Chaucer*. 2nd ed. Boston: Houghton Mifflin, 1957.

Robinson, Ian. *Chaucer's Prosody*. Cambridge: Cambridge Univ. Press, 1971.

Root, Robert K. *The Poetry of Chaucer*. Rev. ed. 1922; rpt. Gloucester, Mass.: Peter Smith, 1957.

Rosenblatt, Louise. *The Reader, the Text, the Poem: The Transactional Theory of the Literary Work*. Carbondale: Southern Illinois Univ. Press, 1978.

Ross, Thomas W. *Chaucer's Bawdy*. New York: Dutton, 1972.

Roth, Cecil. *A History of the Jews in England*. 3rd ed. Oxford: Clarendon, 1964.

Rowland, Beryl. *Blind Beasts: Chaucer's Animal World*. Kent, Ohio: Kent State Univ. Press, 1971.

———. "Chaucer's Dame Alys: Critics in Blunderland?" In *Studies Presented to Tauno F. Mustanoja on the Occasion of His Sixtieth Birthday. Neuphilologische Mitteilungen*, 73 (1972), 381–95.

———. *Animals with Human Faces: A Guide to Animal Symbolism*. Knoxville: Univ. of Tennessee Press, 1973.

———. "Contemporary Chaucer Criticism." *English*, 22 (1973), 3–10.

———. *Birds with Human Souls: A Guide to Bird Symbolism*. Knoxville: Univ. of Tennessee Press, 1978.

———, ed. *Chaucer and Middle English Studies in Honour of Rossell Hope Robbins*. London: Allen and Unwin; Kent, Ohio: Kent State Univ. Press, 1974.

————, ed. *Companion to Chaucer Studies*. 2nd ed. New York: Oxford Univ. Press, 1979.

Ruggiers, Paul G. *The Art of the* Canterbury Tales. Madison: Univ. of Wisconsin Press, 1965.

————, ed. *A Facsimile of the Hengwrt Manuscript of the* Canterbury Tales. Norman: Univ. of Oklahoma Press, 1978.

Sayles, G. O., ed. *Select Cases in the Court of King's Bench.* 7 vols. London: Quaritch, 1936–71.

Schlauch, Margaret. *English Medieval Literature and Its Social Foundations.* 1956; rpt. New York: Cooper Square Publishers, 1971.

Schoeck, Richard J., and Jerome Taylor, eds. *Chaucer Criticism.* Vol. I. Notre Dame, Ind.: Univ. of Notre Dame Press, 1960.

Schulz, Herbert C. *The Ellesmere Manuscript of Chaucer's* Canterbury Tales. San Marino, Cal.: Huntington Library, 1965.

Scott, A. F. *Who's Who in Chaucer.* New York: Taplinger, 1974.

Segni, Lotario dei. *De Miseria Condicionis Humanae.* Ed. Robert E. Lewis. Athens: Univ. of Georgia Press, 1978.

Shannon, Edgar F. *Chaucer and the Roman Poets.* 1929; rpt. New York: Russell and Russell, 1964.

Skeat, W. W., ed. *The Complete Works of Geoffrey Chaucer.* 2nd ed. 7 vols. Oxford: Clarendon, 1899.

Southern, R. W. *The Making of the Middle Ages.* New Haven: Yale Univ. Press, 1953.

Spearing, A. C. *Criticism and Medieval Poetry.* New York: Barnes and Noble, 1972.

Spencer, Hazelton, Beverly Layman, and Donald Ferry, eds. *British Literature.* 2 vols. Lexington, Mass.: Heath, 1974.

Spurgeon, Caroline F. E. *Five Hundred Years of Chaucer Criticism and Allusion, 1357–1900.* 3 vols. 1925; rpt. New York: Russell and Russell, 1960.

Statius. *Achilleid.* Ed. Paul M. Clogan. Leyden: Brill, 1968.

Stemmler, Theo. *The Ellesmere Miniatures of the Canterbury Pilgrims.* Mannheim: Univ. of Mannheim, 1977.

Sumption, Jonathan. *Pilgrimage: An Image of Medieval Religion.* Totowa, N.J.: Rowman and Littlefield, 1975.

Tatlock, J. S. P. *The Mind and Art of Chaucer.* 1950; rpt. New York: Gordian, 1966.

————, and Arthur G. Kennedy. *A Concordance to the Complete Works of Geoffrey Chaucer.* 1927; rpt. Gloucester, Mass.: Peter Smith, 1963.

Taylor, Henry O. *The Medieval Mind: A History of the Development of Thought and Emotion in the Middle Ages.* 4th ed. 2 vols. Cambridge, Mass.: Harvard Univ. Press, 1962.

Thompson, James W. *Economic and Social History of the Middle Ages.* 2 vols. 1928; rpt. New York: Ungar, 1959.

————. *History of the Middle Ages, 300–1500.* New York: Norton, 1931.

————, et al. *The Medieval Library.* New York: Hafner, 1957.

Thompson, Stith. *The Folk Tale.* New York: Dryden, 1951.

————. *Motif-Index of Folk Literature.* Rev. ed. 6 vols. Bloomington: Indiana Univ. Press, 1966.

Thrupp, Sylvia L. *The Merchant Class of Medieval London, 1300–1500.* Ann Arbor: Univ. of Michigan Press, 1948.

Tobler, Adolf, and Erhard Lommatzsch. *Altfranzösisches Wörterbuch.* Berlin: Weidmann, 1925.

Trevelyan, G. M. *England in the Age of Wycliffe.* 3rd ed. 1900; rpt. New York: AMS, 1975.

————. *English Social History: A Survey of Six Centuries, Chaucer to Queen Victoria.* 3rd ed. 1946; rpt. New York: Barnes and Noble, 1961.

Tripp, Raymond P., Jr. *Beyond Canterbury: Chaucer, Humanism, and Literature.* Denver: Society for New Language Study, 1977.

Tuchman, Barbara. *A Distant Mirror: The Calamitous Fourteenth Century.* New York: Knopf, 1978.

Tuve, Rosemond. *Allegorical Imagery: Some Mediaeval Books and Their Posterity.* Princeton: Princeton Univ. Press, 1966.

Valency, Maurice. *In Praise of Love: An Introduction to the Love Poetry of the Renaissance.* 1961; rpt. New York: Octagon, 1976.

Vergil. *The Aeneid.* Trans. Rolfe Humphries. New York: Scribners, 1951.

Wagenknecht, Edward C. *The Personality of Chaucer.* Norman: Univ. of Oklahoma Press, 1968.

————, ed. *Chaucer: Modern Essays in Criticism.* New York: Oxford Univ. Press, 1959.

Ward, A. W., and A. R. Waller, eds. *The Cambridge History of English Literature.* Vol. II. 1908; rpt. Cambridge: Cambridge Univ. Press, 1967.

White, Lynn, Jr. *Medieval Technology and Social Change.* Oxford: Clarendon, 1962.

————. *Medieval Religion and Technology: Collected Essays.* Berkeley: Univ. of California Press, 1978.

White, T. H. *The Bestiary: A Book of Beasts.* New York: Putnam, 1954.

Whitehead, Alfred North. *The Aims of Education.* 1929; rpt. New York: Free Press, 1967.

Whitmore, Mary E. *Medieval English Domestic Life and Amusements in the Works of Chaucer.* 1937; rpt. New York: Cooper Square Publishers, 1972.

Whittock, Trevor. *A Reading of the* Canterbury Tales. London: Cambridge Univ. Press, 1968.

Wimsatt, James I. *Chaucer and the French Love Poets: The Literary Background of the* Book of the Duchess. Chapel Hill: Univ. of North Carolina Press, 1968.

Wood, Chauncey. *Chaucer and the Country of the Stars: Poetic Uses of Astrological Imagery*. Princeton: Princeton Univ. Press, 1970.

Ziegler, Philip. *The Black Death*. London: Collins; New York: John Day, 1969.

Recordings

Ashcroft, Peggy. *The Wife of Bath in Modern English*. Trans. J. U. Nicolson. Caedmon, TC 1102, 1961.

Bessinger, J. B., Jr. *Geoffrey Chaucer:* The Canterbury Tales *General Prologue in Middle English*. Caedmon, TC 1151, 1962.

————. *Two Canterbury Tales in Middle English: Miller's Tale and Reeve's Tale*. Caedmon, TC 1223, 1967.

Bornstein, Diane. *A History of the English Language*. 3 records. Caedmon, TC 3008, 1973.

Coghill, Nevill, Norman Davis, and John Burrow. *Geoffrey Chaucer: Prologue to the* Canterbury Tales. Argo, PLP 1001, 1964.

————, Norman Davis, Lena Davis, and John Burrow. *Geoffrey Chaucer: The Nun's Priest's Tale*. Argo, PLP 1002, 1966.

————, and Norman Davis. *Geoffrey Chaucer: General Prologue and Pardoner's Tale*. Spoken Arts, SA 919, 1966.

————, lyricist. *The* Canterbury Tales: *A Musical*. Book by Martin Starkie and Nevill Coghill. Music by Richard Hill and John Hawkins. Capitol Records, SW–229, 1969.

Kaplan, Victor L. *Chaucer: Readings from the* Canterbury Tales. Folkways/Scholastic Records, FL 9859, 1966.

Kökeritz, Helge. *Beowulf and Chaucer Readings*. Lexington, LE 5505, 1957.

————. *A Thousand Years of English Pronunciation*. 2 records. Lexington, LE 7650/55, 1963.

MacLiammoir, Michael, and Stanley Holloway. *Geoffrey Chaucer: Two Canterbury Tales in Modern English: The Pardoner's Tale and the Miller's Tale*. Trans. Theodore Morrison. Caedmon, TC 1130, 1962.

Orff, Carl. *Carmina Burana*. Cond. Rafael Frühbeck de Burgos, New Philharmonia Orchestra. Angel, S–3633, 1965.

Ross, Robert. *Two Canterbury Tales in Middle English: The Pardoner's Prologue and Tale, and the Nun's Priest's Tale*. Caedmon, TC 1008, 1952.

Snortum Niel, and Daniel Knapp. *The Sounds of Chaucer's English*. 3 records. NCTE, RL 20–8, 1967.

Trimble, Lester. *Four Fragments from Caunterbury Tales*. With Adele Addison and others. Columbia Special Products, AMS–6198, 1958.

Films and Filmstrips

Bergman, Ingmar, dir. *Det Sjunde Inseglet*. [*The Seventh Seal*.] Svensk Film-industri, 1956.

The Canterbury Tales. 10 films. Univ. of Michigan Television Center, 1967. (Series includes Pardoner's Tale; Knight's Tale; Shipman's Tale; Prioress' Tale; Wife of Bath's Tale; Friar's Tale; Clerk's Tale; Merchant's Tale; Franklin's Tale; and Nun's Priest's Tale and Manciple's Tale.)

Chaucer's Canterbury Pilgrims. Sound filmstrip. Educational Audio-Visual, 1970.

Chaucer's England, with a Special Presentation of the Pardoner's Tale. Film. Encyclopaedia Britannica, 1958.

Clark, Kenneth, writer and narr. *Civilisation*. Dir. Michael Gill and Peter Montagnon. 12 programs. BBC, 1969. (Relevant programs include "The Great Thaw" and "Romance and Reality.")

Kirby, Mary, and Naomi Diamond, dirs. *From Every Shires Ende: The World of Chaucer's Pilgrims*. Film. Pilgrim Films, 1969. (Information is available from International Film Bureau, 322 South Michigan Avenue, Chicago, Illinois 60604.)

The Medieval Mind. Film. Encyclopedia Britannica, 1969.

Pasolini, Pier Paolo, dir. *I racconti di Canterbury*. P.E.A. Cinematografica/Les Artistes Associés, 1971.

The Time, the Life, the Works of Geoffrey Chaucer. Sound filmstrip. Educational Audio-Visual, 1968.

INDEX

172   INDEX